MY SERVICE DAYS

INDIA, AFGHANISTAN, SUAKIN '85, AND CHINA

MY SERVICE DAYS

INDIA, AFGHANISTAN, SUAKIN '85,

AND CHINA

BY

STEWART NORMAN ROBERT SIR

GYAN

ISBN : 978-81-212-1529-9(HB)

First Published, 1908

Published, 2018

Published by

Gyan Publishing House
5, Ansari Road
Daryaganj, New Delhi-110002
Phone: 011-47034999, 9811692060
www.gyanbooks.com
E-mail: books@gyanbooks.com .

Printed at: G. Print Process, Delhi.

MAJOR-GENERAL SIR NORMAN STEWART, BART., C.B., AND STAFF.
Moir Duncan *(Interpreter)*, Capt. T. Jermyn, Capt. D. R. Adye, Capt. R. E. Vaughan, Capt. R. B. Low, D.S.O.

CONTENTS

LIST OF ILLUSTRATIONS

PART I

INDIA AND AFGHANISTAN

MY SERVICE DAYS

PART I

INDIA AND AFGHANISTAN

I WAS born at Lahore, on the 27th September, 1851, in what was then the officers' quarters, but which when I last saw them were occupied by the Eurasian employees of the Government Telegraph Department, a row of bomb-proof buildings on one floor, which were little better than the present day out-houses you give your native servants.

At an early age I experienced my first adventure, when, proceeding home via Kurrachee, in the year 1856, with my mother, we were wrecked on the Indus shortly after leaving Fort Altock, an event I can still remember, as we children (my elder brother and two younger sisters) were delighted with the experience, without being in the least degree aware of the danger, our one anxiety being the safety of a she goat which we all petted, and depended on for our milk supply.

On arrival in England we were all taken in by an uncle who possessed a numerous growing family of his own, to whom we were objects of the greatest curiosity, for coming from India, I feel sure, they were surprised to find their young cousins "white." At first we absolutely refused to converse in any language but Hindustani, which we were made to spout before any friends who happened to visit the house, and I understand were looked on as marvels for being able to speak a foreign tongue with fluency. This did not last long, however, for within two months nothing could persuade us to "give tongue" in the strange language, which was probably completely forgotten inside four months.

From Liverpool we migrated to that beautiful little Irish watering-place Bray, where in 1822 my mother was born in a Martello Tower on the coast close by, her father being an officer of the Royal Navy holding a shore billet, which included these curious old erections for the protection of our Irish coast from smugglers, etc.

I don't suppose we boys were more mischievous than others, but we seemed to be incessantly doing things which ought to have been left undone, such as falling into streams, etc., and generally declining good advice. So it was settled the sooner we went to school the better, and Kingstown was our next place of residence, where we were put in charge of some estimable maiden ladies, as our mother had to return to India to join our father, whom she had not seen for some time, including the terrible Mutiny years, the horrors of which we were too young to realise. This parting was one none of us are ever likely to forget, but the sorrows of the young do not last long, and nothing could have been a better cure than school life.

My brother and I were sent to a very excellent school close by, kept curiously enough by a German, and as well as I can remember we thoroughly enjoyed the change.

No boy possessed higher spirits than my brother who soon became a great favourite; he was good enough at books, but he preferred play, whilst he encouraged me to stick to lessons, and in this way, between us, we more or less held our own in the school room and play ground.

During these early scholastic days our lives were uneventful, but not entirely without excitement, for one winter a terrible storm raged on the coast, and the Kingstown Harbour one truly awful night became a refuge for every conceivable craft that could reach its welcome shelter. Many succeeded, but more failed, and the sight of wreckage outside the next morning was appalling even to our young minds. The entire town and whole country side seemed to have turned out, and many heart rending sights we saw in the shape of general wreckage and washed up bodies. H.M.S. Ajax was in harbour, and as is usual on occasions of this kind the entire crew had worked the night through assisting those in distress, and many a good man and true amongst them lost his life in gallant attempts to save others, amongst them the captain himself.

The weather inside the harbour was so boisterous that small boats could hardly live in the sea, whilst nearly all the shipping were dragging their anchors and being battered to pieces against each other or the sides of the harbour. Close under the Yacht Club Captain Boyd and his boat's crew were employed in the work of rescue when a huge swell lifted the boat on to some rocks, and all were thrown into the water; being a powerful man and swimmer, he thought lightly of this and immediately went to the assistance of others, whilst the remainder righted the boat and scrambled in. Whilst this was going on the captain had seized a drowning man and placed him safely on the rocks, remarking "life was sweet," when another roller came in and washed him off, and this was the last seen of this gallant man in life.

When we reached the harbour the following day the work of searching for the dead generally, and Captain Boyd's body particularly, was going on, and like all boys we wished to help, but with sore hearts we were taken away. The fury of the storm had passed, but it was a grand sight to watch the still angry waves. Weeks passed before the Captain's body was found, and the last I remember of this sad affair was following his body on its way to its last resting place.

Two years later to our great joy our parents came home, and we all went on a visit to our uncle, William Knox, of Clonleigh, where I experienced my first great sorrow in the death of my dearly loved brother, who succumbed to an attack of diphtheria after a short illness on the 12th February, 1862. To me who had never been parted from him for an hour the blow was a severe one, but what was a child's grief compared with that of the parents?

Soon my father had to return to India, and on my mother fell the anxious duty of finding homes for myself and two sisters. We moved to Cheltenham, where a home was found for me, the happiest I ever had away from my own parents. I was sent as a day-boy to what was known as "Gedges," or the Preparatory School for Cheltenham College, whilst I lived with the sweetest and dearest woman I ever met, Mrs. Crofton, and her two children, a girl and boy, who vied with each other to make my life happy and bring me up as one of themselves. Their kindness and love I can never forget. With this charming family I spent three happy years till I was old enough to go to a public school.

At the age of 14 I went to Harrow, where, I fear, I learnt more of the art of cricket and football than the mysteries of the classics. My house master, the Rev. Middlemist, was not the man to win a boy's heart, but in his queer way he was kind enough to the boys of his house, if at times a little tactless in dealing with their faults, for he often punished severely when reprimand would have sufficed, and overlooked the graver offences against discipline—he failed to discriminate between high spirits and wilful wrong doing.

My first "form master," however, was just the opposite. "John Smith," as he was always called, was without exception the finest example of a man to touch the hearts of youth, his devotion, to the last joined especially, was quite unique, and every boy who served under him should have passed through life with credit. The moment you entered his presence all seemed sunshine.

The short prayer over, before one commenced the morning's work, was followed by the words, "Laddies, cleanliness is next to Godliness," a pause, and then in a sharp quick voice, "Show your nails," on which every boy in the class had to thrust his hands out knuckles up, whilst he walked down the ranks, and all dirty nails had to go below the clean ones!

My tutor was also a man as near perfection as possible, the Rev. F. W. Farrar. With two such examples one ought to have grown into something very worthy, but, alas, youth does not always follow on the lines set.

My Harrow days over, I joined for six months the establishment of that excellent "Army coach" Jack Le Fleming, Eton House, Tonbridge, and finally went to Sandhurst as a cadet, obtaining my commission in the 6th L.I. just a year after passing out. The eighteen months at Sandhurst with a year of idleness which followed was so much time thrown away, for had I gone up for a direct commission just about the same time as I went up for Sandhurst I would have joined the Army in

'69 instead of '71. By this I do not mean to infer the training at Sandhurst was useless, far from it, but the years lost were far more valuable.

Like all youngsters, I was very pleased to receive joining orders, and as the regiment was about to proceed to India, where I was particularly anxious to serve my start in life, it was from a personal point a propitious one.

The 68th were stationed at Cork, and the 9th February was the date fixed for embarkation, and as my commission dated from 31st December, '71, there wasn't too much time to get uniform, etc., and join.

A raw winter's night saw me at Euston applying for an "Officer's" ticket for Cork, and I was glad to find W. G. Mansel similarly employed, he and I had been Harrow boys together, also cadets, and now we were about to join the same corps.

Railway travelling in Ireland was slow at this date, compared with England, besides which there was no provision made for satisfying the inner man on the train, so by the time we reached Cork the next evening we were famished, and looked forward to getting a square meal at the Mess, as we stood.

When we arrived at Barracks we were directed to the Mess-house and shown into the ante-room, whence we could hear the welcome sounds of knife and fork, and the "buzz" of cheery conversation. A message was whispered to the Adjutant that two youngsters had arrived, and another brought back that he would come to our rescue as soon as possible. Unfortunately for us a big guest night was going on, so it was some time before the Adjutant came out, and assured us that later on our turn would come, in the meantime hoping we would make ourselves at home, and pass the time with a whisky and soda and cigar.

Left alone, we came to the conclusion that if all the other officers were like the one whose acquaintance we had just made we were indeed fortunate. Nothing could have been nicer than our reception, and by the time the officers and guests trooped out we were fairly at ease, or as much at ease as our travel-stained garments, in the midst of men spick and span in mess kit, would admit of. All the younger officers had a cheery word for us, whilst the seniors gave us a bow or nod which completely assured us, and in a few minutes, under the guidance of the Adjutant, we were doing justice to an excellent, if late, dinner.

It was pointed out to us that as the Regiment was about to embark in a few days and a new regiment coming in to take our place, there were no available quarters in Barracks for us, so rooms had been engaged at the "Pig and Whistle," a "pub." facing the barrack gates, where we would find the accommodation quite comfortable. The meal over, we once more repaired to the ante-room where our kind friend introduced us to some of the seniors, who were not engaged at one of the several whist tables, and after another whisky and soda and smoke we started for the "Pig and Whistle" with mixed feelings. "Pig and Whistle" didn't sound attractive! However, we were pleasantly surprised, for when we reached our rooms we found all our belongings neatly arranged round the sides, convincing us that better men than ourselves had put up there before us.

The next morning, as proud as Punch, in bran new uniform, we made our way to the orderly room to report ourselves officially and enter the presence of the C.O., who was a very senior officer, and a bit "stand offish" in his manner. He did not keep us long and sent us to the "right about" with "The Adjutant will give you orders, gentlemen." In another hour we were on the Barrack Square with a squad of recruits, with the watchful eye of Hood, the Adjutant, on us.

The training we had undergone at Sandhurst came to our rescue, and as we both made up our minds to do our level best, we were soon pushed into more advanced squads and felt that our recruits course would be cut short, as it was.

On the 9th February we marched out of Cork Barracks carrying the Queen's and Regimental Colours for the first time and very proud we felt.

As the Regiment had been stationed at Cork for some time, the march through the town to the docks was quite a triumphal affair, and the send-off was a grand one. The majority of the men were light hearted to a degree, but some of the scenes were heartrending and pathetic. Women struggling to get on board the tugs which were to take us to the big white transport at Queenstown, children in arms being held up to kiss, for the last time, fathers, they would possibly never see again, sweethearts hanging on to lovers, and lovers rushing back to their sweethearts for one more embrace, knowing full well that in a few weeks these same sweethearts would through force of circumstances have to transfer their affections to men of the incoming regiment. Such was the scene, a very familiar one to those who have to superintend the embarkation of troops departing on foreign service.

Midst deafening cheers, the engines were set in motion, and soon waving handkerchiefs disappeared from sight, and one had hardly realised we had left our home shores perhaps for ever.

Once on board the Euphrates, one of Her Majesty's Indian transports, all was bustle and confusion, but in a marvellous space of time this was changed to order, and the officers were able to look for their quarters. In the pandemonium, the bowels of the ship far below the water line, I discovered the bunk allotted to me as a resting place for the next five weeks. One glimpse was sufficient, I vowed I would be the last to turn in and the first to turn out. The whole cabin was not more than eight feet square, and I had to share it with three others! It was too early to think what it would be like in the Red Sea!

Back on deck for roll call we found in addition to the Regiment that we were taking out a few details and a considerable number of officers belonging to units at Malta and in India, besides many ladies and children. Without further delay we weighed anchor and were soon passing through the mouth of the harbour, receiving the cheers of the garrisons in the forts that protect the entrance, which were heartily returned.

In a couple of hours we learnt the "Bay" was going to treat us with scant courtesy, and never shall I forget that crossing which kept us in absolute misery till we passed "The Rock," when for the first time you saw a smiling face or two, at all events that is how it appeared to me! It was wonderful to behold the change a calm sea and bright sunshine made, and it was a truly pleasing sight to watch the children running about quite unmindful of a week's sufferings. During the storm in the Bay there were a few accidents amongst the men, but nothing very serious, in fact the most serious happened to our Colonel, who had some fingers crushed by the slamming of a door.

We all looked forward with delight to our arrival at Malta, which meant a day's run on shore, and as I had several friends there who were on the look out for me, I intended having a good time of it. This, however, was considerably marred, for the moment we anchored we heard the terrible news of the assassination of Lord Mayo at the Andamans, where my father was Chief Commissioner, and my thoughts naturally ran to him, for I could well realise how this awful tragedy must have affected him.

It was nice to see old friends of Sandhurst days and hear their experiences of the service, and compare notes, for by this time I have no doubt we looked on ourselves as quite "old soldiers."

After doing the shops, and being properly done, in the matter of purchases of lace and cigars, we managed to put in a fairly pleasant day at the club and in sight seeing, till it was time to embark.

Our next halt was at Port Said, which appeared to me "a sink of iniquity." Most of us tried our luck at roulette, but I did not hear of anyone returning with more money in his pocket than it contained on landing. We managed, however, to pick up a cheap and plentiful supply of cigarettes besides rare (?) stamps, which turned out to be faked. After coaling we were none too sorry to enter the canal, which we looked forward to as a real "laze," but in this we were sorely disappointed, as we appeared to stick in the banks every five miles to the disgust of our captain, D'Arcy Irvine, who was without doubt at "boiling" point. In '72 the passage of the canal was a different undertaking to what it is now, and sometimes we stuck so fast that it looked as if we would never get out of this ditch. On more than one occasion we smashed every hawser we possessed, and the "music" was fairly loud! At each smash the "watches" working the windlasses were hurled in all directions, and the soldiers had a bad time of it, they were blamed for all mishaps, and for the time being sailors and soldiers were ready to go for each other's throats! After a couple of days we managed to get through, and all were glad to enter the Red Sea, which was, to put it mildly, a bit balmy. Half way to Aden we passed H.M.S. Glasgow with her flag at half-mast, as she was carrying the remains of the late Viceroy with Lady Mayo on board.

Without touching at Aden we continued our course to Bombay, and dropped anchor in that loveliest of lovely harbours, I think, on the morning of the 13th March. The view was absolutely superb, and it didn't require the soul of an artist to appreciate it.

Hours passed before anyone on shore troubled their heads about us. At last a launch came off, but it was only to take Spencer, of ours, on shore, his father, Sir Augustus, being Commander-in-Chief of the Bombay Army. We lolled about the decks all day with nothing to do till the afternoon, when the Chief came on board, and informed us we would not disembark till the morning.

A party of us went on shore after dinner to discover a deserted town, for barring a few natives no one was moving about, so our first impressions of life in India were doleful. We managed to find Watson's Hotel, and after a game of billiards slipped back to the ship to snatch a few hours' sleep. Long before daylight the lighters came alongside, and the serious question of disembarkation commenced. It was precious slow work and sultry. After a very inferior breakfast we entrained about 10 a.m., and did not reach Poona till dark, a journey which now takes some four hours.

Poona.

A march of two miles brought us to Barracks about 9 a.m., and the men were not long before they threw themselves down on their cots and were fast asleep. Dirty and tired, I was just about to follow suit on a pile of kit bags, when I heard my name being shouted out, and was more than delighted to find my friend, Cleveland of the 83rd, the bearer of the welcome news that they were waiting dinner for us at their Mess, and were putting us up for the night. In this way all our officers were carried off to the Messes of the 56th and 83rd, the two other British Regiments stationed at Poona. Never have I enjoyed a dinner more than that of the night of the 14th March, 1872. We kept it up till it was nearly time to think of a bath, and a voyage to our lines to look after our men. At Bombay we all picked up servants, who by some means or other discovered our temporary abodes during the night, and were in readiness at the break of day with "Master's" cup of tea! At this early stage we had to admit that Indian servants had good points about them.

By 9 a.m. every man in the Regiment had got outside a really good breakfast, which spoke well for the Indian commissariat. Order reigned in the barrack-rooms, by mid-day we had secured houses, hundreds of coolies, male and female, were arriving with furniture, which was procured on hire, and by night our Mess was in full swing! as if by magic.

I shared a house with Tyndall, commonly known as "Chang" in the Regiment, owing to his 6 feet 4 inches, who was in great request on account of his knowledge of horse flesh. Nearly every charger and pony purchased during the first fortnight passed through his hands.

Everything was new and strange, and therefore interesting. The conjurors and snake charmers were reaping a rare harvest, as they invariably do out of new comers, and up to now we had hardly left our lines. Most of our body servants being Mahomedans they were all excitement as the Mohurram was approaching, and told us a visit to the city to watch the procession of Taboots must not be missed, so on the eventful day "Chang," Deane Drake of the 56th, Cleveland of the 83rd, and myself chartered a "phaeton gharry," and toured the city under the guidance of our "coachman," who was a Moslem.

To "griffs," like ourselves, the Oriental crowd was most fascinating, the varied colouring, so different to the sombre black and grey of the West, was pleasing to the eye, and left us no time to think of the odour prevailing from the masses packed like sardines in the narrow streets we traversed at a foot's pace. Some of the Taboots were real works of art, which must have taken months to make, and what for (?) to be thrown on the last day of the festival into the river. The heat was very trying, and it was only when we got back to our bungalow we recognised how fatiguing six or seven hours of a carriage could be. After some light refreshment, I fell into a deep sleep till the first mess bugle sounded, when my friends roused me, and discovered me in a burning fever. I was popped into bed again and next morning had my case diagnosed as "Dengue" fever which is somewhat rare, very infectious, and particularly disagreeable, as it attacks the joints, and during the convalescent stages the feet and ankles, making walking not only painful, but ridiculous, for all the world like one suffering from an exaggerated form of St. Vitus's dance. In a few days nearly the entire Regiment was down with it, so the laugh was now on my side, as at first my pals thought I was "foxing."

The hospital was full, and the men had to be marched up in companies to get their morning and evening physic. Watching the men was quite comical, but they took it in good part, and cracked many a joke as they went along the roads like a lot of hopping idiots. In time the whole garrison suffered, and the disease spread all over the Bombay Presidency, causing several deaths among the ladies and children in some places.

In the matter of sociability we soon found India far in advance of Europe. Everyone knows his neighbour, and as the social position of each Government servant is laid down in the precedence code no mistakes are made in the matter of "who is to take in who."

The general rule of the country expects the "new comer" to call on the older resident, but in Poona it was the reverse as far as the married people were concerned; bachelors, however, had to do the round, a no easy matter in a large station. For some unknown reason, the two hottest hours of the day, from 12 to 2, were the visiting hours, and fortunate the man who could get through four calls in the day, for a visit entails driving up to the front verandah, where, as often as not, there is no servant in waiting to take your card, so sometimes you have to shout yourself hoarse, and in the end learn that it is a case of "darwaza bund," which being interpreted means the "door is shut." Whether you see the lady of the house or not the call is quite sufficient to secure you an invitation to dinner, and very pleasant functions Indian dinners are where all know each other well.

Poona being the largest military station on the Bombay side, was very gay, and the man who could not find recreation in the cricket, racquets, boating, racing, and riding was surely a waster and good for nothing. It had one drawback, however, the shooting in the vicinity was very poor, in fact you might say there was none. For a man it was about the best station I served in in India, and in the season I think the ladies thought the same, for they flocked there during and after the rains solely for the purposes of pleasure.

In the early seventies few subalterns dreamt of keeping a trap, so everything had to be done on the "Tat," and the subaltern's Tat was a marvel, day or night in all weathers he had to be in waiting; there was no time for the poor beast to even get lame or ill, for his master could not afford a second one! In those days I think mess bills must have been higher, for there are no signs of affluence now to account for the smart dog-carts you see every youngster the proud possessor of. The servant question, for the impecunious subaltern, was a difficult one, not because they were scarce, but on account of the huge slice they took out of his pay. The recognised establishment consisted of a butler on Rs. 30/-, dressing boy Rs. 10/-, syce Rs. 20/-, grass-cutter Rs. 5/-, Dhobi, or washerman Rs. 5/-, and barber Rs. 5/-, whilst you shared the following out-door servants with your friend: Mali or gardener Rs. 5/-, sweeper Rs. 4/-, Bhistie or waterman Rs. 6/-, and Ramoosie or night watchman Rs. 5/-. Add to these items your share of house rent Rs. 25/- and hire of furniture Rs. 15/-, the grand total came to Rs. 125/- per mensem, just 50 per cent. of your pay! As your butler invariably produced a bill of Rs. 30/- at the end of each month for Master's morning tea, needles, thread, and pipeclay, pay day was a most anxious one. The servants knew the exact hour Master would return from the pay office, and all would be in waiting dressed in their cleanest garments, wondering whether the bag he carried contained enough silver to go the round!

Without private means it seemed to me a physical impossibility for the British subtaltern to do ought else but get into debt. With experience officers are able to cut down their establishment, but for the three years we were at Poona this was not possible, for servants would not serve you for less pay, nor would any of them undertake double duties.

Taking it all round boating was the most popular form of recreation at Poona, the Club was well managed, and the boats were quite up to date. It had one drawback, however, as it entailed a ride or drive of three miles to the river, which meant a scramble to get back in time to dress for Mess. Nearly everyone used to row up to Kirkee, where the Gunners were stationed, and back, and by the end of the season these outings were responsible for most of the year's matrimonial alliances. About a mile up stream there was a glorious stretch on which all the regattas took place, and where an excellent view of the races was obtained from the spacious grounds of the Sassoon's, who threw these open and hospitably entertained all comers.

Next to boating the cricket ground attracted most people, and during the North and South match the whole of Poona assembled, and a very gay scene it was.

The races were invariably good, for men came from all parts of India to compete.

In the early seventies there was no polo to attract the general public every evening, so they crowded to the band stands, where there was no room for walking about, so the ladies sat in state in their carriages, whilst the men stood and chatted. Very dull affairs these were, made more dull by the strict rule of the day that all officers had to appear in uniform. This was, I believe, on one occasion resented by a gallant Highland Regiment, the officers of which appeared mounted in their kilts! Talking about uniform reminds me of the A.A.G. of the Poona Division, who was a perfect stickler for it—to go anywhere you had to pass this officer's house, and rumour had it that he spent his evenings watching for officers who dared to go out in mufti. Every week some officer was hauled up to orderly room for this offence, but the invariable excuse was the delinquent was on his way to the boat-house, but in spite of explanations of this kind he never wearied of handing men up.

The Club of Western India was, as it is to this day, quite the best in India, and many a cheery night I spent under its roof. One particularly festive occasion I well remember. Our party was

C

not a large one, only six in number, and after trying cards, billiards, supper, etc., till the small hours of the morning we decided to walk home with one of our number, who lived close by, just have one more "peg" at his house, and then see him between the sheets, as he appeared to be more sleepy than the rest of us. On entering his compound we spotted a harmless donkey grazing off his best flower pots, for there wasn't much else. Inside the house he immediately proceeded to prepare for bed, and before we had time to finish our whiskies and sodas had fallen into a dead sleep, when we thought of the donkey, which we seized, and after securing its legs, lifted bodily and placed it under the mosquito curtains alongside our friend, then taking our departure.

Soldiering at Poona was easy work, as it chiefly consisted of ceremonial parades on the race course, with possibly half a dozen field days in the year, due no doubt to the fact that the Artillery portion of the command was stationed at Kirkee, 5 miles off, and without guns field days are rather tame affairs. At first we were much interested in the native troops, which were astonishingly well drilled. The cavalry were particularly smart and excellent horsemen. Camps of exercise were rare. However, during our three years stay we had one for about three weeks at a place called Chinchwud, which was a delightful change for everyone. The scheme was not an ambitious one, but for all that we put in a lot of hard work in the way of marching and out-post duties, and were all sorry when it broke up.

One evening in March, '73, whilst most of the station were listening to the band near our lines, the "Regimental" and "Officers" calls were suddenly sounded, so all our fellows present dashed off to quarters to learn that four companies were to be in readiness to move off by train at the earliest notice. My company was one of the selected ones; it didn't take long to pack a uniform case and swallow a hurried meal at the Mess. An hour later we were marching to the station, and by 10 p.m. in the train en route to Bombay, for what purpose we did not know. There is always a good deal of mystery on these occasions, and this was no exception. Had a mutiny broken out greater reserve could not have been observed. We reached Bombay at dawn, and full of "importance" marched to a ready pitched camp on the Maidan, where we were told what the row was.

The Mohurram was on, and the Mahomedans as

a body were in that excited condition to take offence at the slightest provocation. The mild and usually law abiding Parsi supplied the want, through, I believe, the accidental fall of a Moslem woman or child from a top storey, which was exaggerated into an intentional push; anyhow, the authorities were quite unprepared for anything serious, for by the time the reinforcements arrived entire streets occupied by Parsees had been completely gutted, the sacred fires in their temples extinguished, and their community, generally, in a state of panic.

The European garrison of Colaba was quite unable to cope with the situation, and the Marine Battalion, composed chiefly, if not entirely, of Mahomedans was, for obvious reasons, not the most desirable body of men to call out, so they were confined to quarters, and matters were left to the Police.

Two of our companies were sent off at once to picquet different parts of the town, and later in the morning further troops came in, consisting of two guns R.H.A., one squadron 1st Bombay Light Cavalry, and 4th Bombay Rifles, whilst the Colaba garrison were fully occupied looking after that portion of Bombay. In addition some 500 N.C.O.'s and men from the different European

Regiments in the Presidency were quickly enrolled as special constables, and armed with truncheons. These men saw most of the fun, besides receiving extra pay.

The unrest lasted for a full month, as the pot was kept boiling by the Parsees enlisting city budmashes to do their dirty work.

Large Mahomedan crowds collected daily and "clamoured" to get at us, whilst we looked on till a Magistrate gave the order to "clear the street," after reading the Riot Act. It was a case of forming up across the street, fixing bayonets, quick march, and then the "double." The next minute empty streets with numberless sticks, pugarees, and old shoes clearly marked the lines of retreat.

The only time things looked really serious was the afternoon the Taboots were to be carried in procession and deposited in a selected tank. The authorities decided on prohibiting this "march," though they permitted the Taboots to assemble in a particular street with the strict injunction that no sticks were to be carried. Hindus and Parsees were warned to remain indoors.

An enormous crowd of Mahomedans with their Taboots collected at the appointed rendezvous, which was in front of the famous Pydhonie Temple. Here I was stationed with my company, two R.H.A. guns, one troop 1st Cavalry, four companies 4th Bombay Rifles.

Without doubt the crowd was a hostile one, and we were warned they intended to defy authority. A few isolated cases of assault began to occur, and then a rush was made, and the first person to suffer was the Commissioner of Police, who was knocked off his horse, and at the same moment several sentries were overpowered. For a short time it looked as if the men would be carried off their feet by the weight of numbers unless orders were given to use the bayonet or fire. Not an instant too soon we were told to go for them, and we went, without making much impression. In the twinkling of an eye, however, all was changed, the unsuspecting mob were attacked by the 500 special constables, with drawn truncheons, in reverse, and the butts of rifles did the rest. The two R.H.A. guns were ready loaded, and had they been fired there would have been a nice butcher's bill. As it was the damage consisted only of broken heads and limbs, whilst we secured quite 1,000 sticks, varying from the bamboo lathi to the swagger cane, amongst which there were several dozens Brigg, of St. James's Street, would have given a lot for.

Feeling ran high for some little time, during

which we were kept busy day and night, especially the latter, protecting the Parsees and their property. Gradually quiet was restored, and after a week's rest in camp, which most of us sorely needed, for the heat was intense, we returned to our respective stations.

The most interesting, if most unpleasant, post I was personally on, was that over the "Towers of Silence," situated midst a forest of cocoa nut palms on the southern slope of Malabar Hill. Here "Tommie's" remarks about the habits of the vultures, which infested the spot, were most instructive, and worthy of a professor of anatomy, for in time they recognised every joint of the human frame.

The Parsees were cunning enough to ingratiate themselves with "Tommy" by playing cricket with those not on duty, and relieving their thirst under cover of darkness with poisonous alcoholic drinks with disastrous result, especially when supplied to sentries on isolated posts. This hospitality had of course to be put down with an iron hand. With the help of a trusty sergeant and a couple of old soldiers I managed to catch some of these gentlemen red handed, to whom I administered justice in the corner of a quiet compound close by, much to the delight of "T. A." himself.

On our return to Poona we were much chaffed on our bloodless campaign, and the prospect of receiving leather medals; an outburst of jealousy on the part of those who had not had this slight change from the monotony of station life at a time when "Atkins" was not as well cared for as he is now.

The leave season was now open, so I obtained five months to visit my people at the Andamans. This entailed a journey by rail to Calcutta, whence a British India steamer left once a month for Port Blair, the head quarters of the settlement. Having a few days to spare at Calcutta I put up with the 14th Regiment in Fort William and did the City of Palaces as well as it could be done at about the hottest time of the year. The fort, as a fort, was a poor show, but it was spotlessly clean, and the glacis and surroundings as green as the most perfectly kept lawn to be seen in any part of the world, a relief to the eye not often obtained in the plains of India. Fort William was not popular, but to the subalterns of the British Regiment it had one attraction, for when on duty at the main guard they received a "gold mohur" extra for the 24 hours' work. The story goes that in days gone by some old gentleman took shelter in the verandah of the guard room from a heavy shower, and was entertained by the subaltern in command. The "old boy" was much struck with the scanty furniture provided, so in his will left a sum of money, the interest on which provided the "gold mohur a day" for the officer on duty.

Until I arrived in Calcutta I had no personal knowledge of jealousies between the Armies of the three Presidencies, so could not at first grasp the position or take in the inuendos! These jealousies were carried to the absurd extent of including British corps! The fact of being stationed in the Bombay command made one almost an object of pity!

Whilst one could understand a Bengal officer considering Bengal troops (native) superior to those of Bombay and Madras, my dull intellect could not follow the argument which implied that a British regiment in one locality was superior to that in another!

It did no harm to remind my hearers that during the mutiny, the loyality of the native armies of Bombay and Madras played an important part and lightened the task of the British troops to such an extent that we were in duty bound to stick up for them rather than run them down, and I should bear this fact in mind for ever and a day.

After a most enjoyable week I secured a passage on the British India steamer which visited the Andamans once a month, and on the 5th morning found myself at Port Blair, the Head Quarters island of the settlement, and on my way to the Chief Commissioners bungalow more grandly termed "Government House" in later years. It was a great pleasure to be once more with my parents, but after looking round the place and "doing" such sights as the islands could furnish the next thought was "what on earth is one to do here for the next 5 months?" The answer was "collect shells!" Oh, ye gods, had it come to this? Without doubt I was in a Penal Settlement! Like other new comers I scorned the idea, but no one cared and the subject was dropped till the next "spring tide," when I found myself joining a "shelling" party. How little we know ourselves—By the time I returned to Ross Island that evening I was as keen a "sheller" as any of them. I was not dressed for the enterprise, but quite regardless of this I entered the water waist deep and secured what proved to be absolute rubbish. In time, however, I gained knowledge, and before my departure had quite an interesting collection, containing many of the rarest shells.

It was an ideal place for boating, and I had my

fill—I visited every corner of the settlement and spent many happy days in those forests teeming with bird life seldom seen, and only heard of in books on Ornithology—When I say seldom "seen" I had forgotten the creations from Paris and elsewhere, which remind one of the destruction of nature, and I trust some day it will be put down.

Of course I visited that fatal spot where Lord Mayo was assassinated and heard the ghostly details of that tragedy which was still fresh in the minds of the many officials who witnessed the sad scene some 15 months previously.

These five months surrounded by nature in the tropics were as happy as any I can recall, so full of peace, repose and indolence, yet withal we were in the midst of thousands of the greatest cut throats India could provide, and aboriginal savages one couldn't get "forrarder" with on account of their unknown tongue.

With many regrets I said good-bye to all, and returned to Calcutta in the Government steamer "Undaunted" a paddle wheel tub one would think twice at boarding to cross the Thames at Westminster!

Fortunately we had a calm voyage which took some seven days only, giving me time to drive across Calcutta, catch my train, and eventually reached Poona, without an hour to spare, the end of September, '73.

'74 saw us still at Poona, but for two months before the break of the rains I was sent to Khandalla on the edge of the "Ghats" with a party of convalescents belonging to my regiment: there were similar detachments from the 7th Fusiliers and batteries at Kirkee. There were only two other officers, a Captain from the 7th, and a Medico. We were strangers to each other, but soon became friends. The Captain was one of the most entertaining men I ever met. He had served many years in that grand old corps "The Canadian Rifles," which had just been disbanded, and was quite new to the 7th. In appearance he was the double of "Lord Dundreary," the same whiskers, stammer, mannerisms, and abnormally large eye-glass.

The Medico was also a bit of a character, as he was, by repute, the original trumpeter who sounded the Light Cavalry Charge, with what truth I can't say, all I know is he never denied it when the question was put to him. Life at Khandalla was decidedly dull, though panthers were to be got by sitting up for them at night. We tried this frequently without success however. Excitement at last came in the shape of a telegram asking me to meet a certain train the same afternoon, and receive a pack of fox hounds, which the Poona hunt had just purchased.

At first I thought it was a hoax, but looking at the sender's name I knew this could not be the case. Amongst the men I thought it quite possible "one or two" might have had some knowledge of kennels, but when I mentioned the subject every man seemed to have been a kennel-boy. I picked out two of my own men and two more from the Artillery, and then set out to find a temporary kennel, which turned out to be a dilapidated bungalow well apart from the Bazaar. We soon had this place cleaned and the broken-down doors attended to. Three whips, five ponies and twelve couple of hounds had to be housed in the course of a few hours in a place where you could hardly purchase a nail.

At the appointed hour we met the train, and drove the "pack" through the Bazaar, much to the astonishment of the natives, who had never seen a hound before, to their new and strange home. The whip and his assistants were natives, but even they objected to such kennels; it was the best that could be secured in the time, so they had to lump it. The pack were distributed in different rooms, and the doors and windows made as secure as possible, leaving alterations and improvements for the morrow.

After the hot train journey the dogs were quite ready to settle down for the night after a meal. Having seen to their wants we dined and turned in later. The weather was warm, and all slept outside, but shortly after midnight we were startled from our sleep by shrill blasts that no "bugler" could have been guilty of. What was it? These were repeated over and over again, when we suddenly remembered the "hounds." We slipped on some garments, and half-dressed made our way in the dark to the kennels, where all was confusion. Three couple of hounds were trying to break out of a room, which fortunately had a sound door, and these with one dog-boy was all that was left of three whips and twelve couple hounds. The boy was so frightened he could hardly speak, but from him we learnt the house had been surrounded by "tigers," and the hounds were in full cry!

You can picture the utter helplessness of our position. Here we were in the dark with precipices and dense jungle on all sides. We could hear both hounds and horns, so made for the high road in the hope that the whips had done the same. When daylight came we were all well separated, but by 10 a.m. we had collected, and a more miserable gathering you can hardly conceive. Leaving man out of it, we mustered eleven hounds cut and torn by stones and thorns, three fearfully wounded, whilst two were known to be dead, and two were never seen again.

The wounded ones in spite of every attention died inside the week. All this was the work of probably two panthers.

The question of new quarters had to be decided, when Captain "Lord Dundreary" suggested the cells! a bright idea which was soon seized. One cell was turned into a hospital, where our medico did all he could to save the wounded ones.

This very sad beginning made the remaining hounds all the more precious; every man in the depot seemed to think he was personally responsible for their welfare, and soon they would have become lap dogs and no longer fit for the chase. Discipline was established, and indiscriminate feeding prohibited. In the evenings we used to give three or four Tommies a treat, and allow them, mounted on "Tabs" from the Bazaar, to take them out for exercise along the one solitary road we possessed. All went well till the "General" inspected us. Having no prisoners, we did not expect him to visit the cells, but occupied or not he *had* to see them, and the captain was solemnly asked to produce his authority for the "misappropriation"! After the best lunch we could give him and his staff, he took me aside and told me I must pay for the whitewash!

With the break of the Monsoon we all returned to Poona and Kirkee, and the following October I said good-bye to Poona and proceeded to join a garrison class at Mhow, the regiment following some two months later. This "class" kept me going till April, '75, when I was ordered on detachment to Asseerghur, a curious old fortress on the top of a solitary hill, standing out in a jungle that was at all times famous for its big game.

This was the dullest place I ever struck; my captain thought of nothing but shikar, and the consequence was I could never get out except for the day. The garrison boasted a commandant and fort adjutant, one company of ours, and a wing of a native regiment, with two medical officers, and what for? To look after some six State prisoners who were kept in solitary confinement, but well fed. In the evenings they were allowed an hour's walking exercise on a measured 100 yards between sentries. These men were Kookahs, a sect of Sikhs who in 1872 had given some trouble in the Loodiana district of the Punjab, and splendid specimens they were, who bore their confinement with the dignity of kings. We always felt very sorry for them, as we visited them daily to ask if they had any complaints. At one time Asseerghur was impregnable, and remained so for centuries. Where they got the labour to build those walls, those gateways, and those tanks cut out of the rock is as great a puzzle as the pyramids of Egypt. In addition, there was a very fine musjid, which was converted into a barrack. The perimeter of the fort could not have been more than a mile, and yet it contained some capital bungalows, with good gardens, in which an excellent grape grew.

There were two entrances to the fort, one by a flight of some 500 stone steps and the other by an elephant road, which any engineer might have been proud of. The walls of the fort were almost perpendicular natural rock. The vast jungles round were full of big game, including tiger, bison, panther, bears, samphur, nilghai, and cheetah, but the officers on duty had no chance against those men, who during the hot weather obtained two and more months' leave simply for shikar purposes, and secured the services of the best shikaris, without whom the hunter is nowhere.

There were men in the Bombay Presidency who came here every year, and had the monopoly of the sport, as every local shikari of note was in their pay. Not very long before we arrived two men of the regiment we relieved on this detachment were walking through the jungles, and their conversation turned on the Indian Mutiny, particularly the slaughter of the innocents. Their indignation rose to such a pitch that one of them remarked, "Let us kill the first nigger we see," said probably without a thought of doing such a deed. Unfortunately, at the moment, a harmless Bunia happened to come up with them on his pony, and without hesitation they pulled him off and murdered him in a thick part of the jungle. On the way back to the fort one of them showed signs of nervousness, on which his comrade threatened to do for him unless he swore by all that was holy to keep the secret. Having given his solemn promise, they continued their way, but on arrival at the main guard the repentant one rushed into the guard-room and gave the story away, and in the end both were hanged.

In the month of December we rejoined regimental headquarters at Mhow, and proceeded by route march to Nusseerabad, dropping a wing at Neemuch.

At this time India was astir; for the first time in the history of the country the natives were realising that the land of their birth was in truth a portion of the dominions of "the Great White Queen," who had sent her son out to tour their land, and let them know through him how highly she prized her Eastern possession and subjects. The Prince of Wales, with a brilliant staff, was the guest of the country, and no one could have represented better the throne the natives more than "professedly" looked up to.

This visit was the greatest compliment Her Majesty could pay the country, and the people felt this. Natives of all castes and creeds travelled hundreds of miles, regardless of toil and expense, to catch even one glimpse of the "Shahzada," their future King and Emperor.

The very poorest in the land flocked to the towns, and even to the smallest railway stations through which the Royal train would pass. It mattered not to these poor, loyal souls whether it was day or night, whether they saw his face or not, they made the effort, they did their duty, and they trudged wearily back to their villages, satisfied if disappointed.

We were on the march to Nasirabad, so were quite out of it, and not one of us set eyes on H.R.H., which was a bitter disappointment to us, as, according to the original programme, we were detailed for escort duty during one of the visits to a Native State in Rajputana, but a change of the "menu" knocked this on the head.

The march of some 300 miles took about a month, and was most enjoyable. As a rule we started at 3 a.m., and reached our camping ground in time for breakfast, thus having the days free for shooting, which was not good, though we managed to get a few bags of snipe and duck, with an occasional black buck, whilst the men shikared "doves" and a few hares. The "families" under the tender care of the quartermaster were always a march ahead of us. As we approached our new ground the tail of carts carrying the women and children was disappearing, the husbands forming the escort. In this way the women and children always had their nights in bed. There is something very fascinating about camp life in spite of the everlasting packing and unpacking. Sundays are always halting days, and with one other halt during the week all had a welcome rest, to wind up with a camp fire and sing-song after dark. The only drawback I can remember was the cost, as the officers have to pay for their "carriage," which also hits the families, as the Government allowance was insufficient. The married soldier in India, besides his "Penates," carries a menagerie which is truly wonderful, and, curiously enough, he doesn't mind spending his money in this way.

After a month of the "road" most are fed up, but given a week in barracks, I believe all would be happy to start again!

Well, having arrived at Nasirabad, there isn't much to say, beyond its being one of the most God-forbidding places you can imagine. One broad road called "The Mall," dilapidated houses on each side, within compounds of some three to five acres, containing nothing but the milk-bush to catch the eye, not a flower, not a blade of grass, excepting the general's compound, where the Peepal and the Banian grew as if to distinguish "Master" from "Man." Besides the general, there were two celebrities, the "Cantonment Magistrate" and "Bhimraj." All military stations have a cantonment magistrate, usually a Staff Corps officer, though in rare cases a civilian, attached to the staff of the general or other officer commanding, who looks after the civil and criminal administration of the cantonment; but here we discovered he was something quite superior to the "article" we had been accustomed to, and found him to be a "Political," a satellite of the Indian Foreign Office, with a "Boss" he spoke of as "The Chief," and who possessed the high-sounding title of "Agent Governor General for Rajputana and Chief Commissioner of Ajmere Merwara." That is not a bad mouthful, is it? He was No. 1 aforementioned celebrity; No. 2, Bhimraj Chogalal, house owner, horse racer, moneylender, subaltern's friend. He owned every house in the station, and was therefore everyone's landlord. Reports says he came into his possessions after the Mutiny, when most natives bolted. From that day to the present the houses have remained the same, barring the actual wear and tear of fifty years. He died, poor old chap, about 1896, to the last a subaltern's friend.

In his affluent days his acts of kindness were numerous, and those who knew him well always think of him with respect. I last saw him a few days before his death, and his last words were, "My lord, I'm poor man," and I know he spoke the truth.

After a sojourn of only three months I was appointed A.D.C. to my father, commanding the Lahore Division, so said good-bye to the Bombay Presidency, little thinking that later in life I would spend nearly ten years of my service at Ajmere, a civil station only fourteen miles distant.

The month of April saw me at Meean Meer, and now I had an opportunity of getting an insight to the famous Bengal Army and see soldiering under more serious conditions. From the first I discovered the further you went north there was less play and more work. By this I do not mean to insinuate that an A.D.C.'s life was overburdened with the latter in the piping times of peace, but without doubt the training of the troops was much more severe than in the Presidency I had just left. In some ways this was accounted for by the climate, which is ideal during the five cool months when soldiering is the order of the day, after seven months of heat which makes this quite impossible.

Just at first life in the Punjab seemed tame after Poona and the other stations known to me, but the hot weather was just commencing, so it was not quite fair to make comparisons. We thought it was fairly balmy at times in the Western Presidency, but after a month or two of Meean Meer one realised what hot weather really meant. As nearly all the ladies leave for the hills, the station was practically a man's station, but we managed to make the best of it at the racquet court and swimming bath, with a visit to one of the messes after dinner for a rubber, till it got cool enough to make sleep possible, if it ever did get cool even at night.

As soon as the hot weather was over and people returned from the hills, Meean Meer was quite transformed by its closeness to Lahore, where every man and his wife spent their evenings in the delightful gardens, and where hardly a week passed without a dance at the Montgomery Hall, for the civilian element of Lahore entertained their soldier friends right royally. A good deal of my cold weather, however, was taken up with touring with the general, the out-stations being Mooltan, Ferozepore, Amritsur, Bukloh and Dharmsala. All the troops in the Punjab were in a high state of efficiency owing to the frequent calls on them for active service on our frontier. Seeing so many different troops added to one's knowledge considerably, and the desire for active service was almost a craving, so no one was sorry when rumours of Russian aggression filled the air.

In the early half of 1878 a contingent from India was sent to Malta, including Bengal Cavalry, apparently with the object of frightening (!) Russia, who at the time had a victorious army in the field threatening Constantinople.

In reply to this demonstration Russia immediately despatched troops towards the Afghan frontier. To the uninitiated British subaltern this move to the west on our part was difficult of solution, for in the event of any serious trouble in the East involving a war with Afghanistan and Russia, it was well known, even to him, that the forces in India would not only require the presence of every available fighting man, but heavy reinforcements from home. So, on the face of it, the Malta contingent struck youngsters as being nothing more than "bluff," whilst the newspapers of the day pronounced it a case of "checkmate" on the part of "Dizzy." We in India did not care whether it was bluff or not; all we wanted was active service.

Personally, I felt anything but happy, as my father was proceeding, or had just proceeded, home on six months' sick leave, and I was a sort of nobody's child. The air was full of rumours, and I was more than pleased to learn towards the end of September that my father was returning, with every chance of being selected for one of the commands, in the event of our declaring war against Afghanistan, which seemed inevitable from the moment Neville Chamberlain's Mission was turned back.

He arrived in Bombay the middle of October, proceeded straight to Simla, and by the end of the month was in Mooltan superintending the concentration and despatch of his division, which at the time was called the Mooltan Division, to distinguish it from General Biddulph's or the Quetta Division, which was concentrating at that point, and which combined were to form the Southern Afghan Field Force, under my father, so soon as they met in the Peshin Valley, before crossing the frontier. At the same time the Khyber Force, under General Sam Browne, and the Kuram Force, under General Roberts, were assembling with the intention of attacking at those two points, whilst the Southern Force had Candahar as its objective.

We left Mooltan on the 17th November by rail, went into camp at Sukkur the next day, and on the morning of the 19th commenced our long march to Candahar. Our transport consisted entirely of camels, and a wild, untrained lot they were. Never shall I forget our start. These beasts had never seen soldiers before, so the troubles of loading were endless, and when this was over and the beasts rose with their loads the fun began, bucking, kicking and wriggling until they got rid of everything, and the country round was strewn with every description of article, private and public, you could think of. It had all the appearances of a camp which had been taken by surprise. All had to be reloaded, and it was only when we reached our next camp we discovered our losses and breakages. This sort of thing continued for some days, until we faced a thumping march of thirty miles, across the "Pat," two or three marches beyond Jacobabad, which seemed to tame man and beast, for after that both got on better together; and by the time we reached the foot of the Bolan Pass, when our serious work commenced, all were glad of a day's halt.

If our camels did well in the Pass, the bullocks drawing the artillery wagons completely broke down, and the consequence was these had to be dragged up by the infantry, who in spite of the fatigue took it all in good part without a murmur, though all were thankful when they reached the top.

After a bitterly cold night we started for Quetta on the morning of the 8th, in the teeth of a biting wind which cut our cheeks till they bled, and convinced us of the wisdom of discarding razors. Here some of the elephants died of cold, a most serious loss at this juncture.

After a march of some twelve miles we reached Quetta, the headquarters of the Biluchistan Agency and our most advanced frontier station. After a halt of a couple of days we continued the march across the Peshin Valley to Killa Abdullah, where Biddulph's Division was encamped, on the 14th.

The situation was anything but pleasant for a commander about to enter an enemy's country, for in addition to our own losses in transport we found General Biddulph's were far heavier, and how to replace them at once was beyond the conception of man. The almighty dollar was also scarce. However, treasure was coming up, and Sir Robert Sandeman, the Resident, was scouring the country for camels. During the delay which followed, the troops were employed improving the road up and over the Khojak to Chaman, where we had an outpost.

The Lorna River, which runs through the Peshin Valley, gave some trouble to the artillery, as there were several quicksands, into one of which one of our guns blundered, necessitating the turning of the stream.

By the 31st all the troops had concentrated, and the 1st January saw both divisions in Afghan territory, Biddulph's by the Khojak and the other by the Gwaja Pass. On the Afghan side of the Khojak a "slide" had been cut, down which the guns were rolled.

As we emerged from the Gwaja Pass all was desolation; to the west nothing but a rolling sandy desert, and to our front and east rocky hills and stone-strewn plains, without a sign of a tree or vegetation, as unforbidding a country as you would wish to see.

On the fringe of the desert there were a few pools where we found thousands of Imperial sand grouse, as tame as barndoor fowls, and in a very short time we secured a nice addition to our commissariat. They were in grand condition, and so tame or frightened that you could knock them over with sticks. It was quite a remarkable sight. When you fired at them they only rose to alight at your feet like tame pigeons. With time and ammunition the worst shot in the world could have made a record bag!

On the 4th the advanced guards of the two divisions, marching on parallel lines, came in contact with some 500 Afghan horse, who were soon dispersed with a loss of some 100 killed and wounded, whilst we had only seven wounded. Major Luck, of the 15th Hussars, in a personal encounter, nearly lost his sword arm, which was only saved by a thin chain rein which his servant had stitched inside the sleeve of his jacket. These Afghan horsemen after the scrimmage rode straight for Candahar, and after a rest made tracks for Herat, never to be seen again. The Governor of Candahar, Mir Afzul, having no money at his disposal, and the troops being in arrears of pay, could not persuade more troops to come our way. On the dead we found Russian gold roubles, which had been given these horsemen to come out and stay the advance of two divisions! One felt sorry for the poor beggars.

The 6th saw us encamped outside Candahar, after a portion of the troops of each division had marched through the city, and lines of evil-looking Candaharis, who stared at us in a surly manner with no signs of emotion or even curiosity.

Candahar itself is hardly worth describing, a collection of flat-roofed, mud-built houses, with a high and rather formidable wall round it, and a large gateway in the centre of each face. There are only two main streets, one running north and south, the other east and west, and where these cross covered by a large dome, which forms a sort of bazaar and octroi office, a shelter in bad weather, a meeting-place for merchants to discuss business, or Ghazis to plot their evil designs. You see Candahar at its worst in mid-winter; from a distance it is picturesque enough, and when the summer approaches no doubt it will look attractive owing to the numerous gardens well-stocked with all sorts of fruit trees. The Citadel, or "Ark," near the Cabul gate, is quite "fine" compared with its surroundings, and provided us with good and substantial quarters for two companies of British troops, a hospital, officers' quarters, and gardens. In front of the citadel there is an open space, inside which no Căndaharis were allowed, except on business.

We had not been many days in the place before we made the acquaintance of the local Ghazi, who selected Major St. John, our senior Political Officer, and Lieutenant Willes, to operate on, without result, I'm glad to say, as the gentleman either forgot to put a bullet in his pistol or the bullet was so much smaller than the bore that it fell out.

It could hardly have been a "miss" in the case of St. John, as when the man fired the muzzle was within a foot of his body. The man was at once overpowered, and in the course of a few hours was hanged on the spot in the presence of the townspeople, the gallows being formed of three scaling ladders, whilst the drop was a couple of rum barrels, which were jerked away as soon as the knot was adjusted.

The execution was carried out with due solemnity, and the crowds looked on without the slightest concern from the streets and the tops of the houses in the vicinity; women and small children gazed on the scene as if it were an everyday sight. They are a cold-blooded lot. The only persons who felt any concern were the officers on duty and the guard surrounding the gallows.

The situation was a peculiar one, as there was absolutely no government, so there was nothing left but for the general to assume full powers, which he did with the help of the Political Officers.

After a few days it was decided that Biddulph's Division should proceed in the direction of Herat as far as Giriskh, whilst my father and the other division marched to Khelat-i-Ghilzi. We started on the 15th and reached Khelat-i-Ghilzi 22nd January, which we found completely deserted. The fortress, if held, would have given no trouble to modern guns, and would have proved a death-trap to the garrison, as there was no means of escape. During our stay the general presented the Order of British India to the Subadar Major of the 12th Khelat-i-Ghilzi Regiment of the Bengal Army, much to this old gentleman's surprise and delight, as forty years previously he formed one of the garrison which held the fort during the first Afghan War. After the presentation he showed the general round, and pointed out the different points of interest. The weather so far had been most friendly, but on the return march rain and snow fell, which made camping anything but pleasant, and our losses in transport were enormous.

For weeks we had to content ourselves with our daily ration of rum, and many were reduced to smoking dry lucerne for baccy. Shortly after we got back to Candahar I paid £1 for quarter of a pound of golden leaf at the auction of a deceased officer's effects.

On the return march of Biddulph's column his rear-guard, composed of some 250 men of the Scinde Horse, had a very pretty brush with the enemy, 150 of whom they placed *hors de combat* with a loss of only some six or seven men killed and wounded.

The serious question of rationing and replenishing our transport had now to be considered, but these difficulties were overcome by degrees, though I expect we had to pay a price. The Engineers had their hands full building quarters for our division, which was to remain, whilst Biddulph's returned to India, and most excellent quarters they rigged up on most economical lines, with a rapidity that was quite marvellous, for before the hot weather came on every man in the force was comfortably housed.

Hardly a week passed without a Ghazi springing

up, so a permanent gallows was erected outside the Cabul Gate, where I have seen as many as three men at a time executed.

At this time I was a candidate for the Indian Army, so was posted to the 15th Sikhs, quartered in the Citadel, to go through the term of probationership, and a very charming time I had with this splendid corps. The colonel, Barter, commanded one of our brigades, so the regiment was under the command of Major Hennessey, with Inglis, Smyth, Abbott and Hadow as his subordinates, and Surgeon-Major Cunningham in medical charge, a better lot of fellows you could not meet. Being quartered in the Citadel, and having sole charge of the town, we escaped all convoy duties, so were more fortunate than others, as the regiment was never broken up. With the officers doing duty with the detachment of British troops and several departmental officers who were also stationed in the Citadel we formed a very pleasant coterie of our own, and managed to pass the time playing most vigorous games of rounders, hockey, etc., with the men in the square by day and "poker" in the evenings. We had a few guns between us and a limited supply of ammunition, which we expended on a "jheel" outside the Shikarpare Gate, where we found sufficient snipe to keep our mess going. When our ammunition began to fail we made use of country powder and shot, which Abbott very cunningly manufactured. The pellets were not always round, but they were equally destructive!

As the hot weather approached and we knew our stay was to be of some duration, garrison life in Candahar became duller, but the British soldier is a sportsman by instinct, and he is quite happy looking on at a good game of football or cricket, or even wandering through a bazaar, when he airs the few words of Hindustani he happens to know, mixed up with his mother tongue. He keeps up a running conversation with an Oriental who does not know one word of his language, and goes away quite happy and satisfied. Many and many a time have I watched T.A. walking alongside of a Pathan conversing in English, and being answered in Pushtu or Persian, whilst both seemed to be thoroughly enjoying themselves and in some unaccountable manner understanding each other. Similarly you see T.A. and Jack Sepoy palling up. This is markedly so amongst the Tommies and Goorkhas and Sikhs. The native soldier is always a happy man on service, which is about the only time he can accumulate wealth, for with his free ration he can send his monthly wage to his family, knowing that on his return an extra field or well will have been purchased or dug.

The unmarried British soldier is also happier on service, for he loves new scenes and environments, and is also able to save a bit.

So putting everything together I do not think our force was in the least sorry to remain a year in the country after the months of hard marching and work. With spring the place began to look attractive, and the fruit season brought a change of diet that made up for a lot. The grapes, apples, apricots, and nectarines were a dream, which could be purchased for a few coppers. Last, but not least, all ranks were well housed, and barring convoy work the duties were not too heavy. The health of the troops was excellent till that awful scourge cholera put in an appearance and carried off the strongest and healthiest, whilst it seemed to skip over the weaker ones. No other disease causes depression amongst soldiers so much as this scourge, and the only way to battle with it is by exerting oneself to the utmost by getting up amusements of all kinds, if you are unable to move your men about by frequent changes of camp. A disastrous engagement is *nothing* compared with the funerals of a few patients who have died from cholera for lowering the spirits of soldiers.

When we were first attacked we were fortunately not unprepared. It approached by steady marches from the plains, and we almost knew to the day when to expect it, and when it did attack us it was with relentless fury; but we also could guess within a week when it would probably disappear. Like all epidemics of cholera, the unforeseen occurred. Whilst it was raging in the healthier cantonments the 15th Sikhs, quartered in the confined Citadel surrounded with cases, remained untouched. Our largest cholera hospital was in their midst; every guard on the gates had to keep a count of the dead bodies of Candaharis streaming through, who had succumbed to the disease, for purposes of record, and still not a man was touched. Why, no one could say! unless it was due to the fact the men pulled themselves together and, like holding the post of honour, were determined to face that ordeal and do their best. If other troops were in any way depressed there were no signs of this amongst the 15th Sikhs, one of the grandest regiments that ever carried arms.

They rose to the occasion like men, and they had a just reward. On one day alone I remember attending the funerals of five officers, one of whom, a young doctor, I spoke to in apparent health a few hours before he was carried to his last resting-place.

There was one particularly sad case of a sergeant in the 59th who was employed in the Cholera Hospital for British soldiers, where he had attended nearly every patient, having a cheery word for each. The epidemic was on the decline, in fact it had nearly worn itself out, when this N.C.O., who had been resting for an hour or so on his cot, suddenly got up, rolled his bedding, said good-bye to his comrades present, and walked to the ward where there were a few convalescent cases, and died in a few hours, apparently without making a struggle for life!

Many men do die from nervousness, but here was a man who saw the worst of the epidemic and for weeks, night and day, cheered those who appeared despondent, without any sign of fear, and who when seized himself made no effort to pull himself together. Without doubt this man had overworked himself, and would not admit he was ailing until it was too late. He lay down on a cot in the ward, collapse followed shortly, and before evening the end had come. The devotion of the medical officers and their subordinates no words can do justice to.

The last week in August, with a clean bill of

health, we were only too pleased to think of packing our belongings and preparing for an early return to India, resigned to the fact we had practically seen no active service, which was a bitter disappointment to all, when rumours began to circulate that things were going wrong elsewhere, the details of which were mere guesswork. However, we were not kept in suspense long. Some important event had taken place in Cabul, but no one was prepared to hear of the awful tragedy at the Bala Hissar, where Sir Louis Cavagnari and his entire escort were massacred on the 3rd September. It was some days before the details reached us, but that something very serious had occurred was beyond doubt, as orders were at once issued for all troops to return to quarters from camp. When the particulars were given out, we naturally thought our force would be relieved without delay and Cabul would be our destination. So it was with further disappointment we learnt we were to stand fast, whilst an army from India, under Sir F. Roberts, was to have the privilege of avenging our comrades who had been so basely massacred. Luck was dead against us, but we kept up our spirits by speculating on an early march to Herat, only to be once more disappointed.

Early in October I obtained three months' leave

to India, and having been promoted Captain in the 68th L.I., I proceeded to Meean Meer the end of December to join my regiment. On arrival at the railway station I received a wire from my father, saying, "Join me at once. Ayub is advancing; I meet him on the Helmund."

So instead of joining I replenished my oufit and set out for Candahar once more, full of hope and excitement, after enjoying a cheery Christmas dinner with friends and relations.

The rail was now open as far as Jacobabad, so telegraphed to Colonel Nuttall, commanding, to kindly secure me a good riding camel for myself and four baggage ones for my belongings, orderly and servant, and to arrange for these latter to be relieved by four fresh camels at each stage up the line, as I purposed marching through day and night without a halt. On arrival at Jacobabad in the evening of the next day I found all ready, so sent all off in charge of Bolaka Sing, my orderly, a sepoy in the 15th Sikhs, with instructions to push on as many stages as possible till I caught them up. Having a 350 mile march in front of us I naturally meant my servant and the orderly to ride the very lightly weighted camels, but when I caught them up the next evening I found Bolaka Sing steadily "footing" it, and nothing would induce him to accept a mount, his argument being he would fall asleep like the others, and one morning we would wake up to find ourselves separated. Nothing I could say had any effect on him, and the result was this man marched 57 miles a day for six days, carrying a rifle and 90 rounds of ammunition, without a halt day or night, in mid-winter. The only rest he had was when the baggage was being changed to fresh camels at each stage. As regards food, morning and evening cooked rations were ready for him and my servant.

Sixteen miles out of Candahar I found a horse waiting, so got in in time for dinner on the sixth day, and by midnight my things had arrived. I asked Bolaka Sing how he felt and how much further he could have gone. His reply was to the point and short, "Two more days, sahib, and then I would have died." It was a remarkable performance, and before dropping the subject I must mention one incident that occurred on the road.

One morning, just as the sun was beginning to get warm and we were about to start after changing the baggage camels, I asked Bolaka Sing for my helmet, which during the night was always put inside a "morah," or cane seat, which was slung to one of the camels upside down, thus forming an excellent "hat case." The helmet was not forthcoming, so on thinking the matter over I came to the conclusion it must have been jerked out when crossing one of the streams or dry beds of streams during the night, and mentioned this to him. All were ready to move on, when I was surprised to see Bolaka Sing standing strictly at "attention" and saluting, so asked him what was up? He replied that he was going to *run* back for the helmet and would soon catch me up! As the missing "headgear" was anything from fifteen to twenty-five miles behind it was hardly probable I fell in with the proposal, so with a smile told him not to bother about it, that I would telegraph to India for another on arrival at the nearest post where this was possible.

The man was quite unhappy, and as the day got warmer he seemed to think of nothing but my "cranium," and looked sad and wretched. At the time we had covered over 200 miles of our journey, so the man's devotion was of a high order and typical of the Sikh.

If I was glad to get between the sheets and enjoy a comfortable night's rest, what must his feelings have been when he turned in that night for the first time since leaving Jacobabad, 350 miles off?

I was now re-appointed A.D.C. to my father

and soon learnt that the prospects of excitement and service were not far off. It did not come from the direction of Herat, nor did it come quickly, for not until the 30th March did we turn our backs on Candahar and commence our march to Cabul. The weight of baggage allowed each officer was reduced to a minimum, for we were terribly short of transport, without any prospect of picking up any animals to take the place of casualties. As far as Kelat-i-Ghilzi the march was familiar and uneventful, but as forage was scarce our animals were growing weaker, so in response to an appeal we began to throw away every article we could dispense with. This was possible, as each day the weather was milder, though still cold at night and in the early mornings. After leaving Kelat we all felt happier with the increasing prospects of at last meeting an enemy, who could be seen in the distance hovering on our front and flanks.

In the valleys we found a certain amount of green crops, which came in very useful as far as filling the bellies of our hungry camels was concerned. Other supplies were almost unprocurable, as the villages were not only deserted but in flames, the work of the Hazaras who hovered in large bands on our flank doing as much damage as they could to their hated rivals, the Afghans.

Barter's Brigade, which had been marching on a line to our right parallel with us, joined us at Mookur on the 14th April, after which we continued as a compact division of all arms ready to tackle anyone, but it was not until we reached Mooshaki on the 18th we felt certain a fight was near at hand.

At daylight on the morning of the 19th April we left camp Mooshaki with A/B R.H.A. and 2nd Punjab Cavalry leading, under General Palliser, followed by the 1st Infantry Brigade, under General Hughes, consisting of the 59th Foot, 2nd Sikhs and 3rd Goorkhas, behind them the 19th Bengal Lancers, G/4 R.A., with escort of 19th P.I., the General and staff, with escort of one company 2/60th Rifles and one company 25th P.I., followed by the baggage, at the head of which were three companies 19th P.I., the baggage guard and Heavy Battery, whilst the 2nd Brigade, under General Barter, composed of the 2/60th Rifles, 15th Sikhs and 25th P.I., with the 1st Punjab Cavalry, brought up the rear, the head of the 2nd Brigade being some five miles from the advanced troops of the 1st Brigade.

After covering some seven miles the advanced cavalry sent in word the enemy were in sight to the left front of our advance. At this moment we were peacefully enjoying a halt and eating breakfast.

The country being open the troops were ordered to advance with a broad front, if my memory is correct "in line of columns" till we reached a point some 1,600 yards from the position held by the enemy, where we found A/B and the 2nd P.C. halted just to the right of the road along which our right flank had been marching. The infantry were now ordered to deploy to the left in a more or less crescent formation in keeping with the general run of the position of the enemy, A/B and the 2nd P.C. still slightly in advance of the right of our line.

In rear of the right of our line and slightly to the right of the road rose a small knoll of about 60 or 70 feet high, on the top of which the General took up his position to obtain a better view of the Terrain, and with the aid of glasses watch the parking of the baggage and advance of the 2nd Brigade.

At this moment the force was as follows: A/B in action facing the enemy, with the 2nd P.C. in squadron columns on its right both slightly in advance and to the right of the 59th, in prolongation of which came the 2nd Sikhs and 3rd Goorkhas to its left in partly crescent formation with the extreme left thrown back. G/4 in rear of the right of the 59th and the 19th Bengal Lancers in rear of the left of the 3rd Goorkhas, one company of 19th P.I. escort to G/4, and the General's escort companies in rear of these again, whilst three companies of the 19th P.I. were near the 19th B.L.

Now a sudden flutter was observed amongst the enemy, who began to show up on the crest line in greater numbers and disclose many standards, which no doubt meant the "blessing" of the same by their Mullahs, and it looked as if they intended upsetting all the General's plans by atackingt him. So to give them no excuse for this he ordered me to go to General Palliser and warn him "on no account open fire." I delivered this very distinct order, and returned in haste. It was now a question of "intention." Did they intend swooping down on us or were they considerate enough to await our attack? The General's idea being to close up the baggage and wait the arrival of the 2nd Brigade.

We were not kept long in suspense, for I had barely reached my father, who was descending the knoll on the reverse slope when bang went our first gun, and then another! He looked at me as much as to say "What the devil have you done?" but before he could speak I repeated the order as I had

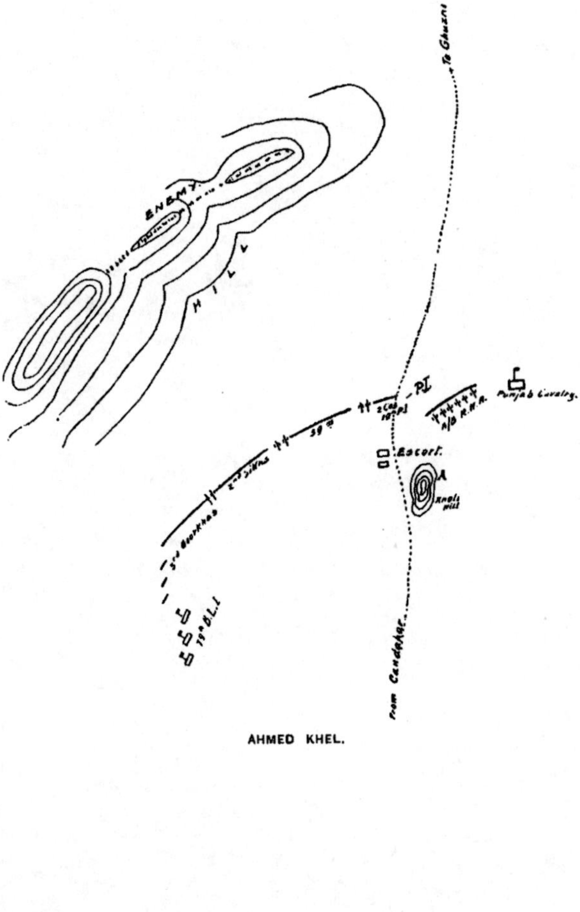

To Ghuzni
ENEMY.
HILL
P.I
2 Cos 19th P.I
A/B R.H.A.
Punjab Cavalry.
59th
2nd Sikhs
3rd Goorkhas
19th B.L.I
Escort.
A
Knoll Hill
From Candahar

AHMED KHEL.

conveyed it to General Palliser. We scrambled down the slope as fast as our horses could carry us, and swept round the base of this knoll to a position in rear of the centre of the 59th, and at the same moment saw A/B taking up a better position a little in rear of their original one. Apparently the very first round decided the Ghazis, who by this time were swarming down the hill side straight for us as hard as they could tear, and before you could say "Jack Robinson" every gun and rifle of ours was blazing away as fast as the men could load, whilst Sir John Campbell, commanding G/4, brought two of his guns into action on the right of the 59th, and detached two more to the right of the 2nd Sikhs and 3rd Goorkhas respectively.

It was a glorious sight to watch these swordsmen advancing under such a withering fire without a thought of halting; on and on they came till they actually struck our line.

In the excitement of the moment the right company of the 59th advanced a little, thus masking for the moment the fire of some of our guns, on seeing which I rode up to the captain commanding this company, and told him to throw his right back, which was carried out by the men *stepping back* without relaxing their fire, just as if they were on parade, although so hard pressed that Lieut. Twynam with half a dozen men had to make a rush forward into the thick of the leading group of fanatics, one of whom this gallant young officer ran his sword through, the action of only a moment. Whilst this "stepping back" performance was going on a small opening was created, which gave Arthur Davidson, now on the staff of H.M. the King, who was commanding the general's escort, an opportunity to push his men of the 2/60th and 25th P.I. into it, and in doing which he lost six men killed; it was just as pretty a bit of fighting any man would wish to see.

On the extreme left things were also humming, but the 3rd Goorkhas rose to the occasion and, by forming their three left companies in echelon, gave the Ghazis a hot time of it. Here the Ghazis were mostly mounted, and now the 19th B.L. had their chance. Unfortunately the officer commanding started slow, and as the mounted Ghazis were coming down at a mad gallop the first squadron of the Lancers received a heavy blow, which unhorsed a good many of their men, but the remaining squadrons made up for this, and precious few of the enemy escaped. It was in this affair Teddie Young's horse was wounded and he, poor fellow, thrown, when Ghazi after Ghazi slashed at him and severely wounded him in some twelve places, including two bullet wounds from pistols.

Now riderless horses and ponies were galloping about in rear of the infantry and amongst the staff, in fact getting in everyones way!

Having come to close quarters all along the line the end was not far off, for the bayonet completed what the bullet had failed to stop. The enemy fought till not a man was left standing, and their dead lay actually in our line, and when you come to think that some of these warriors, for warriors they certainly were, had nothing more formidable than "bullis" (rafters from native huts), the actual piercing of our line was truly magnificent. The majority of course carried the murderous Afghan knife, tulwar, and pistol, whilst many had guns of sorts.

Our guns continued busy, and the whole of our cavalry were pursuing in all directions, so few if any escaped. The cease fire was sounded, and a short time later the 2nd Brigade came up.

We now began to collect and attend our wounded and dead which, considering the circumstances, was small. Our losses were six officers wounded, 17 men killed, and 115 wounded.

On our side the commencement of the action without orders was a fatal mistake. But the mistake made by the enemy was much more serious, for had they kept out of sight and stuck to the higher hills till our 1st Brigade had passed, and then swept down on our transport and baggage, thus cutting our forces in two, they would have inflicted heavier losses on us, with a much better chance of slipping away only to attack us another day. Attacking us as they did after a sprint of 1,600 yards with only some 3,000 fanatics out of a force which was probably 15,000, made their case a hopeless one from the first, for our men after a tedious wait of some 16 months were not likely to refuse the opportunity all were so eager to get. If ever men were spoiling for a fight the men of the Candahar Division were.

The enemy, in spite of the awful knock they had received, were still full of pluck, for when the order was given to advance, an hour after the "cease fire" sounded, wounded men gripped their tulwars tightly and slashed right and left, wounding several. To have feigned death all this time suffering from the most terrible wounds imaginable without moving a muscle till we marched over them was an experience as novel as it was grand to behold. Some of these men had been lying within a few feet of our line, so close that the movement of an eyelid would have been at once detected.

Once more bayonets had to be fixed, and every "body" closely watched, till all had passed over the scene of the late conflict. In all we counted upwards of 1,000 dead bodies without going out of our course.

In the whole history of this war there has never been an instance of such a rush of Ghazi swordsmen.

During the thick of the fight the General was for some moments in imminent danger, seated calmly on his horse with sword drawn, and quite alone, as every member of his staff was carrying orders to different parts of the field. I was returning myself from carrying an order when I saw this, and only reached his side with Lieut. Dickie, R.E., when the pressure in front of him was at its height, for the enemy were then only a few feet off!

The slowness of the first charge of the 19th B.L. was no fault of the men themselves, the C.O. and the C.O. only was to blame. He being a great dandy, was thinking more of the polish of his boots when he gave the order to "trot," which should have been followed by "gallop," but it was at a trot the first squadron met the enemy, and were thus sorely handicapped. However, the men made up for this afterwards.

At this time the British troops were armed with

Martini Henri rifles, and the native with Sniders, both being weapons of destruction which inflicted ghastly wounds, more especially the latter. How these poor wounded fanatics bore the pain without moving a muscle for upwards of an hour, by which time shattered limbs must have stiffened and the loss of blood from flesh wounds must have weakened them to a condition of only semi-consciousness, and then attacked our men in the determined manner some of them did, was truly marvellous. No doubt some people will call it mean and cowardly, and at the moment I may have thought the same, but when I look back on the scene and realise that these men were acting under the influence of their Mullahs, I cannot help thinking they were heroes, undeniably they were brave.

We continued our march to Nani, making a total of 18 miles, much hampered by our wounded, many of whom, or to be more correct most of whom, had suffered severe sword cuts, and when in camp I was much horrified to learn a rumour had already spread that the "stepping back" incident of the 59th had been turned by some malicious persons into wavering, which I indignantly denied, and I hoped "crushed," for a more unfair and unjust accusation I never heard. This evil rumour was the outcome of jealousy.

No troops could have fought with greater steadiness all along the line, whilst most of them if judged by the standard of steadiness might have been on parade; this was particularly evidenced by the conduct of the 3rd Goorkhas on the extreme left, who went through the parade movement of forming three of their companies into echelon just to give their men a little more elbow room for the benefit of the mounted Ghazis as they swept past their left flank! No matter how good your men are, no matter how well they fight, there is always some evil-minded beast who, denied the pleasure of the fight, is ready to come forward and start some lie regarding the conduct of some individual unit. Jealousy! what a curse this is in our Army.

As soon as our camp was pitched my father visited all the wounded in turn, and had a cheery word for each. Even poor Teddy Young, who was at the time supposed to be in a hopeless condition, heard the sounds of our feet outside his tent, and seemed to cheer up when told it was the General come to enquire after him. He asked for me, so I sat by his side and spoke to him, though I could see nothing of him, his face, head, both arms, and legs, as well as back were swathed in bandages. If he pulled through it would have been by his own pluck, for we did not find his body for a long time, and the loss of blood must have been enormous. His belts, pouches, etc., were cut to ribbons; some of the Ghazis went so far as to try and pick him up by his belts, failing which they each gave him another slash. His sufferings in the dooly were terrible, and this he had to put up with daily till we reached Cabul.

After we had finished with the Ghazis at Ahmed Khel, I believe many Hazaras swept down and had their revenge on every Afghan they could lay their hands on, whilst they doubtless robbed the dead and tortured any wounded they came across in their usual style. It is sad to think that any of that gallant gang who swarmed down on us should have been maltreated later, though I hope the curs who would not follow the Ghazis got their deserts.

On the 21st we reached Ghuzni without opposition of any kind, only to find the place deserted, and hardly worth the name "fortress" in strength or position, for it is commanded from all sides, and could be knocked down by field artillery. Here we enjoyed a few days' rest which all wanted, including our transport. On the 23rd, however, a gathering was reported at Oorzoo, a village some five miles off, but hidden to view by a razor-backed spur running down into the plain. Barter's and Palliser's Brigades were despatched for this job, whilst the General waited at a spot about one mile out, when word came back the enemy were too strong for them, so once more we felt quite cheered up. Hughes' Brigade, which was in waiting, was set in motion, and the General started off himself. When we reached the hill overlooking Oorzoo we found it too steep to make riding pleasant, so we climbed to the top and got a splendid view of the country around. The village was a fairly big one, built in the usual Afghan style, high windowless houses forming nothing but a blank wall on the side facing us, the intervening ground was cultivated, and the only obstacles we could see were the bank surrounding the cultivated part to our immediate front, and a nullah running with a slight bend outwards towards the village, whilst to the right of this all was open and apparently good firm going.

Our cavalry scouts were in the cultivation, which was quite low, and with our glasses we could see the ground had been inundated, for the horses were floundering about. A few of the enemies' mounted men formed a semi-circle round the village, from which we could hear a good deal of tom-toming, and occasionally see bodies of men, mounted and foot.

All was taken in at a glance, and the order was

given to attack it over the firm ground to our right front, the advance being covered by a heavy shell fire from the foot of the hill, the distance being some 2,000 yards. There was really no difficulty in the attack, as it was quite unnecessary to go over the inundated ground, which stopped our cavalary at first and caused the message to be sent back. It was a pretty affair, but disappointing. The moment the artillery commenced firing a good body of men came out and looked as if they meant business, but they soon retreated to the cover of the village, from which they blazed away at us without doing any harm. A few hundred men did make a stand to our right of the village, but this did not last long, and by the time we reached rushing distance they made a clean bolt of it with our cavalry after them.

Altogether their losses must have been something near 400, our guns knocked all the spirit out of them, and accounted for nearly all the losses in the village itself judging by the ghastly wounds I saw. Rumour had it they were expecting a large reinforcement which failed to come up on hearing our artillery fire, thus completely "letting in" those who occupied Oorzoo. On the whole it turned out a long day's work, for the first troops started before daylight, and we didn't all get back till dark. After our arrival the General was very busy with the Afghan Governor and other notables with a view to persuading the different elements to patch up quarrels and live in peace with each other. Before leaving Ghuzni we were once more called on to get rid of everything we could possibly part with as our transport was not improving as we went along. I chucked away an old "razai," which doubtless some one else picked up and added to his load.

The troops were given a halt on the 24th, and on the 25th we continued our March towards Cabul though still uncertain we were to go there. This question, however, was settled when we reached camp, for a dak came in bringing letters from the Viceroy ordering my father to proceed to Cabul. On the 27th General Ross and a number of officers from his Division rode in to our camp at Hydea Khel, and we received some news of the outer world. Of course they were full of congratulations and wanted to hear all our news, whilst we were far more anxious to receive theirs. It was very pleasant seeing new faces and meeting old friends from whom we had been separated since November, '78.

On the 1st May, at Argandeh, my father and General Roberts met. Nothing could have been more cordial, but soon the two generals moved away from the surrounding officers, and seated by themselves on a grassy slope, plunged into earnest conversation.

It didn't require a very critical eye to notice that in spite of all efforts one looked somewhat crest-fallen whilst the other was full of sympathy, that an unpleasant position had been suddenly created, which was only saved by the extraordinary friendship which existed between these two famous generals. No matter how large the body of troops close by there is always to be found a creeping, inquisitive Afghan prowling about, outwardly innocent looking, but under whose cloak there may be the dangerous dagger, so whenever I saw my father seated by himself or with only one or two equally unsuspecting officers I invariably kept one eye towards him with a view to stopping any of these gentry, and it was while so mentally employed I watched at the same time the faces of these two generals, and almost read the thoughts of both.

They were left undisturbed, and the conversation over they joined the groups of officers and chatted till a more comfortable feeling reigned, and all were at ease.

We march into Cabul to-morrow, and many officers are fishing for new billets, but I don't think they will gain anything by this, the General is not likely to consider this question on the line of march. It won't be an easy job to please everyone, and doubtless there will be some heart-burnings. It is evident the Cabul heroes think no "small beer" of themselves, and are quite satisfied they are going to get all the plums! It is really most amusing to hear some of the remarks, and already I know who is to get this and who that. Judging from the men here, Sir Frederick Roberts' staff seems to be a formidable one.

On the 2nd May we marched into Cabul, where the General got a very great reception. Some miles out my brother, Donnie, met us, and as I had not seen him since '71, when he was only eleven, it is needless to say I did not recognise the big Highlander he had grown into,. The circumstances made our meeting all the more joyful, and one's inclination was to forget all else. He was a very fine looking youngster, and had much news to give me of a more than interesting nature, so I thoroughly enjoyed the ride in. On arrival the general was received by a grand guard of honour of the 92nd, which was followed by the usual introductions, etc. The officers were so numerous and the uniforms so varied you might easily have imagined the whole Indian Army were present, for every corps seemed to be represented. Our camp was just outside Sir F. Roberts' quarters in Sherpur, and until he moved out into camp to join his command we were not able to shake down. Lepel Griffin and a number of politicals met us at the same place where Donnie chipped in, so we made a fine cavalcade as we approached Cabul, which at first sight seemed to be full of interest. For some days one was kept pretty busy dancing attendance on officers calling, and visiting places of interest too numerous to remember, but one can never forget the view from the Assenai heights, and the Bala Hissar, the scene of the Cavagnari massacre. The place seemed to be full of "Sirdars," who had to be received and interviewed; in this way the General, or, as some called him, the Chief, never had a moment's rest. The topic of conversation was divided between the change of ministry and Abdul Rahman's bona-fides. The City of Cabul covered an immense amount of ground, but had no attraction for the European, with its dirty narrow streets, and the people looked the same cut-throat lot, though probably more robust than the ordinary Sandahari. Some of the Sirdars were fine looking men, armed to the teeth, so one felt much happier when they had taken their departure; their hangers-on looked capable of any intrigue, mischief, or treachery. How easy it would have been for these gentry to whip out a dagger and make use of it! My stay in Cabul was doomed to be short, for on the 22nd inst. I was ordered to Safad Sang to take up the Brigade Majorship of the 3rd Section Khyber Line Force, under the command of General Bright, whilst another Section was under the command of Brigadier-General Rowley Sale Hill, Colonel of the 1st Goorkhas. To leave my father was a great blow, but it would have been madness to refuse promotion of the kind, so after saying good-bye to him and Donnie and all old friends, I once more took to tents and marched down the Khyber till I reached Safad Sang on the 25th inst. and took over the heavy duties of the Brigade Office. I found General Hill quite charming in every respect, and the work most interesting and pleasant. It could not be otherwise with a man who had an opinion of his own, and never shirked responsibility. After I had been there some time an objectionable article appeared in a paper regarding the conduct of the 59th, which led to some correspondence with the regiment and my father, who seemed to think I was responsible for it, but I very soon put this right by pointing out how entirely opposed it was to my notion of what had taken place, and secondly that in the course of my life I had never sent a line to any newspaper, directly or indirectly. I looked upon the 59th as one of the finest regiments I had ever seen, and considered their conduct at Ahmed Khel beyond reproach. My father was quite satisfied with my answer, and was much relieved in mind when I put the true facts of the "stepping back" incident clearly before him. At the time I knew perfectly well who was responsible for the evil rumours, which was nothing but the outcome of jealousy originated by a man who was well to the rear during the fight of the 19th April, and I let him know what I thought of him.

Barring occasional sniping and numerous scares of gatherings our stay at Safad Sang (or Gundamuk as it was often called, being the spot where the famous treaty was signed), life was uneventful. In addition to the troops of the section we always had a moveable column in camp on the spot, one unit of which was the Carabineers, at whose mess I spent many a happy hour. For some time I was confined to my tent with a sprained ankle, so missed an excellent gymkhana got up by the Carabineers, to which General Hill and his orderly officer, Lieut.- Barchard, of the 14th Foot, went full of determination to pull off something in the shape of lime cutting or tent pegging. When they returned in the evening both seemed unusually quiet, so I could not resist commenting on this, when the General replied "So would you be quiet if you had cut off your best charger's tail!" One returned with a tailless horse whilst the other had either hacked off an ear or inflicted a deep wound in the stifle, I forget which. I was more than sorry for the suddenly Manx-made horse, which was really a fine beast, and of course quite ruined as regards appearance. It was only natural they should both be sad, as they were men who loved the "dumb animal."

Just as all preparations for the rolling up of the forces and our return to India were completed came the news of the disastrous affair at Maiwand and the proposed despatch of a force which I hoped would be under my father's command, in which case I felt sure a place would be found for me, but this was not to be, and once more luck favoured Sir F. Roberts, who started from Cabul on the 9th August on his memorable march in command of a mixed force of some 10,000 in the pink of condition and perfectly equipped! The doings of this force are now history, and therefore known to everyone. The route taken was identical with that of the Candahar column to Cabul in the earlier part of the year, and was accomplished in 21 days against

34, but the conditions were so different that comparison would hardly be fair. On the upward march the transport consisted of camels the feeding of which, at the time of the year, was a great anxiety, whilst the horse, field, and heavy artillery over an indifferent road, which was bad in many places, made the going slow, and lastly there was an enemy hovering on our flank whose strength was an unknown quantity. On Lord Roberts' march he had picked troops, mule transport, no artillery on wheels, improved roads, an ample supply of fodder everywhere, and no likelihood of any armed resistance to face till he arrived at his destination.

During the earlier march the people at home were too much taken up with electioneering to give a thought to affairs in Afghanistan, whereas in the case of the Candahar march the eyes of Europe were on the column moving to retrieve the losses sustained at Maiwand. Under such circumstances it was only natural Roberts' splendid performance with a successful engagement at the end should have caused the excitement it did at the time. As a military feat, however, I'm inclined to think the march to Cabul was quite on equality with the one to Candahar, and if the history of the war is ever written by an independent military critic, the

Candahar-Cabul march will be recognised in the terms it deserved. To have given a special decoration to one force and not to the other was a distinction which clearly showed the feeling at the time, and one of those ill-judged acts on the part of the Government towards its gallant soldiers which causes discontent and makes the Army unpopular. I don't suppose any member of the old Candahar Division who did not participate in the return march, gave the subject a moment's thought, certainly none grudged the heroes of the Candahar march any of the honours bestowed, but after years have rolled by and you have time to think and compare notes, you begin to see injustices and grasp how differently some men are treated, and wonder which pays best, "luck or success?" As matters stand every school boy will be taught the march to Candahar, while none will hear of the march to Cabul.

Simultaneously with Roberts' departure the "rolling up" of the troops at Cabul and in the Khyber commenced, and was carried out like clock-work without the loss of a single man.

In a few days I found myself at Peshawur with General Hill, and together we journeyed to Umribsur, whence he went to Dharmsala, and I proceeded to Kussowli and Simla to interview Sir

Paul Haines, the Commander-in-Chief, who received me most kindly, and told me that in an early gazette I would be posted to the 4th Goorkhas, which at the time were marching with Roberts' force on Candahar. I was much pleased at this news as no finer regiment in the Indian Army existed.

The month of September opened with the glorious news of Lord Roberts' brilliant victory over Ayab, but this was partly marred by the intelligence my brother Donnie was amongst the "severely wounded." By the end of the month, however, he was able to join me at Kussowlie on a short visit, looking none the worse for his wound, which kept him on crutches for many a month. He was fortunate in having seen so much service his first year, besides gaining two medals.

Whilst on three months' Afghan leave, I had the misfortune to meet with an accident, through the bursting of a soda-water bottle which cut my ankle joint so severely that I had to go before a Medical Board, and was on crutches for some months, till I was able to join the 4th Goorkhas at Bakloh. My stay with the regiment was doomed to be short, for in the month of June, '81, I was posted to the Sangor District, with Headquarters at Jubbulpore, as D.A.A.G. The station was a delightful one socially, and as far as climate was concerned, but the command being much broken up and having no D.A.Q.M.G. the work was very heavy; it was not particularly attractive, from a soldier's point of view, the garrison being a small one, only six companies British troops, one troop Bengal Cavalry, and one Native Infantry Regiment. As regards office work, the training was excellent, for I obtained an insight to the department of Q.M.G. During the years '81-'85 I had no less than five Generals to serve under, which was unfortunate for all concerned. Generals have their peculiarities, and no sooner had one got into the ways of No. 1 than No. 2 arrived, and so on to the end, it was a case of orders and counter-orders, on minor points, certainly, but nevertheless trying for those who had to carry them out. We were fortunate, however, in finding all five really good men, who knew their work, so it was a pleasure to work for them. The out-stations of the command consisted of Sangor, Nowgong, Banda, Sutna, and the hill station of Pachmarhi, and as only Sutna was on the line of railway there was plenty of knocking about, and the duties were anything but dull. Having to perform Q.M.G.'s work, I made a tour of these stations once a year during the hot weather by myself, and in this way was able to do a bit of shooting, though could never remain long enough in any one spot to secure a bag worth noting. Without professing to be a very keen shikari I dearly loved a shoot. The district, in almost any direction, was an excellent one for big game, which the civilians were very jealous of, so to secure a bag it was wise to make friends with them, as many of the regimental officers did. A staff officer does not get the same opportunities, his periods of leave are few and far between, and seldom does he get away for the 10 days the regimental officer so often takes advantage of, and which should be encouraged as much as possible, if the time is going to be spent in sport. Nothing does a soldier more good than a stay in the jungles.

Talking of shikar reminds me of meeting a man named Hughes, of the Geological Survey, one of the finest sportsmen in India, as far as big game shooting is concerned. During the years I was at Jubbulpore his work brought him there every rains. One day he asked me to run over and see his trophies, or, as he put it, a few of them. He was taking advantage of a bright sun to dry some of them. It was a sight I shall never forget, for he had upwards of 30 tiger skins and many specimens of the black bear, stretched out in rows, and before he left India had raised his bag to over 100 tigers! At the time I am speaking of he was recovering from wounds inflicted in a tough encounter with a bear, which he fought armed with only a large shikar knife to help him till assistance arrived! He was a man of extraordinary strength or could never have escaped with a whole skin.

The circumstances of the case I have forgotten, but I remember this much, he was startled in his sleep and rushed out of his tent with the knife in his hand, not dreaming anything so formidable as "Bruin" was the disturber of his slumbers. With him was a pet dog, which made for a bush, and it was soon evident to my friend, the terrier had found something more than his match, so to save the poor little beast he rushed into the bush without thinking of danger, and in a moment the bear was on his hind legs embracing and clawing him alternately. Fortunately his right arm was free, and soon the shikar knife was buried up to the hilt more than once in Bruin's sides, when the shikari appeared on the scene, and with the help of a lantern shot the beast with one of his master's rifles. The skin made a splendid trophy, which was much valued by poor Hughes, who, I regret to say, joined the majority a few years ago, after many years of patient suffering, the result of a gun-shot wound, which destroyed the sight of both eyes, caused by carelessness on the part of a companion who was out partridge shooting with him. But for this sad accident I have no doubt he would have bagged 200 tigers before the close of his Indian career. On one occasion when beating through a teak jungle in Central India, I came across the dead bodies of a tiger and boar. One of the beaters noticed the ground in front of him in a very disturbed condition, so drew my attention to the spot. Without doubt a struggle to the death had taken place, for the ground was torn up in every direction. Getting the beaters together we advanced very cautiously, and soon came on the pug of a tiger, which we followed up to find Master Stripes stone dead about 50 yards off, with what looked like one huge rip running nearly the whole length of his belly, a truly awful wound. We then circled, and eventually found the body of the boar, and a splendid specimen he was, literally torn to pieces, and one side of his skull smashed in. The fight must have been a grand one, and a sight worth watching; judging from the condition of the bodies it could only have taken place during the previous night.

During the time General Wilkinson commanded he broke the monotony of the annual inspection of the out-stations one year by marching through the district. We trained as far as Sutna and then took the main road at Nowgong, and across country to Saugor.

After leaving Sutna we found ourselves at a small deserted cantonment named Nagode, which had last been occupied by, I think, a Madras Cavalry regiment, several years previously. Curiosity took us into some of the compounds, which at one time were well kept gardens, but now overgrown with weeds in which quail were abundant and afforded us an excellent morning's shoot.

The houses had evidently been respected by the natives of the village, for in some of them we found chairs, tables, children's toys, and pieces of fancy work which had been left behind as not worth taking away. In some cases there were even photographs on the walls, which vividly reminded us of accounts of houses hurriedly vacated during the days of the Mutiny.

The head official of the village assured us the natives never entered these compounds out of respect for those whose presence not only afforded them protection in days gone by, but added to their prosperity. The loss to these poor people when Nagode was abolished as a military station was considerable, and the General's appearance raised hopes of a re-occupation, which pained him to dispel. The official begged the General to do all in his power to persuade the "Sirkar" to once more send troops there, and thus bring back the trade which at one time made it a flourishing little town.

From Nagode we marched to Punna, where the Raja had made great preparations to give us three days' sport after tiger; but, alas! the elements were against us, as the rain came down in torrents, and never ceased during the three days we put up at the Guest House.

This was a sore disappointment, as the Raja's shikaris and beaters had been in position for days and nights round a strip of jungle which contained more than one "Stripes." Instead of sport we had to content ourselves with visits to the Palace, and such sights as his small capital could afford.

The Raja with much pride paraded his unique army during a short break in the rains, and showed us some perfect specimens of the famous Punna diamonds. These gems have a peculiar yellow tint, which detracts from their value, but if anything adds to their beauty.

We were treated with the usual Oriental hospitality, which after a time becomes embarrasing to the European who is unable to make any adequate return.

In spite of the weather our stay at Punna was full of interest, and a break in the everyday life of India which one will always be able to look back to with pleasure. The Chief was one of the old school who could not understand a word of English, so different to the present day Potentate who lives in polo breeches and highly polished brown boots, with the everlasting cigarette of abnormal dimensions between his lips, and speaks to you with the familiarity of the West, and the absence of the courtesy of the East.

The road to Nowgong being an excellent one we had no anxieties about our baggage, so each day was devoted to shooting such small game as quail, partridge, hare, chinkara, and buck. The General being an excellent shot and a really good sportsman, enjoyed the uncertainty of what *might* jump up in front of his gun much more than the organised beat, in fact this kind of sport appealed to us both, and with many regrets we said good-bye to our small camp and a most enjoyable outing.

PART II

SUAKIM, '85

PART II

SUAKIM, '85

A SOLDIER's life is full of surprises. The end of February, '85, saw me on tour of inspection with my General (A. H. Murray), and on the very day we reached Banda, he received a wire from Army Headquarters, Simla, directing me to report myself at once to Brigadier-General John Hudson, who was appointed to the command of an Indian contingent about to start for Suakim, and with which I was to proceed as D.A.A.G. This was truly joyful news, but it was a great upset to our plans; as Banda was off the line of railway, and the General's health was indifferent, I disliked leaving him. However, he was not to be persuaded to return with me, so after sending my horses off by road, I said good-bye to him the same night, and never saw him again, as he died very shortly afterwards, to my deep regret. On arrival at Jubbulpore I found a telegram from General

Hudson ordering me to proceed to Bombay to superintend the embarkation of the troops.

Two days and one night I devoted to my affairs, and the third morning saw me in Bombay, where I soon discovered this embarkation job meant seeing everyone else off and leaving by the last transport myself. The embarkation staff at Bombay did all the work, but for the 10 or 12 days I was there I had to spend all my time at the docks, and constitute myself as a sort of "Court of Appeal" in the event of disputes between the regimental authorities and the local embarkation officers. My time came at last, and I found myself on board the Indian Marine steamer Tenasserim with a detachment of the 9th Bengal Lancers, the Madras Sappers and Miners, and any odds and ends, in the shape of departmental staff officers, as companions. After an ideal passage we reached Suakim on the evening of the 14th March, and were ordered by signal to join the other transports at anchor some miles down the coast, where we would receive further instructions regarding disembarkation, which took place the following day.

On landing I was put in charge of the water supply of our contingent, the arrangements for which were in the hands of the Naval authorities. It turned out an easy task, as every evening certain tanks were told off to brigades, and one had merely to pass the *number* of the tank on to the unit concerned, and see that the regimental authorities carried out their orders. The bhisties, or water carriers, drew water morning and evening, by which time the supply was exhausted, when the condensing ships set to work and refilled all the tanks during the night. The arrangements were carried out with mathematical precision, and not once was there any failure, which speaks well for the Naval system. The supply provided was a liberal one, and was quite sufficient for that luxury, "the daily bath"; but when it came to marching, the labour was great, as the water had to be carried in zinc cylinders holding 10 gallons each, two of these forming a mule load. In filling these cylinders the fatigue parties had to be very carefully watched to prevent waste, as we only carried the exact ration for each man for drinking and cooking purposes. The rule was to fill up these cylinders over night, and so have all in readiness for the march. Each cylinder had two strong bands, to which rings were attached, corresponding with hooks on the pack saddles, so all that had to be done was to lift two at the same moment and hook them on to the pack, and then pass a rope round the ends of both under and over till a compact load was made well up on the animal's back. All ranks understood how precious the supply was, so took particular care in adjusting these loads. In addition to the supply carried on mules, each unit had a water cart or carts, drawn by mules, at the end of which was a tap which enabled water bottles to be refilled on the line of march if the same turned out particularly distressing or prolonged. These carts were invariably under special guards with instructions that no water was to be drawn except under the orders of the responsible officer in charge of the regimental supply. Only on one occasion did I see these orders abused, and that was by the Australian Contingent on the march to Tamai, which was a real corker, and the lesson they learnt was one not to be forgotten, for on reaching their destination they found themselves short, whilst others were enjoying the benefits of their untouched supply. However, we managed to spare them a drink all round, with the warning they were not to expect the same consideration again—a warning which to their credit they bore in mind.

Just at first there was a good deal of "shifting" of camps, as every night we received visits from "snipers" and others, who crawled in on all fours and speared many an unwary sentry or follower in a manner which was truly astounding, considering the precautions taken. One night these gentlemen grew bolder and rushed a large guard of the Berkshire Regiment, well in rear of the entire camp, and under the very nose of one of our gunboats. They managed to kill several of our men, and got off themselves with slight loss, but not without leaving behind one of Osman Digna's most important Lieutenants, a loss which caused that chief considerable regret, for the next day he sent in a letter offering a sum of money for the man's body, which I need hardly say was not complied with.

Later on we tried every device we could think of to put a stop to the sniping, but with poor results. On one occasion a mine was laid on a spot surrounded by a low wall, from behind which the Arabs frequently took up their position to pepper a searchlight on the walls of the town. This mine was so laid that anyone entering the enclosure must assuredly be blown up, and we thought we had caught them at last, but to everyone's surprise it was again made use of, and no explosion followed! The next morning a party of Engineers went out to ascertain the cause of the failure, and on approaching the spot the officer in charge halted his men, whilst he advanced to inspect the wires, the slightest touch of which would explode the mine, but with fatal results, for the next moment there was an explosion, and the poor fellow was blown to atoms. After this accident the ground was carefully examined, and two points were clearly demonstrated. Without doubt men had been there the previous night, and had not only disconnected the wires, but re-connected them before leaving, and this on a pitch black night! proving to us that not only had they, through spies, learnt our plans, but possessed men thoroughly conversant with the handling of electric wires. It was well known that amongst Osman Digna's following there were several mechanics and others who had served under the Egyptian Government, and whose education he was now apparently making good use of.

On the 19th a reconnaissance was made as far as Hashim, which was entered by the cavalry and mounted infantry, and at whom only a few shots were fired.

The following day practically the whole force, with the exception of the Shropshire Light Infantry, paraded at daybreak, and advanced on Hashim about 6.30.

With the Cavalry Brigade and Mounted Infantry in front and on the flanks, the 2nd Infantry Brigade in line of columns formed the front of a three-sided square, with the Guards'

Brigade and Indian Contingent in columns of companies forming the right and left faces respectively, inside being the Gardners, rockets, Engineers, and animals. On reaching some lows hills due East of Hashim the Engineers and East Surrey Regiment occupied these, and proceeded to form a zareba, whilst the remainder of the 2nd Brigade, supported by the Indian Contingent, with the Guards in reserve and the cavalry on each flank, were ordered to attack the Dhilibut Hill, which was occupied by the enemy.

The Berkshires formed for attack, with half a battalion of Marines in support, the remainder of whom advanced to the right of the Berkshires, followed by the Indian Contingent, with the 15th Sikhs extended in line, and the 28th Bombay Infantry and 17th Bengal Infantry in column in rear of right and left flanks of the 15th Sikhs.

The hill was so steep the Berkshires had almost to "crawl" up some of it, so the advance was necessarily slow. The summit was held by the enemy's riflemen, and it was quite impossible to form any correct estimate of their strength. Without a halt the 49th advanced inch by inch, as it were, whilst we all looked on, and a prettier piece of work I never saw, as they were under a hot fire all the time. The enemy clung to the heights to the last, and eventually bolted along the spurs in rear and across the Khor behind the village of Hashim, under the heavy fire of the Berkshires, who had gained the hill.

As soon as this was accomplished, the Marines and Indian Contingent swung half right and occupied the ground south of Hashim.

Whilst this was going on two squadrons of the 9th Bengal Lancers were engaging the enemy making for Tamai, and others who were apparently coming from that direction with the intention of getting round our left and rear. One of these squadrons being dismounted had to resist a nasty rush of the Fuzzies at considerable disadvantage, hampered as they were with carbine, lance, and sword, till the mounted squadron came to its assistance, but not before it had lost nine men and a water cart with its followers, some of whom were killed, whilst the rest were made prisoners.

On the extreme right the 5th Lancers and remaining squadrons of the 9th Bengal Lancers made several effective charges at bodies of the enemy who were attempting to turn our right.

After remaining in the Khor for some two hours under a dropping fire, which knocked over a few men, the Indian Contingent was ordered to retire, covered by the 2nd Brigade, followed by the

Guards and Horse Artillery, who kept up a heavy fire on the enemy, who seemed to spring from the bowels of the earth in all directions, occupying the ground we vacated within an interval of time that was astonishing even in thick bush.

Our losses were one officer and eight men killed, and three officers and 36 men wounded. What the enemy suffered is impossible to say. They appeared and disappeared as if by magic, and only in a few cases did I see any fall to our withering fire. The cavalry, on the other hand, claimed having killed many, and one Sowar of the 9th B.L. is reported to have slain seven to his own cheek!

The troops returned to Suakim after a long day of 12 hours, leaving the East Surrey Regiment in zareba, which turned out a very happy move, as it practically put a stop to sniping at night

This was the first occasion our Indian troops had experienced what bush fighting meant, and on the whole they seemed to enjoy it. Considering the conditions, the work of the mounted troops appeared excellent.

On the 21st the force was given a day's rest prior to breaking up Osman Digna's gathering at Tamai to the South-West of Suakim. For this purpose the following troops paraded on the morning of the

22nd, under the command of Major-General Sir John McNeill:—

1 Squadron 5th Lancers.

1 Battalion Royal Marines.

Berkshire Regiment (49th).

1 Field Company R.E. with Telegraph Section.

Detachment Naval Brigade with 4 Gardner guns.

Ammunition column.

15th Sikhs.

17th Bengal Infantry.

28th Bombay Infantry.

1 Company Madras Sappers and Miners.

Sir John McNeill's Staff:—

A.D.C., Lieut. Hon. A. D. Charteris, C. Guards.

Brigade-Major, Lieut.-Col. W. F. Kelly, Royal Sussex Regiment.

Commanding Indian Contingent, Brigadier-General J. Hudson.

Staff Indian Contingent, Maj. R. McG. Stewart, R.A., A.A. and Q.M.G.; Bt.-Major N. R. Stewart, D.A.A. and Q.M.G.; Major A. J. Pearson, R.A., D.A.A. and Q.M.G.; Major J. Cook, Brigade-Major; Captain C. Muir, A.D.C.

The force was formed up before daybreak, and marched at day light, the 5th Lancers scouting in front, followed by the British and Indian troops in two squares in the order named.

The object of the advance was to proceed some seven miles and there form a zareba, to be held by the British troops, on the completion of which the Indian Contingent were to return to Suakim with the empty transport, this zareba being the first of a series to be built on the way to Tamai or Tamanib.

Inside the Indian Contingent square were all the animals carrying water and provisions. It marched in echelon to the British square, which being more compact and mobile, had to halt continually for the more cumbersome square in rear. The "going" was so slow we hardy seemed to make any progress, and Suakim was still in sight when we began to feel the effects of the sun, and by the time we had covered five miles man and beast seemed to have had enough, so it was decided to halt and build the first zareba where we stood.

The precautions considered necessary having been taken, fatigue parties from each unit were sent out to cut the bush, the loads were removed from all animals, and the work of building the required zarebas was commenced. These were three in number, the leading one for the Berkshires, the centre one for animals, followers, stores, etc., and the rear one for the Marines. At the corners of the Berkshire and Marines' zareba, pointing towards Tamai and Suakim respectively, it was intended to have two Gardner guns in position.

Personally I was engaged erecting canvas tanks and looking after the water supply generally, so did not pay much attention to what was going on elsewhere. The work I was superintending was completed a little after 2.30, when I rode up to General Hudson, who with his staff was eating lunch, and reported to him accordingly. Being mounted, he ordered me to warn the regiments of the Indian Contingent to fall in where they stood preparatory to marching back to Suakim. At the time the 28th Bombay Infantry and two companies of the 17th Bengal Infantry were facing North, the 15th Sikhs West, and six companies 17th Bengal Infantry South, the intention being to march back in a hollow square with the animals inside, it being known at the time that communication with Suakim was being kept up by squadrons of the 20th Hussars and 9th Bengal Lancers.

The Marines' zareba was complete, the Berkshires nearly so, and the one for animals only partially so, though enough bush had been cut to complete it and join up all three. The Marines were inside their zareba, and half a battalion of the

Berkshires in theirs, but the Gardner guns were not in position. The other half battalion of the Berkshires were in the bush some distance S.E. of the Marines' zareba, and between them and the left of the 17th N.I. were picquets of that regiment. In front of all facing Tamai were the 5th Lancers. The animals were in front of the 17th N.I.

Major von Beverhoudt, commanding the 17th N.I., had just drawn his regiment up in line some 50 yards clear of the Berkshire zareba when some of the 5th Lancers came galloping in by the left flank of the 15th Sikhs and right of the 17th N.I. and on in the direction of Suakim. As no enemy was to be seen, and all was quiet, the last thing to enter my mind was an impending fight, more especially as only a few minutes before I had seen General Hudson at lunch and noticed Sir John McNeill chatting with a group of officers. For these reasons it is hardly surprising little or no notice was taken of the galloping Lancers. The next instant, however, the Arabs were rushing us from every direction. In front of them were soldiers in shirt sleeves running to the cover of their zarebas for all they were worth, and quicker than thought there was a fire which was absolutely deafening, and a scene that beggars description.

All seemed to grasp the situation except

the 17th Bengal Infantry, who only had to open fire as they stood, instead of which this regiment for the moment seemed paralyzed, remained at the slope, and actually watched their Commanding Officer being killed by an Arab, who jumped up behind him on his horse's back and plunged a spear through his body! Still the men fired not, and appeared incapable of action, so great was their consternation. The next instant they began to look about, and then step back, breaking their formation, and lastly they went. It wasn't a case of a stampede, it was more "a bolt at a walk." Anyhow, nothing could be done with them, and God knows their British officers did all in their power as well as many of their native officers and non-commissioned officers. After a few yards had been covered the walk broke into a run till the mass of these men got jammed in the gap on the right of the 28th Bombay N.I., where two companies of their regiment were, and the Marines' zareba, where some of them did use their rifles. A great number, however, went through the gap and joined the runaway followers, who had been in the first instance carried by the force of the Sepoys of this regiment, a force I had myself experienced, for they nearly lifted me and my horse bodily off the ground. The whole affair was only a matter of seconds, and in describing it, it would be untruthful to call it by any other name than "panic"; without doubt the regiment was panic-stricken and useless. The men being drawn up for the purpose of marching quietly back to quarters were completely taken unawares, and seemed incapable of pulling themselves together or realising a "battle" had started. In spite of the excitement it was painful to watch the look of astonishment, despair, or fright, whichever you like to think it, on the majority of the faces one could take in at a glance. A few men certainly did shake themselves free of their comrades and open fire, but it was too late, and they were too few.

The Arabs, although on the heels of the last men, had now to face the fire of both zarebas, and a small body of Madras Sappers and Miners, fortunately brought up by their C.O., Captain Wilkieson, at a most critical moment, were checked just long enough to prevent the mass of men getting through and attacking the 15th Sikhs and 28th Bombay Infantry in rear. Had this rush not been checked at the "biscuit boxes" the fire from the South and West faces of the Marines' square must have caused many casualties to our own side. To give some idea of how rapidly all this occurred, I may add Sir John McNeill had barely time to seek shelter inside the Berkshire zareba, whilst his A.D.C. was wounded by a spear thrust.

When the first shots were fired some men in their shirt sleeves who had been cutting scrub, and others belonging to the picquets on the left or Southern flank made a rush for the zarebas past the 17th Native Infantry, which may have started the panic, but the excuse is a poor one, as the majority of these men were merely rushing to get their arms. What would have happened had the enemy pushed their attack home at this point is mere speculation, but the story of McNeill's zareba would be incomplete if I omitted all reference to the fortunate check the enemy received by the few rounds fired by the Madras Sappers and Miners, for had they followed in great numbers—and there was some danger of this happening for all we knew—the fire of the Marines would have taken the 15th Sikhs in rear, and the result would have been too awful to contemplate. As soon as all the Arabs who had penetrated the ground between the two zarebas had been killed, I found my way to my General behind the right flank of the 15th Sikhs, whence one was able to watch the fight to the end.

The 15th Sikhs and 28th Bombay N.I. had no protection in front of them. The fight was now at its height, and only a few yards separated our men from the Arabs, who were pressing the attack home to such an extent that more than once the Sikhs had to use their bayonets, charging out by companies a few yards, to enable them to make their weight tell, and back again into the line to pump in more lead on the next rush. It was a truly marvellous sight. Our fire was simply terrific, it was impossible for men to load faster, and yet it didn't seem nearly fast enough, for several hand to hand fights were going on all along the line of these two regiments, and at the same time every face of the two zarebas was engaged nearly as heavily as our two regiments in the open. The bush was so thick, in spite of the large quantity of scrub we had cut down, that it was quite impossible to guess how much longer the fight would continue. It was a very anxious moment, practically the whole of our reserve ammunition had been carried away when the mules stampeded at the commencement of the fight, and the men were already asking for more, in fact some had fired every round. Another very serious matter was the condition of the men's hands, as the rifle barrels were now almost red hot. As regards ammunition, the Marines and Berkshires were better off, as they had their regimental reserve to fall back on.

In front of the 28th Bombay Infantry the scrub was thicker than elsewhere, besides being only a few yards off, giving absolute cover to the Arabs. Any unsteadiness on the part of this regiment would have been fatal to us.

We now had time to look round and see what had occurred in other parts of the field. Beginning with the Marines' zareba, all had gone well there, the zareba had been rushed on every side, but not an Arab managed to get inside. The site of the animal zareba was full of our dead, the enemy's, and at least 100 camels, but the saddest sight of all was inside the Berkshire zareba. The majority of the Berkshires who were outside cutting scrub rushed for the corner where the Engineers were putting the finishing touches to the sand-bag parapet for the Gardners, and with these men jumped at least 100 Arabs, who first attacked the Naval Brigade men with the Gardners, and practically killed all. Here also Lieut. Newman, R.E., superintending this work, was killed. To wipe out these 100 Arabs the rear ranks of the Berkshire were obliged to turn about and fire point blank, and the consequence was in slaying the foe many comrades were also sacrificed. The face of the Berkshire square was only 65 yards, so it is easy to realise the effect of the fire of the rear ranks turned about.

The firing ceased as suddenly as it commenced, and hardly a man was to be seen. The stillness after the deafening noise of our fire was almost unbearable. Fortunately there was lots to do. The work of completing the zarebas had to be restarted, the wounded and dead had to be sought and attended to, and lastly the fate of the half-battalion of the Berkshires in the open had to be ascertained, as well as that of the picquet of the 17th N.I., and we were glad to find both had come well out of the fight, and had accounted for many of the enemy, besides escaping the murderous fire of some of the faces of the Marines' and Berkshires' zarebas.

The Arabs attacking from the South, after clearing the scrub, made use of our camels as cover, and in this way advanced right up to the biscuit boxes and South face of the Marines' zareba till all the animals were shot down by our fire. The sight of these poor wounded and killed camels and mules was enough to sicken the strongest—poor patient beasts that had not the sense to bolt, or tell friend from foe.

At the outset of the fight most of our mules carrying ammunition and medical stores were collected outside the E. and N. faces of the Marines' zareba, and stampeded at once towards Suakim. With these were many followers, private and public, medical subordinates, warrant officers, and war correspondents, who once the firing commenced could not possibly retrace their steps on account of our fire, so bolted after the mules, and soon met their fate, excepting thost who were able to outrun the Arabs till they met succour in the shape of the squadrons of the 20th Hussars and 9th B.L. patrolling between our force and Suakim. The line of retreat of those fugitives who fell marked the road for many a day.

The loss of medical panniers was a very serious matter, and many ghastly operations had to be carried out without anæsthetics.

We managed to recover a few boxes of ammunition, which when issued gave each man, I think, some 10 rounds for further attacks!.

Considering the fight only lasted some 20 minutes, our losses were heavy, eight British officers killed and three wounded. Including these our total amounted to 150 killed, 174 wounded, and 148 missing. The company of the Madras Sappers and Miners suffered the severest losses. Out of three British officers one was wounded and two killed.

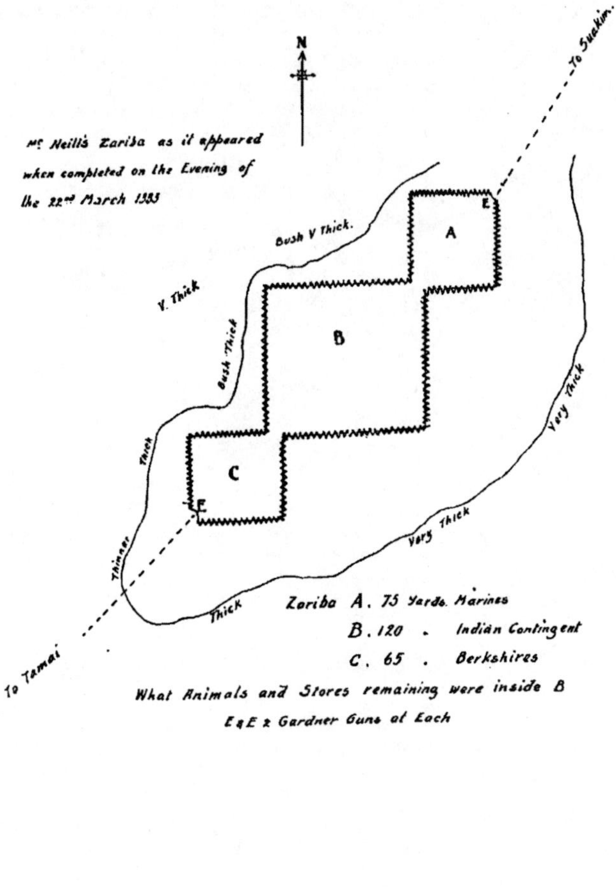

What Animals and Stores remaining were inside B

E & E 2 Gardner Guns at Each

Before dark the zarebas were completed, and the different squares were told off (as shown in plan opposite), and, excepting one alarm, when a few precious rounds were fired at nothing, the night passed quietly. The Indian Contingent being without food and great coats, were not sorry when relief arrived next day.

Besides our own dead, we buried hundreds of the enemy in long, deep trenches. Lieutenant Swinton, of the Berkshires, was buried in a grave inside their zareba, and the rest of the officers in a separate grave from the men outside on the morning of the 23rd. Over Lieutenant Swinton's grave a cairn of stones was erected, which curiously enough was respected by the Arabs after the zareba was finally vacated some weeks later.

During the evening the telegraph line was cut, so communication with Suakim was suspended till darkness admitted of our using lamps, when fuller particulars of the engagement were signalled.

On the morning of the 23rd General Graham relieved the Indian Contingent with the Coldstreams and Scots Guards.

The whole story of McNeill's zareba spells "Surprise," for without doubt it was a complete surprise, and no one was more surprised, I should say, than our gallant commander, a man who would sooner have risked his own life a dozen times over than recklessly thrown away that of the last-joined recruit. Sir John McNeill was the bravest of the brave, and brave men are not careless of the lives of others.

Later it was stated the 70th Regiment, occupying the hill well to the north of our line of march, from their elevated position, watched the movements of the enemy, and reported the same by "helio," but who to? I remember seeing the flashing, on the march out, and I also remember shells being fired, from one of the vessels in harbour, ahead of us and to our right, which certainly pointed to an enemy being in view of someone. But putting these facts together, I personally came to the conclusion the 70th were sending messages back to Suakim, and the guns were firing in response to these messages, which were unconnected with us. For us, marching through thick bush, it would have been no easy matter to flash back to the 70th Hill.

One thing which did surprise me very much was the little use made of our staff officers to procure information from the front. One or more might easily have advanced with the cavalry. The job would not have been a very pleasant one, but two or three dismounted men by stooping down could have gained the requisite information and then have withdrawn in ample time to prepare the force against surprise. It was certainly not the country for cavalry to remain seated on their horses, as the Lancers apparently did, for mounted men could see nothing of foot-men moving rapidly through the bush with "cat"-like precision and noiselessness.

If the story is true that Osman Digna did send in a written threat of his intention to attack our troops if they attempted to zareba, and this intelligence was not repeated to Sir John McNeill, all I can say is, it was a most regrettable omission on the part of someone. But apart from this, in my judgment the methods adopted by our force up to the time of the attack were of the "happy-go-lucky" order, as the precautions were meagre in the extreme.

I don't think the fight of the 22nd March has ever been treated with the importance it deserved. Had more troops wavered, it seems to me highly probable the entire force would have been annihilated, and under the circumstances of the case we have much to be thankful for that the 15th Sikhs and 28th Bo. Infantry stood their ground as they did. Judging from the rewards which were bestowed on the units which composed this force,

I am inclined to think this day's fight was officially reported on in terms quite inconsistent with the gravity of the situation. Looking back to that day, after an interval of 23 years, I am more convinced now, than I was at the time, that McNeill's zareba was as fine a fight on both sides as any during the long years our troops struggled for supremacy in the Soudan. The only excuse I can find for treating this fight as a small matter was a reluctance to admit it was "a complete surprise." With no spirit of controversy have I written this account, I am merely expressing my feelings of the day. If others think little of McNeill's zareba let them, but in justice to the troops who stood and fell, I am quite unable to write on the subject in more modest terms. If any of my readers have a thought that this is a self-advertisement let me refer to the opening paragraphs where I point out my duties on that day consisted of erecting canvas tanks and fill-in these with water. For the rest of the time I was merely an onlooker in the same sense as my bhistie, who stood by my horse during the fight as calmly as if he were watching a field day!

The contention that the Indian Contingent were to build an intermediate zareba on the 22nd March on the return trip to Suakim and occupy it with one regiment I am unable to believe for more reasons than one. In the first place I have no recollection that anything of the kind was hinted at; secondly I don't think any arrangements were made for provisioning a second zareba, or were water tanks taken out for this purpose; thirdly, if my memory is correct, no regiment of the Indian Contingent carried either great coats or cooking utensils; and lastly, is it reasonable to believe we would have taken laden animals out eight miles to carry the same loads back four? The first time I ever heard of this suggestion was on reading a few weeks ago the "History of the Soudan Campaign."

The loss of Lieut. Richardson and four men of the 5th Lancers, reported missing, was very sad, and as far as this officer was concerned, romantic in the extreme. The story goes that on the evening of the 21st he received a letter from his bride-wife saying she had dreamt he had been killed. He took this so much to heart that before retiring for the night he said good-bye to some of his brother officers. The following morning he was sent with a handful of men to the front scouting, and I think I am correct in stating he and they were never seen again. Anyhow, they were returned amongst the missing, and not till months after did we come across their bodies, when recognition was only possible through what remained of their uniforms. The telegram announcing the news of this officer's supposed end, when placed in the hands of his wife, caused her to drop down dead.

The Indian Contingent were not sorry to get back into camp on the afternoon of the 23rd, when they received a great ovation from their British comrades. The 17th N.I. were detailed for duty in Suakim, as they were more or less suspected of "nerves."

On the 24th a convoy was sent out towards McNeill's zareba escorted by the 9th Bengal Lancers, 15th Sikhs, and 28th Bo. Infantry, which was met half way by the Coldstreams and Marines, who were attacked on the way back to the zareba, losing one man killed, three officers wounded, and 25 men and followers wounded, besides over 100 camels, which clearly proved the Arabs had some fight left in them, in spite of having lost some 3,000 killed and wounded on the 22nd!

On the 25th the usual convoy went out, but was not molested; but on the 26th a large convoy, escorted by two guns R.H.A., two squadrons 5th Lancers and 20th Husaars, 9th Bengal Lancers, the Grenadiers, East Surrey Regiment (70th), Shropshire L.I., 15th Sikhs, 28th Bo. Infantry, under the personal command of General Graham, was rushed without result, which went far to show the enemy were beginning to think better of the game, for on the two succeeding days the convoys were in no way interfered with. It turned out, however, they were now collecting elsewhere, for on the 1st April the officer commanding at McNeill's zareba, reported that Tamai was occupied by the enemy, having obtained his information from the Mounted Infantry, so orders were at once issued for a force to start the next morning at 3 a.m. This force consisted of 304 officers, 6,884 rank and file, 1,111 horses, 171 mules, and 1,639 camels, and did not move off till 4.30 a.m., owing to some of the troops having paraded at the wrong spot. The whole was under the command of General Graham. The advance was in one large square, the front face being three companies in line, with sides of 700 yards, with all the animals inside the square.

On reaching McNeill's zareba a halt was made for breakfast, dropping stores, etc., and picking up the troops stationed there, who were replaced by the 28th Bo. N.I.

At 10 a.m. another start was made, and a captive balloon sent up, which turned out a complete failure. At 5 p.m. we reached the Teselah Hill, where we at once zarebaed. The cavalry and mounted infantry were sent back to McNeill's zareba to spend the night, with orders to rejoin in the morning. Picquets were posted, and we spent a quiet night, excepting a few rounds which were fired into the square at midnight, which was put a stop to by one round from the Horse Artillery. One private of the East Surrey was killed, two men of the Berkshires, and two Australians wounded. On arrival at the Teselah Hill these N.S.W. men resented the idea of hiding behind a zareba, which they considered a waste of energy. The fact was they were utterly pumped by the march, and had consumed nearly all their supply of drinking water, and only wished to lie down and rest themselves. When the firing commenced at midnight they were all there, and wanted to rush out and engage the enemy!

On the morning of the 3rd the troops were drawn up as shown in sketch ready to march off as soon as the cavalry and mounted infantry arrived, which they did at about 8.30. The ground was undulating and sandy, with practically no cover, excepting patches of grass in the hollows, so with mounted troops in front there seemed no necessity for this "square" formation, which must have been very trying for the four battalions in column form-

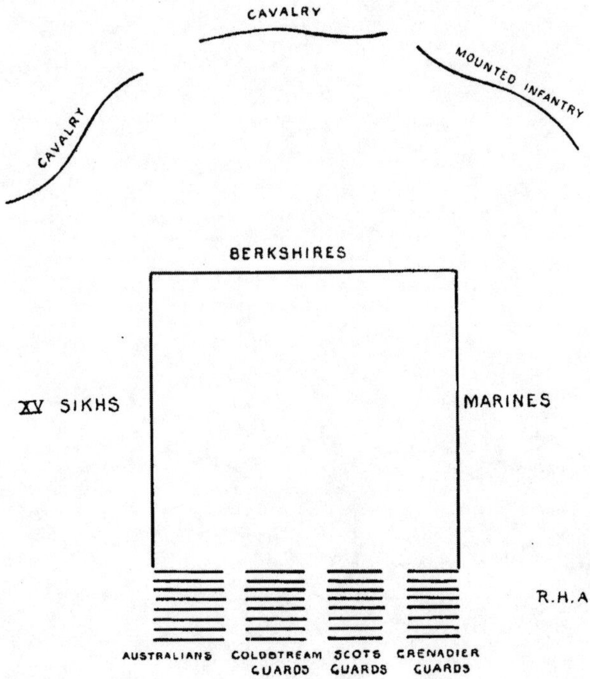
CAVALRY
CAVALRY
MOUNTED INFANTRY
BERKSHIRES
XV SIKHS
MARINES
R.H.A
AUSTRALIANS
COLDSTREAM GUARDS
SCOTS GUARDS
GRENADIER GUARDS

ing the rear face. It had the merit, however, of making "surprise" absolutely impossible.

When we reached the "Khor," which was nothing but the deep broad bed of a river, and quite dry, the square was ordered to wheel to the right, by which time the Mounted Infantry were exchanging shots with the Fuzzies. This change of front brought us over the wells, the only water supply of Tamai, a place consisting of a number of mean-looking huts with grass roofs. The square halted, the Berkshires and the 15th Sikhs were ordered to occupy the heights on the far side of the Khor, from which they were able to scatter the few hundreds of the enemy in sight, and there was nothing left for the force to do but march back, as the water supply was quite inadequate for our wants. On the return march the huts were set on fire, and soon there was a continuous "popping" of ammunition, which had been secreted in the grass roofs, proving the Fuzzies had made a hasty bolt of it. It was a most disappointing day, as we were led to suppose the Arabs would certainly put up a good fight at Tamai; but that old fox Osman Digna had no intention of being caught in the open. The only place they could have made a stand was in the Khor, but our artillery would have soon shelled them out of this. On arrival at the Teselah Hill the men had their dinners, after which we started for McNeill's zareba, which was reached about 6 p.m., after a fatiguing march through sand nearly the whole way. Our losses were one man killed and one officer, 14 men, and one follower wounded.

General Graham and his staff rode on to Suakim, whilst the force under General Freemantle spent the night at the zareba, and returned to Suakim the next day, the 4th, leaving the 28th Bo. N.I. with two Gardners manned by the R.N., under the command of Colonel Singleton, 28th Bo. Infantry.

On the 6th a large convoy, escorted by four battalions, went out to McNeill's zareba to remove all stores prior to the evacuation of that post, whilst the Coldstream Guards, N.S.W. Infantry, 17th Company R.E., 2 guns 5/1 R.A., and 2nd Company M.I., a total of 68 officers, 1,649 rank and file, 54 horses, 190 mules, 327 camels, and 349 followers, proceeded to No. 1 post under General Fremantle and zarebaed. This formed the first of a string of posts to be occupied along the projected railway line. During the rest of the month the force was entirely employed building posts and on convoy work. As the posts were occupied the troops at Suakim were continually shifting camp to remain as compact as possible, and by the 26th the force was distributed as follows:—

	Officers.	Men.	Followers.	Horses.	Mules.	Camels.
Base - -	108	2063	1890	231	1018	2126
Head Quarters	169	3857	2041	1195	1701	1077
Handub -	96	2004	2301	642	195	2076
No. 1 Post -	1	34	3	5	2	—
Head of Rail	46	1116	30	72	88	70
Ootao - -	63	1511	911	162	405	644
Tambuk - -	43	905	138	42	80	76
Total -	526	11490	7314	2349	3489	6069

To supply so many men and animals with water in a country where there was practically none was no light task, considering it had to be carried to the posts.

The navvies brought out from England to build the line of railway to Berber caused us much amusement. Every shovel-ful of sand they threw up seemed to bring down two with it, causing many unique expressions of disgust; but the climax was reached when our Indian coolies were formed into gangs to work with their British comrades. The Indians could not realise the use of the wheel-barrow, which when filled they immediately hoisted on to the heads of two and carried bodily off to the bank under construction. This completely beat the British workmen, and produced remarks which I wish I could repeat.

The navvies were certainly splendid specimens

of manhood, and looked their best in the suitable working kit provided for a tropical sun, but which was completely disregarded on the Sabbath, when one and all turned out in small cloth caps or bowlers, corduroys, and the thickest blue cloth double-breasted pea-jackets I ever saw! How they existed in garments of the kind under a sun so fierce was beyond understanding.

One day we received warning that our camps were likely to be attacked at night. Special guards were placed round the camp of the navvies, who were warned what to do in case of attack, and at the same time advised to arrange amongst themselves for one man per tent to be awake during the night. The scorn with which they received the advice was more than comical; they merely pointed to their picks and shovels and said, "To hell with your niggers!" Not a man among them missed his full night's sleep. They were there to work, and if anyone interfered with this they would know the reason why!

They were capital fellows, but a great anxiety to the authorities, and no one was sorry when they were safely put on board homeward bound. Their camp songs at night before they turned in were truly delicious.

The 28th Bombay Infantry, looking ahead, and thinking the regiment might be employed in these particular parts for a period of three years, which, I believe was the estimated time for the Suakim-Berber Railway, very wisely determined to make themselves as comfortable as possible, so brought over with them the whole of their mess property, including mess tents, shamianahs, etc., as used in India during peace, as well as a complete active service equipment. The consequence was their mess was the centre of attraction, where any morning you might see officers from all the British regiments enjoying a quiet read of the papers in comfort, and soon became known as "the Guards' Club." Later, when we were turned into an army of occupation, this foresight on the part of the officers of the regiment was well rewarded, as they were able to cater for a large number of honorary members, who otherwise would have had to live in discomfort on the food cooked by the one body servant allowed by Regulations, and spend a miserable, lonely existence. Here again could be seen the handiwork of Westmacott, an organiser whom nothing defeated! It was always a pleasure to dine at this mess, where everything was done well, and where you were sure of a hearty welcome from a particularly go-ahead body of officers, who were equally good in the field. For their services at Suakim the regiment was turned into "Pioneers" in '88, gaining further laurels on the Punjab Frontier and in Tirah.

After the break up of the Headquarters and the departure of Sir Gerald Graham, Sir George Greaves assumed command; to him was left the final arrangements connected with the force of occupation, which was to remain in Suakim under Sir John Hudson. Sir George was a man who made things move, a rapid thinker and worker himself, intolerant of delay and shilly-shallying in others, during his short command all were kept fairly busy, and in record time he had all in order, after settling every conceivable point mortal could think of in the interests of those remaining behind. The result was Sir John found everything in working order.

The troops were hutted, arrangements for ice machines (chiefly for the use of the hospital), and water supply had been carefully thought out, and we were left in comparative comfort to face the hot season. The ice machines were not quite a success at first as we only managed to make the water cold, so the British India ice ship "Bulimba" was chartered for a further term till mechanics, who thoroughly understood the machines, could be spared from the Nile, where similar ones were turning out ice regularly.

The command now devolved on Sir John Hudson, which consisted of the original Indian Contingent excepting the 9th Bengal Lancers, only one squadron of which remained, besides the 1st Shropshire Light Infantry, wing of the Sussex Regiment, some guns, Mountain Battery, and the newly-formed Camel Corps. The heat during the day was terrific, and used to go up to 125deg. in our Headquarters' house.

Owing to the scarcity of vegetables, scurvy broke out amongst the Native troops and followers also a very fatal disease called berri-berri. Special arrangements had to be made for the supply of green food from Suez and Aden, which improved the health of the men considerably.

We still had a very large camel transport, the feeding of which caused much anxiety. To an army of occupation they were of no use, whilst the difficulties of grazing were enormous and extremely harassing to the troops, necessitating large guards, in spite of which camels were lost and men and followers were killed by the ever watchful Hadendowas, so it was decided to get rid of them at any price.

Our first effort turned out a lamentable failure, and would have been comical but for the fact it was almost brutal. Some local merchants were approached with a view to purchasing. At first all went well, as we found a ready market at Jeddah, on the opposite coast of the Red Sea, but later the Turkish authorities refused permission to land any more, due no doubt to the fact we were at war with a Mahomedan race. Then a Greek came forward and assured us he could either dispose of his purchases or arrange for their feeding till he could get rid of them, so to this man we sold a batch of 100, as an experiment at, I think, Rs. 25 a head. A few days after the sale he satisfied us he had got rid of them, and we were just handing over another batch of 100 when a report came in from the Water Forts, the stench out there was so unbearable the men could not stand it any longer, as all were sick. On going out this report was found to be only too true. A detachment of cavalry was ordered to proceed at once and ascertain the cause, which was soon discovered. About half a mile from the Forts the troopers came across the skinned carcases of 100 camels exposed to the rays of a burning sun. Our Greek friend had done us. Under cover of night he drove the poor beasts out, skinned them, and made a clear profit of 100 per cent. out of the hides, and we had the pleasure of burying this putrid mountain of flesh!

Our next attempt was not very much better. We sent out a deck load of these poor beasts, on one of our transports, and threw them overboard after first shooting them. This turned out failure No. 2, as it only attracted large numbers of sharks inside the coral reefs where the men used to bathe!

Attempt No. 3 turned out more satisfactory for a time, as they were taken out to sea, and in this way, we thought, the difficulty had at last been solved. Not for long, however, for soon reports came in from Mail steamers running up and down the Red Sea complaining of the many carcases they ran into, which stuck to the bows of their vessels, causing endless annoyance and inconvenience. There was nothing left but for the Government to carry them back to India. As these animals could not have cost less than Rs. 100 each the loss in sea transport must have been a heavy one.

With the hot weather our staff dwindled down. Pearson was invalided, Cook went on leave not to return, and McGregor Stewart's five years of staff terminated, so I found myself promoted to A.A.G. and Chief Staff Officer, with Major Hare as D.A.A.G. for British troops.

The office work was very heavy, as we had to keep up a double correspondence, viz.: with Cairo and Simla, but it was a training and experience any man would have been glad of. I can truly say the General and his staff never knew what it was to be idle for a moment, so time did not hang heavy, and in spite of the intense heat everyone was fit, for after the sun went down the temperature cooled, and all enjoyed the comforts of sleep at night, which made up for the trials by day.

After the excitement of almost daily expeditions of the first months, the duties of occupation were dull, but all ranks found some compensation in the "extra pay," for the authorities were good enough to allow us the choice of drawing our salaries in gold or silver, and as the sovereign fetched locally something like Rs. 15 not many rushed for the familiar rupee. This additional "pay" for the native ranks and followers kept all "koosh," as we say in India, and although leave was open to the officers, not too many availed themselves of the privilege, they preferred to make "hay" under the burning sun, as opportunities of the kind don't often fall to the lot of the "soldier man." On the whole I never remember a happier garrison than the Suakim one of '85.

There was no lack of amusement, the fishing in

and just outside the harbour was excellent, and under the guidance of the cheeriest of the cheery, "Dickie Westmacott," of the 28th Bombay Infantry, hardly a week passed without a gymkhana, whilst polo was played regularly. Cricket on a coir matting pitch was also indulged in, and the mess of the 28th Bo. Infantry was an attraction for all, run on lines other regiments might well copy. Here again one could see the handiwork of Westmacott, who was as good a man in camp as he was soldier in the field; in the latter he was hard to beat, and proved this years later in the Tirah Campaign, when, as a General, he showed *how* rear guard actions ought to be fought, and *where* Generals *ought* to be when these actions are going on, the best loved "soldier" I have ever struck.

Sir John Hudson, in addition to commanding, was acting Governor of the Red Sea Littoral, during the absence of Colonel Chermside, and was fortunate in having as a Lieutenant Brewster Bey, of the Egyptian Customs Service. What he didn't know about Arabs wasn't worth knowing. Nearly all the time we were in occupation, McNeill's zareba, or rather the ground on which the fight took place, for we razed it before evacuation, was held by the Arabs as their nearest outpost. Here they squatted for months, and in defiance, erected a long pole with an empty kerosine oil can on the top, which glittered in the sun to make us aware of their presence. They retained some of the wretched followers they caught on the 20th March belonging to the water carts of the 9th Bengal Lancers, and for the rescue of whom we were most anxious. Brewster amongst his spies had an old Arab lady, to whom was entrusted the delicate duty of securing the escape or release of these unfortunates. We offered a generous reward, and more than once did the old lady nearly succeed. On a small piece of paper I wrote a short message in Hindi and Urdu, which she managed to show the prisoners, and in return she brought back acknowledgments, and on one occasion a slip to say they were, at the moment, being fairly well treated, as their duties chiefly consisted in carrying water from long distances and gathering fire wood, adding that they had picked up a little Arabic, which improved their lot. The old lady was at times absent two and even three weeks, and more than once showed signs of severe treatment. However, she was in no way deterred, and at last returned with the news she had fixed the escape for a particular night. To assist her we were to send a small party out which was to approach close to the camp, with a larger one in rear in case of accidents. She managed so well that a start was actually made, when one of the party lost heart and burst out sobbing, which attracted the attention of that portion of the sleeping guard, which could not be bought over, and the result was failure, much to my sorrow, as it was almost the eve of my departure, and the release of these poor souls before leaving was my one wish. Fortunately for the prisoners, the attempted escape was not suspected. At first we rather discredited the old lady's story, but later she brought in a written account from one of the prisoners explaining the failure. At this moment I forget if the release was effected later or not, but I rather think some of the men did escape.

In the month of October Sir John Hudson heard the Contingent was to be relieved by another, chiefly from the Madras Presidency, as also the staff, so he asked me, as a favour, to remain on, as he did not look forward to the prospect of having no one with a grasp of affairs to help him run the show. After considering the matter 24 hours, I agreed to remain, and he despatched a wire to the H.E. the Commander-in-Chief in India, begging he might retain my services, and in reply received a cable stating the request would be considered if a written application was forwarded by the outgoing mail, with reasons in support of the request. This was complied with, and I settled down to a further spell of Suakim. Some three weeks later I was returning from a fishing expedition down the coast when we noticed with surprise a steamer entering the Suakim Harbour from the Indian side, a rare occurrence. As we entered the harbour some hours later we could see Sir John waiting at the landing stage, and as I stepped off the launch he greeted me with the words, "Your relief has arrived," the explanation being that our Mail boat carrying the request to Simla for my retention struck a coral reef and remained fast for a tide, thus missing connection with the Mail steamer at Aden, and led the Simla authorities to believe either Sir John or myself had changed our minds! After a consultation with the newly-arrived A.A.G., the General sent another cable, explaining the circumstances, and adding the new man much preferred the billet in India he vacated. The answer came that it was too late to make any change, but Sir John could keep me as an additional A.A.G., till the last transport, so in this way I remained an extra month, and was able to go into the working of the office with my successor.

On the 19th November I embarked with almost

the same detachments I went out with, viz., a squadron of the 9th Bengal Lancers and the Madras Sappers and Miners, after taking a regretful farewell of Sir John Hudson, who had now been joined by Lady and Miss Hudson. I think I can safely say the months I served as A.A.G. to Sir John were quite the most delightful I ever experienced as a staff officer. He was a very particular man, but always just and considerate, and in an independent command was extremely strong, and always ready to take any amount of responsibility, and being Governor of the place and district, his hands were considerably strengthened.

Our transport on the return journey was a British India steamer, which proved a comfortable sea boat, but a real bad mover against the head winds we experienced going down the Red Sea, when our average for days was not more than seven knots per hour, and as a consequence there was every chance of our running short of water and fodder, so when off Aden we decided on putting into that harbour for these necessities, and proclaiming our wants by signal, which brought the Commissariat Officer on board in a condition nigh apoplectic. His face was a picture, the idea of coming to a place like Aden for water and grass! I agreed with him it was an uninviting spot, but preferable to dying of thirst at sea, to saying nothing of the loss to Government in the event of our having no fodder for the horses. After a certain amount of haggling he supplied our wants, but took an absolute delight in telling me that "as sure as God made apples" the Government would make me pay the piper, for taking the vessel out of its course and claiming excess rations, as the ship's papers clearly showed we had started with the regulation supply! I thanked him for the supplies as well as his gracious words; but I took the precaution to post a report of my action to Sir John Hudson, and kept my commissariat friend thirsty till it was time for him to clear off! As a matter of fact, when we reached Bombay we had none too much of water or grass.

During the voyage some of the Madras Sappers were attacked by that hateful disease berri-berri, and lost, I think, five men, including a Native officer, who had done excellent work, and was present at nearly every engagement. This company suffered from the complaint at Suakim, but no one anticipated an outbreak at sea. The disease being almost confined to fishermen on the sea coast, who seldom enlist, was hardly known to our medical officers, and was only diagnosed by an officer of the R.A.M.C., who at one time served at

Cannanore on the West Coast of India, and as well as I remember the recoveries were nil, so one could not help feeling anxious when it attacked the men on board. I am glad to say, however, it did not spread.

PART III

INDIA

PART III

INDIA

On arrival at Bombay I received a wire offering me the A.A.G.-ship of either Meerut or Allahabad Divisions, and accepted the latter, as my old regiment, the 68th L.I., were stationed there. After a couple of days at Bombay to make good my wardrobe, I started for Allahabad, picking up my belongings at Jubbulpore en route, and reported myself to Sir Charles Gough, who I found in the midst of packing, as he was about to leave India. He was relieved by General Tom Gordon, whom I found a General hard to beat and a true friend.

Allahabad never was a popular station, but to me there were many worse. Purely military stations are apt to "pall" on one after a time. Here there was a large civil element, and a considerable number of merchants, lawyers, and others whose opinions and conversation carried one outside the official world, and whose society refreshed one. The hospitality of the place was boundless, and the days and nights literally flew. Even in the hottest weather one was never dull. The Club, as Indian Clubs go, was extremely good, and here all met in the evenings. It was delightful seeing the old regiment again, though the changes amongst the officers were many, only some six remaining of those I knew 10 years previously!

After getting the hang of the work I took three months' Soudan leave, which I spent at Bhuj, where sport of every kind was at one's door. I never saw such small game shooting or such splendid specimens of panthers, the tracking which my indefatigable host, Jack Ashby, never seemed to tire of. He made some fine records, the particulars of which I wish I had, but this was not astonishing of one of the best shots in India. On more than one occasion have I seen him make a good bag of quail, representing a bird for each shot fired. The Rao of Cutch and his younger brother, Prince Kaluba, were the most delightful representatives of the bluest blood of India I ever met. In all our shikar parties His Highness invariably took the part of host, so it goes without saying that things were done well. His Highness's country rejoices in being beyond the reach of the "globe trotter," so the lucky guest who has the good fortune to find himself inside this State gets the best sport the country can provide, and takes his departure with feelings of the greatest regret, and the strongest desire to revisit it, knowing the warmth and genuineness of the reception awaiting him.

To watch the Rao Sahib dealing with his subjects was a revelation. They loved him, and well they might, for he was approachable to all, and no ruler I know deserved better the devotion of his followers. The earnestness and excellence of the Rao's work might well be imitated by other Chiefs. He visited England during the Jubilee of '87, and left a mark at home which must have been gratifying to the authorities of the India Office. No "Court" that he received turned his head, as frequently happens in the cases of other Chiefs who visit the West. He lived the life of an English gentleman, and was never so happy as when on the moors in Scotland he shot from Phones. During his stay he saw everything worth seeing which could improve an already superior mind, and seemed to enjoy it, but I would be surprised to hear he ever repeated his visit.

After an absence of seven years I expected to find some changes in the small station, but was not prepared for Swiss châlets and prettily laid out gardens where I remembered rock-strewn hill and hollow. The mess house had sprung into a really attractive building, which might easily have been mistaken for a club. After a cordial greeting from the Colonel (Hay) and Mercer, there was much to listen to and digest.

When the 2nd Battalion was raised the authorities, for reasons best known to themselves, omitted to transfer a single 1st Battalion officer, and to make matters worse not one officer in the new battalion had ever served with Goorkhas. It was a decided misfortune, and the consequence was the new corps worked on lines of their own, and kept much to themselves. Personally, I put this down to the intention of springing a surprise on us, as soon as the battalion felt ready to appear in public, as it were. The officers, of course, mixed freely with each other, as the mess was now a joint one, but owing to the local conditions the men's lines and parade ground of the 2nd Battalion were some little distance off, completely hidden in a forest of pines. So without being curious it was impossible to say what progress had been made, and as the Commander-in-Chief was expected in the course of a few weeks, the secrecy of the doings of our comrades was understood and respected. The arrival of a Commander-in-Chief in a large station causes a stir, how much more so in a small one perched on a hill top of the Himalayas. The red letter day arrived, and on the first morning His Excellency inspected the 1st Battalion, and then invited all the officers to accompany him to witness the more important function of inspection of a newly raised corps which had hardly reached the first year of its birth. With considerable interest we joined the staff, and rode to the parade ground of our comrades, to find the battalion drawn up in line as steady under arms as the oldest soldiers. The inspection was very minute, and the result most satisfactory, judging from the words His Excellency addressed to the officers. If we, of the 1st Battalion, were critical, it was only because we looked on them as one of ourselves. We formed opinions, but we kept our thoughts to ourselves, and were more than pleased to listen to the words of praise and encouragement from the highest in the land. Later in the day, however, a "bomb" was thrown. It came about in this way. The Chief was talking to one of our senior officers about the wonderful progress the new battalion had made and its general efficiency, when he turned round to this officer and asked him his opinion. He very correctly obtained permission to speak without reserve, which was at once granted. He pointed out certain minor defects he noticed, and wound up by saying he could not understand why the battalion had failed to drill all the morning as a rifle regiment! There was no getting over this, the point had not been noticed by His Excellency, the Adjutant General of the Army, who was himself an infantry soldier, or by any member of his staff, although one of these was an officer of a very distinguished rifle regiment!

After His Excellency's departure I obtained three months' leave in India, and during my absence received a wire from "Bill" Beresford (Lord William Beresford), Military Secretary to the Viceroy, offering me the officiating second in command of the Meywar Bhil Corps, which I accepted, as promotion in the Goorkhas was at the time hopeless. On making enquiries, I found the second in command had to live alone at a place called Kotra, in the heart of the Bhil country, where big game shooting was reported to be excellent. The duties consisted of looking after two companies of the regiment, and the political charge of five small Boomia Chiefs, which entailed a pleasant three months of camp life in the cold weather visiting their estates. On the 20th July, '88, I started for this wild and to me unknown spot.

As I was taking my ticket at Church Gate Station for Rohera Road, a small station in the Rajputina Malwa Railway, whence I had to ride to Kotra, a distance of some 37 miles, I recognised a "back" which seemed familiar to me, and found it was owned by my old friend Captain Creagh, of the Indian Marine, who was in the act of taking a ticket for Ajmere to spend a month with his brother. In a few words I explained where I was going, and begged him to accompany me instead. pointing out that it was more than half-way to Ajmere. He jumped at the idea, and the next afternoon found us at Rohera Road, where we dined, and put up for the night in a tumbled down building which at one time was used by the Engineers when constructing the line. A dak of horses was waiting for me, besides two sowars as escort. My own horses I could not expect for another week, so there was nothing for it but to dismount one of the sowars and give his horse to my friend. On examination we found the saddle looked so horribly uncomfortable that I suggested a riding camel, and to be on equal terms I sent one of the sowars off to Rohera Village to secure two riding camels. These turned up before bed-time, so we felt quite happy, especially as I still had horses to depend on in case of accidents. Having six months' supplies with me, and excellent servants, we loaded up the carts over night, and told them to make an early start at 5 a.m., and have lunch ready for us some 20 miles on the road on the banks of a river which was recommended by one of the sowars, who was directed to accompany the carts.

Just as we were thinking of making a start at 10 a.m. the following morning the rain came down in torrents, and without doubt it was the bursting of the monsoon. There was nothing to be gained by waiting, so made up our minds to face it. The riding camels looked all right, and we proceeded to mount, but as my friend's beast rose he opened his umbrella, and the next instant I saw a wriggling, bucking mass, and my pal stretched in the mud, laughing till I thought he would burst. Fortunately there was a wire fence round the compound, so it didn't take long to catch his mount and readjust the saddle. The second attempt was quite successful, and once across the line we found the going good for the first two miles, when we ran into a perfect network of nullahs with high steep banks and streams that were almost torrents, negotiating which was anything but pleasant. It took us over two hours covering the first five miles, when we were glad to say good-bye to cultivation and enter the jungles. At 2 p.m. we sighted our carts, and could see that cooking operations were going on, but when we got closer we found a river some 100 yards broad, between us and our commissariat, running like a mill stream. The mounted orderly, however, assured us it was all right, so we forded the stream without meeting with mishap.

The rain having ceased, and the spot being an ideal one for a picnic, we soon forgot aches and pains, and after a sumptuous repast lolled about till we were quite dry.

Knowing the regiment had sent provisions to my house at Kotra, we could continue our journey and allow the carts to follow. So off we set at 4 p.m., declaring we felt fresher than when we started. The sun was shining, the late rain had washed the trees of all dust, the scenery was superb and hours passed like minutes; but the going was terribly slow, and when the sun dipped we were still some seven miles from our journey's end. Soon darkness came on, and then only did we realise how bad the road was. We tried conversation, but that soon relaxed into mutterings, as our beasts began to stumble against what might have been rocks, fallen trees or banks of nullahs! Every mile now seemed five; but at last we heard the sound of a bugle, and recognised the tattoo, which cheered us considerably, for we were beginning to think in spite of assurances from the sowar, we had lost our way. Another hour of scrambling brought us into the small bazaar, and a few minutes later we were drinking claret and soda by the gallon. Never shall I forget that thirst.

I had to interview native officers, vakeels, and other small fry connected with the Political Office, to get rid of whom was no easy matter. In the meantime I found my friend had thrown himself on a cot and was fast asleep, an example I proceeded to follow. At daybreak my servants and carts appeared on the scene, and by breakfast time the house was in order and we had time to look round us. The house was not a mansion, but the environments were all that could be desired. It was perched at the end of a spur, and for miles the view in front was exquisite, whilst behind, as far as the eyes could see, was nothing but forest. In the afternoon we enjoyed an excellent three hours' shoot with the quail, and discovered the river which passed the foot of the garden promised considerable sport. My friend had no rifle, so during his week's stay we contented ourselves with small game shooting, which was quite good, for besides quail there were partridges and hares galore.

The only thing to mar our sport was the coming monsoon, which meant flooded rivers and impassable roads, so after a week's holiday my nautical friend had to say good-bye, and I had to settle down to a life of absolute loneliness, the nearest white man in the country being upwards of 50 miles off at Kherwarra, the Headquarters of the regiment. It was a new experience for me, this isolation, but the surroundings were so full of charm I did not find it irksome. I was surprised to find the Bhils such smart little soldiers; some of the companies you might have mistaken for Goorkhas at a short distance. They were very keen, well set up, and really well drilled.

I quite looked forward to seeing the regiment. The work was interesting, and just sufficient to keep one comfortably occupied. I began to make enquiries concerning the sport to be had, and learnt that anything from a sparrow to a tiger could be obtained for the asking. This sounded well enough; but when I began to put it to the test I found that a single rifle wasn't in it. The tigers were there, sure enough, but the jungle was so vast that the chances of getting a shot were remote; so after beating for weeks I gave it up as hopeless, and made up my mind to fire at the first object, rather than let sambhur pass untouched hoping for Stripes to come my way. On more than one occasion I saw a tiger, but never got a fair shot at one. However, I had all the excitement, and contended myself with the smaller game. With two more guns without doubt a splendid bag could have been obtained in the magnificent jungles around.

After a month's solitary existence I was glad of a change to Kherwarra on a visit to Colonel McRea, when I made the acquaintance of the regiment, and learnt that much better shooting was to be obtained from the Headquarters' Station, as the jungles not only held more game, but were easier to beat. On my return to Kotra I began to think of the cold weather tour, and for four months spent a really happy time in camp. Having two sets of camp equipage, supplied by Government, travelling was quite luxurious, for when I moved I had only to ride to the next camp, where I found all in readiness. The work chiefly consisted of settling petty squabbles and boundary disputes. Four out of the Boomia Chiefs were in a state of impecuniosity, whilst the fifth was affluent; but as each of them could trace his origin for centuries, they were as particular about precedence as a Raja with his 10,000,000 subjects, and they would spend a lifetime quarrelling over the possession of a tree growing on the banks of a nullah, which separated their states, whilst the branches projected to the other bank. Sitting in the verandah of my house at night I have suddenly noticed a blaze in the jungle, which would only last for a short time; and when I asked what this meant, my Moonshi would say without concern, "Some Bhil has shot a man, and is burning the carcase!" A common occurrence, no doubt, in days gone by, but I hardly think this was the case in '88, for during the year I was at Kotra I had only one case of murder to deal with. After completing my cold weather tour I found the solitary life, especially during the hot weather, nigh intolerable, and was not sorry one day to hear Colonel McRae was proceeding to officiate as Resident at Oodeypore and I was to command at Kherwarra, where I spent a most enjoyable six weeks, at the end of which I received a wire from Simla offering me the command of the Merwara Battalion at Ajmere. In spite of the loneliness of the place, I was for some reasons sorry to leave Kotra, where everyone did his utmost to make life bearable. The petty Chiefs recognised the solitary life one spent, and often used to come in for a week merely "to see the sahib," and have a little "shikar." We got only one tiger, but this, I regret to say, fell to the rifle of the Punewar Chief, who was an excellent shot and a good sportsman, who would have been much more pleased had the luck been on my side.

After 12 months of the jungles Ajmere seemed quite a gay place. Besides the regiment, the Government officials consisted of a Commissioner, Deputy Commissioner, Executive Engineer, Medical Officer, and Principal and Head Master of the Mayo College. The rest of the community were the numerous officials of the Rajputana Malwa Railway, who really made the place. The command of a regiment is the nicest appointment any officer could wish for, so I was beaming with joy when I took it over. Ajmere itself is one of the most picturesque stations in India, surrounded, as it nearly is, by hills, with the Ana Sagar lake to complete the scene.

Boasting a very good Club near the racquet and tennis courts, practically the entire station met there every evening, and formed quite a family party. Most of the bachelors made use of our mess to our mutual advantage.

Saturdays and Sundays generally brought a contingent over from our neighbours at Nussurrabad, so life was anything but tame. Amongst our small community there were good men and true; sportsmen to the backbone, such as Frank Tebbs, Brian Egerton, Baldock, and Jimmy Tickell were not to be matched everyday. Without "gambling," after dinner whist was very popular, and quite the most ardent player was dear old "B. G.," whose "proof of the pudding was in the eating" always produced a happy smile, even when "a call for trumps" had not been seen by him. Amongst our officers there was one who never failed to keep the table supplied with his wonderful experiences of rod, gun, and rifle. Two of his stories are quite worth repeating. He prided himself on being a particularly good shot with a "scatter" gun, but one day when out with three others, for the life of him, he could not bring down a single snipe, which were plentiful and not too wild, so when a halt was made for lunch he was very crestfallen, as he hadn't bagged one bird. One of the party suggested his ammunition must be bad, on which another proposed fixing to a tree a sheet of newspaper and having a shot at it to see the pattern. He fired at some 25 yards, and on examining the paper discovered a space in the centre without the signs of a pellet, and would you believe it, to use his own words, "When they put a dead snipe against it, it was the exact shape of that bird on the wing." After this discovery he aimed just a little to the right or left and hadn't a miss the rest of the day!

On another occasion when he was at home on furlough he was walking round the "lake" in his father's grounds when he heard cries of distress, which caused him to run in the direction of the sounds, only just in time to save his father's life, for a pike had jumped out and seized the poor old gentleman by the leg, and was just dragging him into the water, when he clubbed the beast over the head, the biggest pike he had ever seen!

I remember his telling this "pike" story some years later to the Bishop of Calcutta, whose breath nearly deserted him!

During my stay in Ajmere we were honoured by visits from H.R.H. Prince Albert Victor of Wales, and H.I.M. the Czar of Russia (then Czarewitch), with whom was Prince George of Greece. These visits were purely informal, and days of rest, whilst touring through the Native States of Rajputana, whose Chiefs were entertaining them as only the Chiefs of India can.

On both occasions these young Princes won the hearts and esteem of all they came in contact with by the simplicity with which they entered into all the sport shown them, and the gracious manner in which they associated with the guests assembled to do them honour.

The chief features of Ajmere were the Mayo College, where the bluest blood of Rajputana is educated, and its Principal, my valued friend Colonel W. Loch, or to his intimates "Lockie."

For 10 years I knew the "boys" of the Mayo College, and every time I met them the pleasure of seeing them increased. Without them Ajmere would indeed have been a poor place.

The "form" of the boys was truly excellent, and the spirit which pervaded the College was equal to the best schools in the world. They were brought up as young gentlemen, and if any of them fail in after life it will be their own fault. Whenever the XI. were playing cricket you were certain to find the rest looking on, and longing for their turn to come when they could uphold the honour of their College at a game, which to the mind of the Englishman, is National.

On the 9th December I received a telegram from H.E. the Commander-in-Chief asking me if I would accept an appointment as Colonel on the Staff, and replied at once in the affirmative. After a connection with the Merwara Battalion of nearly 10 years, during the whole of which time I was commandant, it was only natural I should say good-bye to this fine corps with feelings of intense regret. Considering the regiment had to be worked by only three British officers, one of whom was, as a rule, absent on leave, I consider the condition in which it always was, was highly creditable to the Native officers and N.C.O.'s, and men themselves, and I sincerely trust that in the near future the authorities will see the advisability of treating it more liberally in the matter of officers, in order that it may be brought into line, as regards efficiency for active service, with other regiments of the Native Army, for undoubtedly Merwara is a district from which a fine battalion could always be recruited, in fact I think the district could easily bear the strain of furnishing two battalions of men who would compare favourably with the better known races of India. The men are of fine physique, have proved themselves loyal to a degree, and in years gone by were able to more than hold their own in broken and wild country against the forces of the large Native States, by which they are completely hemmed in, and in fact withstood for years the attacks of Regular troops with so much success, that the Government of the day wisely made terms with them, and guaranteed them protection in the future. Education, or to be more correct, civilization, is only just reaching them, and at first sight they appear below the average intellectually, but soon they pick up sufficient knowledge for the requirements of the soldier. As a body they are good shots, possessed of great marching powers, and extremely amenable. Being tillers of the ground, and inhabiting a wild district, they are particularly keen sighted, and make excellent trackers. They stand heat and cold equally well, and in the matter of pluck are in no way wanting.

As regards "caste," they are inferior, but in my humble opinion this does not detract from their usefulness as soldiers. I have never known men take more kindly to the musketry range than the Mers, who are fond of shooting for shooting's sake. Like a great many of the wilder tribes, they like their "tot," but the records of the regiment show drunkenness is rare. During the Mutiny the loyalty of this battalion, which at the time was an armed police force, saved the town of Ajmere from pillage, and the lives of many Europeans, besides worrying evil-doers, the district round, in return for which the Government of India gave all ranks a special enhanced pension, which was being enjoyed by many men when I joined the battalion in '89.

Owing to the proverbial hospitality of Anglo-Indians my last days in Ajmere were spent in feasting. On the 11th I said good-bye to the men on parade, and in the evening dined with the regiment. The latter function was a cheery affair, but all day long there was a nasty lump in my throat, and more than once I found it no easy matter to control my feelings. Many of the leading Natives of the City called and appeared to be really sorry at my approaching departure, amongst them being men I barely knew by sight. On the 12th my dear old friend "Lockie" gave a farewell dinner at his charming house in the Mayo College grounds, where my most intimate friends were assembled, and who later accompanied me to the station, where I found all the Native officers of the regiment, and other Natives waiting with the usual supply of garlands, "pan," and numerous trays of fruits and sweetmeats, the joy of one's servants, who invariably annex these! Garlanded like an Indian idol, the train moved off, and I finally said good-bye to Ajmere and the many friends I had seen daily for the last 10 years, and a great wrench it was.

My old friends Frank Tebbs and Powell had their carriages on the train, so I was well cared for as far as Sirsa, where they had to leave me.

On the 14th I took over the command of the Ferozepore garrison, from Colonel Bruce, consisting of the 11th R.F.A., No. 4 Western R.A., 15th Bengal Lancers, Oxfordshire Light Infantry, 15th Sikhs, and 28th P.I., besides the fort and arsenal, the latter being about the largest in India. The above force, with a battalion of Reservists who were in camp, made up a very nice body of troops to handle. The whole formed part of the Lahore Division, commanded by that excellent soldier the late Major-General Gerald Morton.

It was very gratifying to me to be once more associated with that fine corps the 15th Sikhs, but alas only one old friend, of Candahar days, remained, viz., Reggie Hadow, who was now Commandant. On the first opportunity I enquired after my old orderly, Bolaka Sing, to learn that he had gone to pension as a Naik.

When commanding at Ferozepore, the L.G.C. notified his intention of inspecting the garrison; dates were fixed on two occasions, and each time countermanded, and finally I was informed the inspection was abandoned. On receipt of this I applied for and obtained 10 days' leave. On reaching my destination a telegram was handed me saying the L.G.C. would arrive at Ferozepore the following morning. I at once wired to his military secretary saying it would be impossible for me to return in time, but would arrive in the evening, in answer to which I received a further wire telling me not to return. Under the circumstances I felt justified in staying on and enjoying the leave, placing my house at the disposal of the L.G.C. and his staff. Later I wrote to one of the staff, hoping they had been made comfortable during my absence and the inspection had gone off well. In due course I heard all was most satisfactory excepting the horses of the 15th Bengal Lancers, which were unsteady under artillery fire. This was very astonishing, so on my return I spoke to the Station Staff Officer and C.O. of the regiment, who were even more astonished. The former handed me a copy of the L.G.C.'s remarks on the inspection, which were most flattering, and contained no reference to the unsteadiness of the horses, so did not know what to make of the letter. A few days later I was in Meean Meer on duty and took the opportunity of reporting the matter to my General, who on reading the letter burst out laughing, and said, "That had nothing to do with you; it occurred at Jullunelur; I was present!" So much for staff officers' notes.

Whilst on the subject I may mention another case. Any unsatisfactory remarks are invariably conveyed to the officer concerned. One day Major —— was informed that the General had reported him as being "Physically unfit for service." Now the Major happened to be a particularly efficient officer, as hard as nails, never sick or sorry, and a "giant" to boot!

After 10 years of a single battalion station it was a delightful change to be once more surrounded by soldiers and have scraped off "the rust and barnacles" which accumulate at anchor, for the command of a corps in an isolated station is very much akin to the command of an old hulk at safe anchorage up stream or in a harbour.

After a stay of only three months, during which time I was either inspecting or being inspected, H.E. offered me the command of the Hyderabad Contingent, which I took over from Sir M. Gerard on the 27th April, with the temporary command of Brigadier General, the Headquarters being at Bolarum alongside the Secunderabad command, one of the largest in India. The contingent consisted of four Field Batteries with obsolete guns, each commanded by a Captain, with two subs., R.A., four regiments of Lancers, three squadrons each, and six battalions of Infantry, all being Natives, and a very proud man I felt the day I signed the "taking over" documents of this fine force. For the first week I put up with the Herberts (Colonel Herbert being the A.A.G.), and then moved into the General's house, which for an Indian bungalow was quite an imposing one. From the first I found the work most pleasant and interesting, but hardly hoped to get much insight to the command before the cold weather, so made up my mind to take a short run home for 60 days, which I did during the summer, and whilst staying with my people at Aldershot Park was able to pay my old regiment, the 68th, a visit in camp, where all was bustle, as practically the entire Aldershot command was under orders to proceed on active service to settle matters with President Kruger. The feeling, amongst the youngsters at all events, was, the force was far too strong; that the whole affair would be over in a few months! After a delightful month spent at Sandersfoot, South Wales, I was once more Eastward bound, and soon back at Bolarum, where the first item of news I heard was "the officers of the contingent were up in arms as their German bandmaster had been taken by the Viceroy!" As the bandmaster was the private servant of the officers, and under a contract to serve them a term of years, I was naturally much surprised, and when I heard the circumstances, annoyed. The story requires a bit of telling, and to make it quite clear I must go back to the history of the band.

For many years the contingent possessed a string band for their Headquarters Mess, which was kept up by donations from each cavalry and infantry unit of the force in return for which musician recruits were trained at what was known as "The Contingent School of Music."

The band itself was composed of musicians who had either served or were serving in the Contingent. In earlier years the services of one of the bandmasters of British regiments in Secunderabad were secured under authority. This did well at first, but as the band increased in size and improved generally, it was considered desirable to engage a thoroughly good conductor, and the result was one of the Colleges of Music in Germany sent out an excellent violinist and conductor in Herr Bückner, who soon worked the band up to such a state of perfection that it became the envy of many corps, and the pride of the Contingent.

During my absence, it appears, the fame of the band had reached the elevated heights of the seat of Government, and the Viceroy had made up his mind to secure this treasure, in the shape of a bandmaster, as a conductor for his own band. The Military Secretary approached Herr Bückner, our private servant, direct; the offer was a tempting one for two reasons. In the first place it spelt

£ s. d., for at Simla and Calcutta a fine violinist like Herr Bückner would pick up many private pupils. Secondly, he was about to be married, and the climate of Simla had many attractions, so naturally he was anxious to accept, but being under a contract which had another two years to run he could not well give a definite reply, and after some hesitation on his part informed the secretary of the Band Committee of the offer which had been made.

As far as Bückner was concerned, no exception could be taken to his conduct, and he was told the matter would be placed before the Committee at their next meeting. I gathered that before this could be carried out the Resident received a communication from the Viceroy in which he expressed his desire to have Herr Bückner transferred to the Viceregal Band! with a remark that any objection on the part of the officers would be viewed as a personal slight to the head of the Government of India! On receipt of this document Sir Trevor Plowden sent for Colonel Herbert, who happened to be at the moment commanding the Contingent in virtue of his being the senior officer present on duty, and to him he *read* Lord Curzon's letter without *showing* it. Herbert accepted the letter as "an order," and informed Sir Trevor Plowden he would see the wishes of the Viceroy were carried out, and merely informed the officers that Herr Bückner was to go. I fancy no one was more surprised than Plowden. It was a matter which did not concern him, but I feel sure he would have seen the justice of a blank refusal to so despotic an act. When the officers heard the news they were justly indignant, for as they very truly said an appeal to them would have met with immediate response, but to have their servant removed without consultation was more than they could agree to. They were quite prepared to oblige Herr Bückner, and break the contract, but they asked for time to secure another man, and naturally expected the Viceroy or the Government to meet them half way by giving the new incumbent a passage out.

In the ordinary course, I called on the Resident, and from him heard the story as repeated by Colonel Herbert, and was also told of a second letter from Lord Curzon to the Resident, in which His Excellency expressed his pleasure on hearing the officers had complied with his wishes, and further implied that he hoped one day to make it up to them! It did not take me long to discover what the Resident's views of the case were, and I think he was much disappointed at heart that no fight was shown.

It was now too late for me to do anything, and the subject was so distasteful to the officers that they avoided it as much as possible. We secured the services of another conductor from the same college of music, which ran the band fund in to the tune of some Rs. 1,000, as the authorities declined all assistance.

Later I heard this regrettable affair originated in some silly remark by a lady at Simla, who compared H.E.'s band with the Contingent one to the detriment of the former.

When H.E. subsequently visited the Nizam he had an opportunity of listening to the soft strains of the Contingent Band, which he graciously praised, but he omitted to allow his praise to take any practical form; perhaps he will remember them one day!

This episode closed, I had time to think of putting my house in order and settling down comfortably before the more or less hard work of the "so-called" winter months, for up to this moment I had only come in contact with the troops stationed in Bolarum itself. As the command was distributed over seven different stations it took me some time before making a proper acquaintance with it, and it was with the deepest interest I made my first tour of inspection, only to discover the excellence of the force. The batteries, through no fault of their own, were practically useless as a modern fighting machine, but they provided a body of native drivers of no mean order. The Lancer regiments were as good as any I have seen, and the infantry, with a certain amount of weeding out of old men and undesirable non-fighting classes were up to quite a high standard, whilst the "esprit" of all was excellent. The Bolarum Garrison of one Field Battery, one Lancer regiment, and one infantry, of course had a great advantage over the rest, cantoned, as they were, alongside the magnificent Secunderabad command, with the troops of which they were always able to exercise. The only drawback I could see to the Lancers was their having only three squadrons instead of four. Taking the officers of the Contingent as a whole they were in all respects quite up to the average of the rest of the Army. They only wanted to be tried, to perform any duty, as well as their more fortunate brethren elsewhere, and their day must come, for they are far too valuable a body to be neglected much longer. A more delightful command it would be difficult to find, and the only misgiving I had was they were too scattered to do them justice. Socially I never struck a more attractive and sporting lot of officers than the Contingent ones. Wherever you went, however, there were a good many who were not entirely satisfied with doing the round of these seven stations; they were longing for active service and a "chance."

But surely that was natural, and in accordance with human nature, and in no way reflected on them. The system was wrong, for everything connected with the Contingent had to pass from the General in Command to the Military Secretary to the Resident at Hyderabad, and from him to the Government of India. The Military Secretary in my time was Colonel E. C. Lushington, an officer of exceptional ability and tact, and who had the advantage of having served nearly all his time in the Contingent, so personally I never felt the somewhat strange position in any way irksome; in fact, I might truthfully say it was quite the reverse, and to Colonel Lushington I owe a deep debt of gratitude, for he added considerably to the pleasures of the command, whilst his knowledge of the men and officers frequently came to my assistance, and relieved me at times of much anxiety. Between us a friendship sprung up from the first which I felt would last a lifetime. He, from his considerable knowledge, was always able to put his finger on the humbug or waster, and did this in a manner that almost made you feel you had made the discovery yourself. A man of presence and great charm who was always ready to help those in trouble, he ably filled a position which with little trouble could have made the life of the General in Command almost intolerable, instead of which he supported the General with a loyalty that was rare, unless he felt he could not do so conscientiously, which I am glad to say during my time was never the case. The position of the Military Secretary was not all joy, for more than once I found the Resident a difficult nut to crack, but a personal interview saved all unpleasantness, which I put down more to the Military Secretary's "preparation" than any personal influence. At times the civilian is inclined to think the soldier man is trying to get round him, which as a rule is a mistake, for my experience makes me think he is more inclined to err on the side of "frankness."

The pleasure of my first cold weather inspection of the command was much marred by the depressing news from South Africa, so on the 27th February we were more than overjoyed to hear of the surrender of Cronje and his force after making a noble stand. On the 13th March Reuter announced my dear mother had been given the C.I. by Her Majesty in person. The only bit of pleasing news in this, to me, peculiarly sad month.

On the 18th my good friend Sir W. Lockhart's death was announced, and on the 26th I received a cable from my brother Donnie telling me of my dear father's death. I little thought when I said good-bye to him on the station platform at Aldershot a few months previously I would never see his face again. A better father never lived; with loyalty and devotion he served his country to the end.

We still seemed to be doing badly in South Africa, for on the 3rd April we heard of the serious loss of seven guns in the Bloemfontein District. On the 20th I heard from —— giving me a very interesting account of their doings in Natal. He seems to think Buller's task too heavy, and adds that Thomas Atkins once under cover is difficult to move. He is very much down on the "staff," who are never to be seen in action, but "all there" in camp. Not nice reading this when you know the author to be a man who would make the best of things. On the 22nd April I was delighted to receive a confidential letter from the Commander-in-Chief offering me the command of the Bengal Brigade for Ashanti in the event of India being called on to furnish troops for the relief of Kumasi. It was almost too good to be true, for I expected the home authorities were not likely to admit they were so hard pressed for men that they could not send a Brigade from home. On the 8th May we heard of a reverse in Ashanti which did not improve my chance of getting there, the news from South Africa being more assuring I felt pretty certain in my own mind any expedition sent to Kumasi would be under some man at home. On 21st June it was decided to despatch a force to China, and on the 24th I received a wire appointing me to the command of the 1st Brigade, and left with Leonard as my orderly officer four days later. This more than made up for my late disappointment, as it was likely to be a long affair. We reached Calcutta on the morning of the 30th, where there was plenty to do in the way of fitting oneself out for a country where the climate varies from tropical heat to arctic cold. Calcutta itself was almost unbearable, in spite of heavy rain at times, in fact the heat was so great the men employed loading our transports struck, as they could not stand it any longer, and it looked as if it would delay our departure.

I was glad to meet Gaselee again, having only seen him once since the old Kandahar days. His command was a splendid one, and to make his position more assured they gave him the local rank of Lieut.-General, not a bad lift for a man who was only Colonel, and junior to myself in that rank. Every day I knocked up against old faces, and hardly an hour passed without a wire from some youngster asking me to take him with me on my staff. We made a start on the 3rd July on an old British India boat called the Naddea which, however, proved to be a first-class "sea" boat. Our party consisted of Colonel Lorne Campbell, Commandant of the Base, with Climo, Cummins, Ellis, Watling, and Furney of the 24th P.I., Major Thomson, I.M.S., Captains Young and Chamier of the Supply and Transport, Jermyn, D.A.A.G., 1st Brigade, besides Messrs. Steer and Newman as war correspondents. For some days we experienced the full force of the S.W. monsoon, and on the 9th our first casualty occurred in the death of Lorne Campbell's charger, a serious loss when you have only one. We did not stop till we reached Hong Kong, where after a stay of two days we continued our journey to Wei-hai-Wei. Here I had to change from the Naddea, which was full of stores for this place, and did not get away till the 24th. In the meantime I had a run on shore, dined with Prendergast, who was Commissioner there, and met Jellicoe, invalided from Tientsin with a bullet through his arm, also Captain Percy Scott, of Ladysmith fame, in command of H.M.S. Terrible, a most interesting man to meet, who was most anxious to see some of his 4.7 with us, and on the 27th we reached Taku.

PART IV

CHINA

PART IV

CHINA

27th July, 1900, Tientsin.

Arrived here after dark after three and a half hours' rail journey from Tang-ku. We anchored this morning early in the Peiho abreast of Tang-ku on the left bank of the river. Rain came down at seven and lasted in heavy showers tiil the afternoon making the disembarkation for troops and animals anything but pleasant.

We experienced considerable trouble walking the horses and mules over the slippery "sleeper formed" causeway to the open trucks on the line, and several fell over, a drop of some four feet, which made them more restive at the second attempt. By 2 p.m., however, we had all entrained, and slowly steamed to the Tang-ku Railway Station, where we were met by the Russian Colonel commanding this railway base, and who was responsible for the transportation of all troops. He paid us an official call in our carriages, during which we "refreshed" as well as our limited cellar admitted. With him was a very smart looking young "sub.," who knew sufficient English to make conversation possible. The band of the Siberian Regiment under his orders played some lively airs, including "God Save the Queen" more than once. I did hear the colonel's name, and made a mental note of it, but for the life of me I cannot remember it, anyhow, he had charming manners, and we spent a pleasant three-quarters of an hour chatting. Amongst other things he asked me if I had any "dead horses." This was a poser. Noticing my surprise, he quickly added his men were fond of "horse flesh," and thought it quite possible a few had been killed during the entraining operations! I regretted I was unable to oblige him, as barring certain abrasions, our only casualty was one officer's charger that jumped out of a truck and disappeared from view. We filled glasses and toasted our respective armies, whilst I wished him better luck in the matter of horse flesh later on, as there were many more ship loads of animals behind us!

At 3 p.m. all was ready so we said good-bye to our first acquaintance with the Russian Army. By this time the platform was packed with officers and men, and I must say these Siberians made a jolly

RUSSIAN GUARD (SIBERIANS).

good show. Led by their colonel they gave us many a hearty cheer, whilst the band once more played our National Anthem, and the Sepoys of the 1st Sikhs heartily responded.

The line to Tientsin is worked by a Russian Railway Battalion some 2,000 strong, and considering all things they do it admirably.

We now had time to examine our surroundings. The carriage we sat in was riddled with bullet holes, and at our first stoppage I examined the rest of the train, and found all the carriages in the same condition, including the engine. Ventilation of this kind for carriages on a sultry day was a bit of "all right," but we were not so confident about the perforations in the vicinity of the boiler of the engine, and on pointing them out to the driver he smiled encouragingly, whilst he thought to himself "What, nervous already?"

The country we passed over was quite level, but for some eight or nine miles impassable as it was under water. The embankment was high and substantial, so our progress was in no way impeded. Then we came to a fine open bit of grass land without obstacles of any kind, an ideal spot for cavalry desirous of indulging in shock tactics.

At each culvert and bridge a Russian picquet is posted, and at the larger ones further protection in the shape of guns; these were covered up, but they appeared to be machine guns. The picquets varied in strength; some consisted of only half a dozen men, whilst others had 50. Small cover was thrown up at each post, and all seemed well supplied with stores and transport in the shape of two and four wheeled carts painted green, which were drawn by one or two horses according to their size.

The men at each post left off what they were doing in order to give the passing train a cheer. At several points there were deep borrow-pits filled with water, where the men were enjoying a bath, and in nature's toilet they looked really fine specimens of manhood. I am much impressed with their physique and their jolly cheery countenances. They look as happy a lot as I have ever seen, and fit to go anywhere. There is a complete absence of cruelty in their looks. They are of the agricultural type, men who have lived all their lives with nature, men who have never known the temptation of a town, such was my impression. As a body they are the fairest of the fair in complexion and colouring, very well built, and muscular.

At one spot we passed a large guard of some 200 men, probably night outposts, who were marching out. When they saw us they were at once halted, and as the train passed they saluted and then cheered, which was immensely appreciated by our Sepoys.

After passing over some miles of open plains we came to cultivation, where the millet was growing to a great height, much to the delight of our native soldiers. There are numerous canals with many cross cuts, but we could see no signs of life. Many villages were to be seen, all apparently destroyed. Dead dogs were much "en evidence," the result of Russian marksmenship, a few wounded ones limping in the distance, and at one spot a solitary old rooster who had evidently escaped detection sums up the life we saw, excepting Russian soldiers, during the three and a half hours' journey to Tientsin.

As we approached the town we passed through the camp of the Russian Army, where we were again received with cheers, while guards turned out and presented arms.

Now we got our first glimpse of the foreign concessions of Tientsin, railway workshops, and depots, and I must say I never saw a more depressing sight; all was ruin and desolation, which looked as if it could only have been caused by some "awful" upheaval of nature; it seemed quite beyond the work of man; it was so thorough and complete, and the nearer we got to the town the greater the devastation of what was once a flourishing and picturesque suburb.

Our Russian railway guard pointed out the battlefield where some of their men had a pretty hard time of it.

At the station we were met by a staff officer belonging to the staff of General Dorward, who at the time was commanding the few British troops in Tientsin, and from him we learnt the Legations were still holding out, but could not hope to do so many more days.

There being little or no twilight, it was soon dark, so we hurried on to find quarters in Victoria Road. We found the road all right, but the front door was locked. However, my old friend "Bond" came to the rescue, and threw his fifteen-stone body at it, and soon we found ourselves in a nice little villa, the drawing-room of which we turned into a mess room and the dining-room behind into a brigade office, whilst upstairs we found ample bedroom accommodation for our party. With the help of our native servants we did not take long getting supper, having previously declined General Dorward's hospitality, as we wished to sample our own arrangements and discover any weak spots.

The troops were guided to their quarters, which

consisted of large godowns on the main thoroughfares or inside the compounds of private houses, the houses being used by the officers.

In our house we have nothing but what we brought with us in the shape of camp furniture, but we are quite cosy, and after another peg and smoke I will be quite ready to turn in, after a long and rather eventful day.

28th. Called on Gaselee, and heard from him the advance would take place "as soon as possible," a safe sort of remark, but with so many commanders one can hardly expect anything more definite. The latest news from Pekin is that they can hold out till the 4th. There is no prospect of our getting there before the 12th, which makes one feel very sad.

My brigade won't be complete for some days; at the most I will only have the 7th Rajputs, 1st Sikhs and 24th P.I., as the Biluchis cannot possibly arrive in time for the advance.

Visited the troops and found them very comfortably housed. The officers are in comfortably furnished houses, one of which I inspected with a view to moving in, but when I saw children's toys and garments lying about, just as the occupants had hurriedly vacated it, it seemed almost desecration to go in and disturb things, so have decided to stick to our unfurnished abode and camp kit.

Till we move there is not much to do, as our troops while stationary are under the orders of Dorward, commanding the line of communications. The men are busy getting accustomed to the magazine rifle. Riding along the banks of the Peiho I noticed a good many corpses, a simple way of getting rid of the dead. We will be a motley crew when we do move.

Have ordered C.O.'s to take their men out daily for route-marching, as all are soft after the sea voyage. The climate reminds me of Bombay in November.

29th (Sunday). An idle day, so am polishing off private correspondence. Parsons, Jermyn and Leonard dined with me at the hotel, a fearful scramble. There must have been at least 300 diners of all nationalities. The room showed signs of the bombardment. We were just thinking of making a move when a Russian officer came in armed to the teeth, making a great noise. He had just come off picquet, and must have had something stronger than water! He made for a group of French officers, all of whom he insisted on kissing, and eventually sat on one of their knees. He refused food, but helped himself liberally to wine. He attracted the attention of all by his loud talk and gallant deeds, flourishing a loaded revolver all the time. Close by was a table of Japanese officers, who were doing justice to champagne. They seemed to take in everything without even a glance round in the din. They were quite unique. Owing to the presence of our Russian friend we ordered further refreshment, but this was cut short by the arrival of an A.D.C. to tell me General Gaselee intended accompanying a Japanese reconaissance at 2 a.m., at which hour he wished me to meet him, so we squared accounts and made off to snatch a few hours' sleep.

30th. Went to Gaselee's quarters 1.50 a.m., and after waiting a quarter of an hour, was told the start was not to be made till 7! As it was raining, we were wet through, so returned to our rooms and dried ourselves as well as we could without a fire. At 7 a.m. we met the general, who was full of apologies; a second A.D.C. had been despatched the night before to tell us of the change of programme, but this young gentleman did not trouble to come on to my quarters when he failed to find me at the hotel.

By the time we reached the Japanese they were already engaged. The reconnaissance was checked by a canal, so the Japs contented themselves with drawing the fire of the enemy, which soon became pretty hot. We pulled up in a village about 400 yards in rear of the firing line. Here we found a battalion of infantry in support and a field hospital. We inspected the latter, and found it perfect in every detail. Soon some wounded came in, so watched the surgeons with much interest. The moment the men were bandaged their first thought was to get back to the firing line, and those who were not allowed to go seemed very unhappy.

The fire was now much more intense, so we returned to the battalion in support just in time to hear the colonel address his men before moving off to the front. He spoke in a low but very distinct voice, which reached every man, as all were "squatting" as close as they could be packed, and eagerly listening. At a signal all rose as one man, and moved off at a quick shuffle, carrying their rifles at a short trail and extending slightly without any further words of command. Every man seemed to know exactly what was expected of him, and in a few moments all were in the firing line. Although we could not see this owing to the crops, it was most evident from the increased fire. Later on we managed to get a bit closer to the men engaged; bullets were now very thick; the fire was heavy on both sides till the order was given to retire.

Up to this the Chinese had not fired a gun, but the moment they discovered the retirement they fired two shells, the direction of which was good; the first fell about 100 yards behind the Japs, but the next one found the exact range. It looked as if they just wished us to know they had guns and could use them. On this occasion the enemy did quite the right thing, for we found out practically nothing about their position.

On the ride back we found a brigade of infantry in "reserve" just in case the reconnaissance turned out to be one "in force." I was much struck with all I saw, and consider the Japanese infantry as good as the best the West can produce. Their coolness is quite remarkable. In appearance they remind me of our best Goorkhas. They hardly looked at our group of British officers, and while they were waiting for orders to advance some were eating grain, others were smoking, whilst others had their needles and thread out making firm a loose button or mending a tear! They evidently love fighting; you could see this in their faces. For small men they seemed to me overloaded, though they made little of this.

Their casualties were some 40 or 50 killed and wounded.

31st. Stored all our heavy kit in the "Gordon

Hall," so have nothing but what we will take on the march. No further news from Pekin.

1st August. The shaves are numerous. We are ready to move, and so are the Japs and Americans, but the Russians and French want further delay. The Japs are very suspicious of the Russians, whom they watch very closely. Was shocked to see —— walking about with his arm round the neck of a Japanese general, much to the latter's disgust, I fancy.

I hear two Japanese officers rode clean through the Chinese lines last night, and obtained some very important information. A real plucky act, but in no way astonishing; they are a brave race.

2nd. Staff officers from the Japanese and Americans joined ours, and selected a bivouac some two miles beyond the Chinese City of Teintsin. This looks like business.

3rd. A conference of commanders is sitting. The 24th P.I. marched into bivouac at 5.30 p.m. Still no orders out.

4th. Marched out 2.30 p.m., and reached our bivouac 6.30. Got soaked to the skin, as the rain came down in torrents just as we were in sight of our camping ground. Real bad luck! The march was abominably slow. Some of the so-called bridges were "hairy" things to cross, consisting as they did of thick broad planks "lengthways" across the streams and canals, making the going most unpleasant for mounted men. However, there were no accidents. We are up to our knees in mud, behind a high bank, with very thick crops beyond, through which any force could creep up and rush us, but the Chinese are not enterprising. We are watching the bank carefully. The men have two days' rations on the person, with emergency rations on mules. We will work junks after to-morrow, which will relieve our animals and always ensure our supplies. Each junk has its own guard of four men, and the whole is under a British officer, with a native officer to assist. We are wondering how things are going in the Legations whilst we smoke our pipes in the stillness of the coming night before we turn in as we stand. There is something very attractive in campaigning.

5th. As it rained considerably during the night, we looked anything but pretty this morning when it was light enough to see. The attack was in the hands of the Japs, with the Russians on their right rear, the Americans and ourselves in support, our troops being the left support. They commenced to advance before daylight, and drew the enemy's fire at once. For the first hour a few shells flew over our heads and into the bank, but one fell amongst our men and did some slight damage, besides killing Scott Moncrieff's (C.R.E.) horse.

As soon as it was daylight it was evident the Japs were heavily engaged all along their line. We were all excitement, for we could see nothing, and could only follow what was going on by the sound of the firing. The 12th Field Battery fired a few rounds, and at last we were ordered to advance, the signal being loud cheering, which denoted the taking of some position. Once over the bank we were in the crops, which was far over our heads, even mounted, and before we had gone a dozen yards we were wet to the skin. The firing in front grew heavier and heavier and the cheering also. On we stumbled, till we passed over the first position. Here we found some twenty or thirty Chinese corpses, and marks of gun wheels showing that the guns had got away, and by the time we reached more open ground on the banks of the Peiho, the fighting was over, the Japs had carried the main positions, which we reached in another ten minutes. The Japs started dressed in white, now they were mud from head to foot. As their different battalions closed up and marched past us they were the admiration of all; but they did not seem to notice this. I never saw men so less conscious. They are truly wonderful infantry. Their cavalry, however, *look* wretched, though I suppose their pluck is the same. They are poor horsemen, badly mounted, and carry a miserable-looking article called "sword." Their artillery is anything but attractive, but they know their work. There is no mistake about this. No other troops would have carried out this morning's work as well as the Japs did. Their losses were over 300. They don't respect the wounded or dead, as far as Chinamen are concerned, and some of the sights were very horrible!

We crossed the Peiho by a bridge of boats, where we found a Chinese camp left standing in a clump of trees, evidently some general's headquarters, and camped ourselves this time on the left bank of the Peiho, abreast of the prosperous-looking village of Peitsung.

On examining the village we found a few wounded villagers and some Chinese dead. The wounded we attended to and protected from the Japanese prowlers, who hovered round our camp in the hopes of picking up something in the shape of a stray pigtail!

Their losses were about 300 killed and wounded, ours 25, and the Russians only some half-dozen. Before retirement the Chinese took good care to flood the country round their position, which interfered considerably with any support being given by the troops on the left bank of the river, whilst the high crops prevented any turning movement by our cavalry on our extreme left, and in this way the frontal attack of the Japanese was deprived of the support which was originally intended. Had the Russians and French been able to advance from their position in the vicinity of the Hsi-ku arsenal, and our Bengal Lancers been able to turn the Chinese right, their rout would have been a very complete one, and their losses would have been enormous. Had this unsupported frontal attack fallen to the lot of any other nation but the Japanese I expect there would have been a fair amount of grumbling; with our very mixed forces co-operation is not to be expected to the same extent as would probably be the case if the undertaking were entirely in the hands of one general commanding the army.

Here the sappers ran up a crows-nest, from which we obtained a good view of the country round, but there was nothing to be seen of the enemy. We leave sixty rifles of 7th Rajputs, whilst the Americans and Japanese leave a company each.

6th. Sha-tu-Chuang and Yangtsun. The

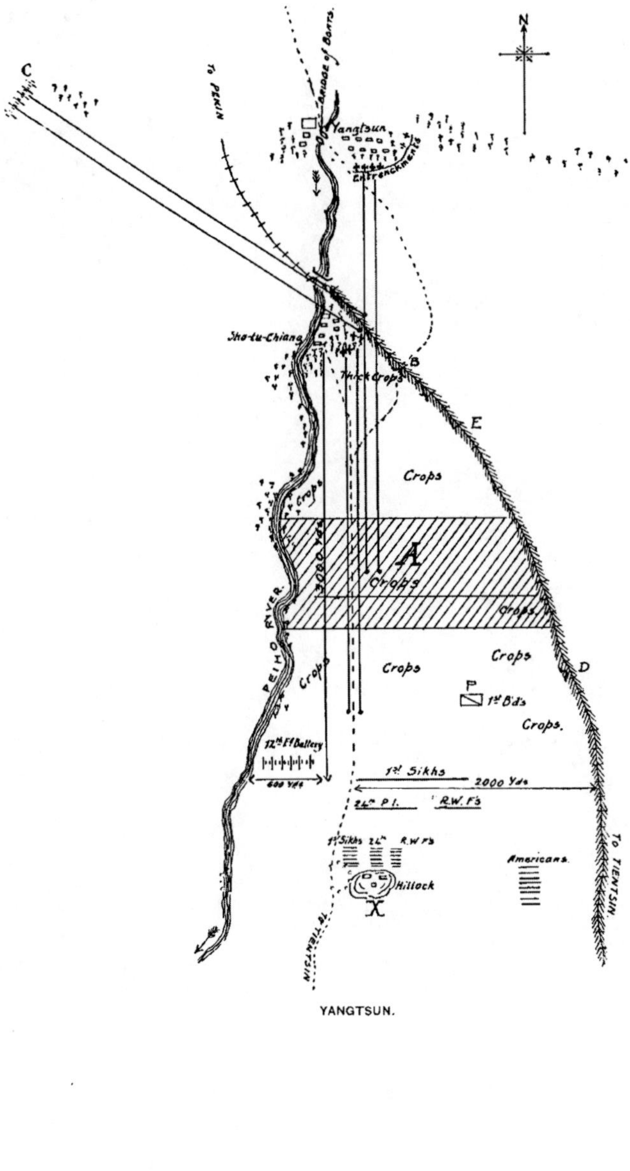
N
C
To PEKIN
Bridge of Boats.
Yangtsun
Entrenchments
Sho-tu-Chiang
B
Thick Crops
E
Crops
A
Crops
Crops
3000 Yds
PEIHO RIVER.
Crops
Crops
Crops
Crops
D
P
1st B'd's
Crops.
12th F.d Battery
600 Yds
1st Sikhs
2000 Yds
24th P.I.
R.W.F's
1st Sikhs 24th R.W.F's
Americans.
Hillock
X
To TIENTSIN
To TIENTSIN.

YANGTSUN.

fight to-day is best described by reference to the map, or, rather, rough sketch, I have made. We started this morning at daybreak, and reached the hillock marked X about 9. Here we halted in line of columns, piled arms, and examined the country in front, whilst the cavalry did a bit of scouting. With our glasses we could clearly make out the village of Sha-tu-Chuang, nestling in the corner formed by the Peiho and railway embankment. It appeared to consist of only a few huts, and there was nothing to indicate it was occupied; on the other hand, it might have been full of men, the crops prevented our seeing anything. Not so with the railway bank from E to the bridge; it was strongly held, and on the far side an army might have been concealed. Yangtsun, some 1,500 yards in rear of the bank, was palpably held in strength, but owing to the height of the bank one had to depend a good deal on guesswork, as the cavalry confined their scouting chiefly to our side of the railway.

After an hour's halt I was directed to make a frontal attack on the village and embankment, and at the same time was warned not to allow my left to extend beyond the track shown by a dotted line.

I at once ordered the 1st Sikhs to advance a couple of hundred yards and extend from the left, which was to rest on the track, the 24th P.I. to extend from its left and the Royal Welsh Fusiliers prolong to the right, thus forming left and right supports respectively and a second line, whilst the 7th Rajputs remained behind as a baggage guard and reserve. Before advancing I warned C.O.'s they had not much to fear from aimed fire, as the Chinese method of defence was by concentrating their fire on a certain piece of ground, which we would discover later on. This being the case, it was my intention to advance without firing, and get through this "danger zone," marked A on sketch, as quickly as possible. The moment we moved a shell or two was fired at us, and some desultory rifle fire, just sufficient to cheer us up and make us feel we were not at peace manœuvres.

We covered some 1,000 yards without casualties when the real business began. We now knew we were entering the danger zone, shells and bullets were falling thick, and our field battery was at work on the enemy. Riding behind the second line I could see our casualties were only slight. After a check which didn't last a minute, on went the two lines, still reserving their fire. Things were going just as I wished, when I unexpectedly found myself being hampered by the Americans coming up on my right, which meant reducing our front as we advanced instead of extending it, so now with my staff got between our two lines to ensure my original orders being carried out, not that there was any need for this, as our men did not hesitate for a second, their blood was now up. A galloper was sent to me with orders to give way to the Americans, but this wasn't good enough. Of necessity, however, we did give way by closing in a little to the left, which, of course, meant a better target for the enemy and more casualties. This was not the moment for argument, so I sent the gentleman back with "Righto," and the Americans wedged themselves in as best they could. After all, it didn't take long to get through the danger zone, but our worst enemy was the intense heat in the Indian corn, which was far above our heads.

The enemy's shells and bullets were now flying and whizzing over our heads, but the sound was much more objectionable, and the bobbing of heads increased. Until you have been under fire this is not easy to understand, nevertheless it is a fact, which the older soldiers well knew. The row and noise was deafening, but on we went, till we were within 800 yards of our objective, when we opened fire and advanced by rushes, till we got to the 400 yards distance, when we fixed bayonets and rushed the village and embankment, after giving them a few rounds of independent firing. The nearer we got to the village the thicker the crops, under cover of which the Chinese made a clean bolt at B. Until we actually reached Sha-tu-Chuang we had no idea there had been any guns there, so admirably were they posted in gun-pits carefully concealed by the Indian corn just in front of the village. These guns got away at B without our seeing a vestige of them, and reached Yangtsun before we topped the embankment. It was real bad luck. Owing to the intense heat the men were done to a turn, and had to wait a minute or so before they could fire steadily at the tail-end of the bolting pigtails, who once in Yangtsun were comparatively safe behind entrenchments and the numerous houses.

The Americans crowded on to the embankment, which was now thick with men from E to the bridge. Whilst examining the country from the railway through my glasses my attention was drawn by some sudden movement or flash, such as might be caused by the sun on, say, a piece of brass, in the direction of C to our left front on the far side of the river, which made me suspect the presence of artillery, so immediately ordered our men to leave the railway and retire quickly to the lower ground in the rear. This was carried out only just in time, for half a dozen shells in quick succession fell on the bank where the men a minute before were lying. One of these plumped into the centre of the left company of the Americans, killing several of their men.

All this time our own artillery were busy shelling Yangtsun over our heads, and a very pretty sight it was. The Chinese battery at C seemed quite satisfied after these few rounds and another half-dozen at the village, which went wide of the mark, but very close to some of our chargers left a couple of hundred yards in rear.

It is easy to be wise after the event, but a glance at the sketch makes it self-evident the ground to the left of the railway should have been given to the British brigade and that to the right to the Americans, whilst our Lancers would have been better employed to their right again. Massed as they were in a dip nearly opposite D, where the crops were thickest, they were practically useless, for they could see nothing of what was going on. In fact, the only persons who had a good view of the fight were our headquarters' people at X. They saw a body of mounted men on the far side of the railway ride clean across the open. Warning of this was sent to our cavalry, but it was too late. Why none of our Lancers were on the far side I cannot conceive; one mounted man on the embankment abreast of where we made our first extension could have given the most useful information. I am almost convinced that at one time I did see some of our cavalry well away to our right, but these men must have been called in before the advance commenced. With allied troops I suppose these mistakes must occur.

Had the enemy been anything but Chinamen we would have suffered considerably; by this I do not mean to belittle the Chinese. But how can you expect troops to fight who are invariably deserted by their officers the moment danger approaches?

This was the first time any of our men had been under shell fire, and, on the whole, their conduct was admirable, though, of course, there were a certain number of cases of "exhaustion"! This, however, was not peculiar to one race or colour; it was fairly evenly divided. Another week of the same "physic" would do us all a heap of good! Considering our casualties only amounted to some 50 killed and wounded we ought to be satisfied. We have only one officer wounded, Lieutenant Costello, of the 1st Sikhs, who was early shot through the knee.

One thing I was very much struck with and which seems to me quite worthy of notice, and that was the conduct of our syces, who walked fearlessly along behind the troops without letting a single horse break away. Those belonging to my staff were at one moment sorely tried, for a shell burst in their midst, killing my orderly officer's (Major Leonard) horse, wounding four others, and carrying away the calf of one syce without disturbing the equanimity of the others in any way. This is not the first time I have known followers behave well under trying circumstances. I must say they stick to "Master."

As my horse was wounded and began to limp I had to dismount, the staff following suit, and very unpleasant we found the walking, for by the time we reached the railway we were completely pumped.

Johnson (commanding 12th Field Battery) tells me he had no idea there were any guns in front of Sha-tu-Chuang; he opened fire on the embankment and Yangtsun village. Some kind friend suggested that the shell which fell amongst the Americans was one of our own; but this is absurd. Met General Chaffee just as the firing ceased; he seems one of the right sort. General Lienovitch also rode up just as the firing ceased; he does not appear to be communicative! This is the first time I have had a chance of looking at the American soldier, who is much the same as our own, but a bit more "mature."

The Welsh Fusiliers are a bit soft, but a month or two of Northern China, with cooler weather, will soon pick them up. Hong Kong is not the place to make a man hard. This headquarters' wing is very short of officers, particularly captains. Speaking generally, they are a very good type of the British soldier. I wish the whole battalion were here. The 12th Field Battery are a splendid lot. All our native troops are good, with plenty of dash in them. The 1st B.L. ride uncommonly well; their horses, however, look very soft, and I fear soon there will be many sore backs.

Our camp is very cramped and irregular.

Yangtsun. 7th August. Halt to give the animals a rest and refill from the junks. The former seems hardly necessary, considering we have only been three days on the march. The real cause is probably due to differences of opinion amongst the commanding generals. This is pure surmise on my part. I have long learnt commanders in our Army do not take their subordinates into their confidence. There is no exception in this particular force of ours! Let us hope the Legations are not too hard pressed. So far the only scraps of news I have picked up are from the Americans! After all, this is only a trifle, and not worth a moment's consideration. Whenever any of my officers ask for news I hope they will believe me when I say, "I have none." Visited the wounded, who are doing very well. Costello quite cheery, and apparently in no great pain, merely complains of stiffness. These small bullets are merciful compared with the old Martini and Snider. The wounded are being sent back to Tientsin.

The Marines are now posted to my brigade. Went over yesterday's field and am more convinced than ever we ought to have done much better. It was a fatal mistake having the Americans and ourselves on the same side of the railway. Had the Bengal Lancers been properly used there is no doubt they would have cut up a big body of the enemy and have chased him to a standstill.

Battles are not cricket matches that finish with the taking of the last wicket, or prearranged hour. They should be pushed home; the retreating enemy should be harassed to the bitter end, and "touch" with him should never be lost. We fought, we won, and we halted! Our cavalry and

Cossacks did nothing. We are not likely to get another chance like it this side of Pekin.

One sees very little of the other troops of this curiously composed multitude of armed men, who look at each other with intense suspicion, if not hatred, in spite of all being employed in the common cause. The Americans keep close to us, but where the rest are Heaven only knows. Each force seems to settle down on its own camping ground, without a thought of the others. If field force orders *are* issued they are not passed on to brigade commanders. If the British and Americans purposely keep in touch with each other, probably a similar understanding exists between the French and Russians, whilst the Japanese keep a watchful eye on the latter, with a view to events which even now are openly discussed.

Without doubt our force is looked down upon by the rest, as our British troops are so ill represented. The ordinary foreigner won't take the trouble to discriminate between sepoy and follower, and speaks of all as "coolies." He, however, is quite unable to disguise his feelings when he deigns to look at our Artillery and Bengal Lancers, for he possesses nothing to come up to either. Before this campaign is over I expect he will have

FRENCH GUARD.

some solid reasons for respecting our Indian infantry soldier.

Of one thing I am quite certain. Our native soldiers consider themselves just as good as any foreign troops in the field. From conversations with our native officers our men are not too impressed with the Japanese. This is not astonishing, as the native of India has great admiration for big men. The Hindustani has no great love for the Goorkha, who reminds him of the Japanese; but he must and does admit the undeniable pluck of both, whilst he professes to fear neither. The Japanese cavalry are most unattractive; the same might be said of their artillery without detracting from their excellence as gunners, and this want of admiration may be accounted for by this very unattractiveness.

The French troops puzzle our men a good deal. This is probably due to the ill-fitting garments of the Marine Battalion, topped by the most unbecoming white helmet, with blue cover, I have ever seen. When their troops from Europe arrive they will see men worth looking at I expect, as we hear of Chasseur d'Afriques and Zouaves.

Our pack mules and carts drawn by mules form the best transport in the field, though the Americans prefer their wagons with teams and their pack animals driven in herds. The Russian transport seems satisfactory, but, like the artillery, the wheels look very light. The Japanese use pack ponies with a man to each, as against our one man to three led mules. They load their ponies very well, but as the majority are entires they give endless trouble, and therefore require the full attention of one man to each animal. In the matter of transport the French troops with us are entirely dependent on country carts.

The uniform of the Americans looks very comfortable and suitable. I don't like the white coats and long boots of the Russians. On the whole, our troops, British and native, seem the best equipped and most suited to the climate, which at this season is very trying for infantry.

Many persons who were present at yesterday's fight doubt my assertion that the Chinese had a battery in position to our left front, and stick to the view that our losses on the embankment were due to a mistake on the part of some of the Allied guns; but in my own mind I have no doubt, as I was standing close by the spot where the shells fell, and am convinced these could not have been the result of any mistake on the part of the Allies, and a personal inspection of the ground, later in the day, where I maintain the Chinese battery took up their position, confirms this opinion, for I followed the wheel tracks till they disappeared in the crops in the direction of the retreat.

The American losses came to some 80 killed and wounded, and the Russians upwards of 100, whereas we only lost 45, due, I am convinced, to the rapidity of our advance in open order. The Americans did not open out as much as our men, and the Russians, as is their custom, retained a close formation; in fact, the casualties illustrate better than words *how* each force advanced and the pace kept up.

The water (Peiho) is like pea soup, and defeats our filters. The fields round are full of vegetables, and in the village of Yangtsun we found a quantity of ice, which was more than welcome.

As far as I can gather, the Japanese advance yesterday on the right bank of the river (our left) was completely stopped during the fight by the flooded condition of the ground forcing them to make a large detour to their left.

From to-morrow the British are to march in rear, so we will be saved endless outpost duties, much to the relief of our men. This arrangement, however, will prevent us seeing the methods and doings of others. I hear the French intend halting till they get more transport. The order of march will now apparently be Japanese, Russian, American and British.

8th. Cha-tu-Chuang. The start this morning was pleasant enough, but in the end the ten miles proved most distressing. 7 a.m. is too late for a start in this climate. The Marines felt it most. As we passed through Yangtsun we had a good look at the Chinese entrenchments, which were more ornamental than useful owing to the absence of a ditch in front. They provide ample cover, but are in no way an obstacle, as the earth in front is only scraped out to a depth of some six inches. The parapet was beautifully made from earth obtained in rear, a matter of no moment to the Chinese mind! This, however, is not always the case, for many of the entrenchments stormed by the Japanese on the 5th had very "up-to-date" ditches in front. During the march we found many wells of water deliciously cool, though slightly brackish. The heat was terrible, but with the help of leaves, handkerchiefs, or towels stuck under helmets and pugarees the men managed to protect their necks and spines.

The junks are working well, and when our camps are on the banks tie up opposite us. Our telegraph line was cut in several places, but this sort of thing we must expect.

9th. Ho-shi-wu, only eleven miles, and yet we took nine solid hours doing it, in spite of many halts! Dozens of men were bowled over by the heat. The Marines suffered more than the Welsh Fusiliers, 37 of whom were put on the junks after only going half way. The 7th Rajputs seem to stand it best. I have never seen native troops fall out as they did to-day. This village is strongly entrenched in places, and many of the houses are carefully loopholed. In front of the village the crops are cut down to about 2½ feet from the ground, bent over and interlaced in a most intricate manner, the sharp points and network forming a most disagreeable obstacle for man and beast, whilst the long ends lying on the ground make walking most unpleasant, being as slippery as ice. It seems a pity to have wasted so much energy, for not a man was to be seen.

One very old lady was the only custodian of the village. She looked me up, poor dear, and gave me a quarter of an hour of her tongue. Perhaps it was just as well I did not understand a word. It was a sad sight, for I fear she was demented. She certainly looked it! The dust added to our misery to-day. The 1st Bengal Lancers got in touch with some of the enemy's mounted men, whom they charged, killing 40 and capturing some ponies and four standards, with a loss of only one man wounded and two horses killed. The high crops sorely interfered with our Lancers, but I hear it was quite a pretty little affair as the enemy made some show at first. When we came up with our cavalry I found them the centre of an admiring crowd of Russians and others, who were examining the men and their lances most minutely, the latter showing evident signs of having been lately "used." We are leaving an allied post here, our contribution being 50 Royal Marines and one Maxim, with a detachment from the Hong Kong Battery, all under an officer of the Marines, who will command the post.

10th. Matao. Started to-day at 4 p.m., reaching here at midnight. This experiment was no better than the 7 a.m. march, for we had to make a long halt, after covering only one mile, till the sun went down. At about 6.30 p.m. we heard a loud explosion. Every man halted whilst we watched a huge circular wave in the sky approaching, and later overshadowing us, when it began to rain a thick black dust, the result of the blowing up of an arsenal or powder magazine at Ho-shi-wu. The men were much pleased when they grasped the situation, and gave a spontaneous cheer. The horses suffered to-day, having started at an earlier hour.

11th. Chang-chia-wan. Started at 6 p.m., so got on better again, reaching at midnight. It was pitch dark, and there was no one to show us our ground, so in the end the brigade trampled down the Kowlian and bivouacked where they stood. We had hardly fallen asleep when the rain came down. At daybreak we moved to our proper ground. As a precaution quinine was issued to all, as the place looked malarial. The Japanese, who were leading, found this place occupied, but not for long! They followed half-way to Tung-Chao, when they fired a few shells without drawing any fire, so returned a short distance and camped.

12th. Tung-Chao, a short march of only five miles, so we did not start till 9.30 a.m. after breakfast. We got in 12.30, including one halt of forty minutes. This is a walled town of some pretensions. The enemy, however, had quite deserted it, leaving in their haste ten guns behind. This will be an important commissariat base depot, as the junks will discharge their cargo here. From here to Pekin there is a paved road and broad canal. Shortly after our arrival we discovered a junk trying to slip up the canal, laden with black powder. In a temple we also found a large quantity of powder packed in tins, over which a guard was placed pending its destruction. We are encamped in front of a backwater, in which there are several bodies floating, near the town, whilst the staff are located in buildings in what you might term the suburbs. My quarters are in a Mahomedan Chinese Mosque, the owners of which raised no objections so long as we didn't prevent their devotions! Their koran is in Arabic, so some of our men were able to converse with the priests in a fashion. These priests seem to be able to read fluently from the koran, but I hardly think they are capable of conversing in Arabic. However, we have no means of testing them, as the knowledge of that language on our side is only limited. A little looting was started in the town which was soon stopped by placing the town out of bounds. This sort of thing cannot be tolerated. The followers have to be watched, but the "cat" is a wonderful cure for all "weaknesses." In the evening it was decided to send out a reconnaissance to-morrow.

13th, Halt. An Allied reconnaissance started this morning. Our contingent consists of two guns 12th Field Battery, three squadrons 1st Bengal Lancers, and the 7th Rajputs, all under Lieut.-Col. Gartside Tipping of the 1st B.L., with orders to take the more southern road running parallel to the canal, and keeping touch with the Americans, who again are keeping the canal on their right flank, the other or northern side being left to the Japanese and Russians, the whole to advance some eight miles towards Pekin, and there entrench without attempting to draw on an engagement or even fire at the enemy if seen, unless attacked. We are leaving 30 rifles from each infantry unit under the command of Captain White with a subaltern of the Welsh Fusiliers and an English speaking native officer from the Hong Kong Regiment, in all 150 rifles.) Fatigue parties are busy building a "post," unloading junks, and foraging generally. Up to now White has been acting D.A.Q.M.G., but having only a mule as a charger he has been handicapped. Leonard also has to depend on a mule, a beast that always walks just in front of me, giving me all its dust!

The heat is great and the water the worst we have struck. We have again found a large supply of ice. The town is full of people, but the suburbs are deserted. From the 150 men we leave behind 60 will be posted inside the town. The men on the junks have been relieved by sickly ones who will return to Tientsin with the "empties." A regular system of water transport with Tientsin will be established. Rain came down in torrents whilst we were at dinner, driving us to the shelter of the verandah. In the morning we are to march to the entrenchments of our advanced post and assault Pekin on the 15th, as we expect a good deal of fighting outside before we can possibly effect an entry. Before turning in I must just add heavy firing is now going on. Are our troops engaged or can it possibly be the Legations?

14th, Pekin. Paraded this morning 3.30, and came up with the advanced party 9 a.m. They had not been engaged. The firing we heard was from Pekin. After unloading animals and eating breakfast we were informed that after a longish halt we would push on to the relief. We have absolutely no news, but by to-night we will know the best or worst! At our halting place not a sound is to be heard, the firing ceased at day break. This silence is ominous, however; we can only hope. Eleven a.m., we are off at last. The crops are thicker than ever, you can't see a yard ahead except down the broad lane, at this season grass covered, along which the staff and mounted troops are marching. The infantry advanced through the crops on the left. After going some five miles we came in sight of the walls of the Chinese city, when the 12th Field Battery came into action and fired

CENTRE WALL, IMPERIAL CITY, showing the Position of the Chinese Gun (where the wall is broken) which Shelled the British Legation, the wall of which is on the left of the picture. The ruined buildings shown on the right are where the British and the Japanese made a gallant defence.

a few rounds at a gateway some 1,500 yards distant, to which there was no response. Heavy firing, however, was going on to our right front, proving the Japs and Russians had stolen a march on us. Owing to the crops the march was painfully slow. However, in due course we reached the S.E. gate of the Chinese city without opposition. On passing through we found three machine guns which had been abandoned, but all component parts were removed. Inside the Chinese city a few shots were fired at us by men dotted here and there. We pushed on till we reached the centre of the right portion of the Chinese city, and there halted to close up and make final dispositions. The Chinese are here in their thousands, the main street is empty, but every lane is blocked with the masses tightly packed, who profess absolute ignorance of what has occurred within a few yards of them. We long for news, but we get none. We wonder what is in store for us. As a rule men about to engage in a struggle are cheerful, but to-day there is nothing of this kind. Each one is thinking to himself what this awful silence means. We can hardly hope all is well for surely the besieged must know we are close at hand! Are we about to witness sights such as were seen at Cawnpore? We don't compare notes, we merely sit with our thoughts with clenched teeth, and wonder whether we are to fight or "butcher." If so much as the hair of a woman or child has been touched it will assuredly be the latter. The "fall in," thank God we are off.

Our force is broken up into four parties. No. 1 remains where we halted, No. 2 advanced by one of the side lanes towards the Tartar city, striking the wall as nearly opposite the sluice gate as possible, No. 3 straight ahead to the paved road which bisects the Chinese city, when it turned to the right, No. 4 followed No. 3, and turned to the left, making for the Temple of Heaven. General Gaselee accompanied No. 2, whilst I went with No. 3. On reaching the paved road we wheeled to the right and formed up across it, there being ample room for a full company in line. In the distance we could see the Chien-men (gate) some 1,200 yards off against the sky or rather the superstructure. We noticed at once that every lane right and left was full of men, when a slight movement of some 50 or 60 men dressed differently attracted us, they were not more than 250 yards off.

They looked at us for a few seconds, and we recognised them as foes; they doubled out and some went down on their knees to aim whilst others stood and in an instant we were blazing at each other. A few rounds and a bayonet charge and all was

ENTRANCE TO BRITISH LEGATION FACING THE SLUICE DITCH.

over. They disappeared as if by magic, leaving seven dead in their Boxer garments. All the while the peaceful inhabitants looked on, or rather the front men at the head of each lane. As we advanced they did not move, they merely gazed as only Chinamen can, apparently perfectly indifferent to their novel surroundings. Not a man ventured on the main road, whilst all appeared to be carrying fruit or water, which they gave to the troops nearest. We rushed the street till we reached the bridge across the ditch in front of the Chien-men (gate); here we were exposed to the fire of some men in the ditch to our left and of others on the wall of the Tartar city to our left front.

The fire was heavy, but wild, and soon we cleared the ditch, but could do nothing with the men on the walls. Had their shooting been only fair we must have suffered somewhat; as it was we only had a few wounded. I now ordered a gun from the 12th Field Battery to be brought up to the head of the street by hand, and told off a party of the Royal Welsh Fusiliers to get on the tops of some houses to our left and open magazine fire on the bastion whilst the gun was run out. After firing five rounds, which sent the masonry flying in all directions, not a man was to be seen. At this juncture some Europeans appeared above the gateway, the first intimation the Legations were saved. Up went a cheer I shall never forget. They turned out to be Russian sailors who had crept along the wall from our right. We could not understand a word they said; they were making desperate signs which had some meaning. They, however, could not remain, as they were being rushed by the Boxers on the wall to our left, at whom they fired a volley or two, and then bolted back towards the Legations. We could see nothing of the movements of either party, but we could follow the sound of the firing. The Russians again were not very sure of us, as they evidently could not understand who our Sepoys were, but the Welsh Fusiliers and gunners reassured them. I was just about to order all six guns of the 12th Field Battery up to knock down the gateway or rather gate when Colonel Scott Moncrieff rode up and informed me General Gaselee with party No. 2 were inside the Legations, where all were safe. Now all was changed, every man was happy, all bitterness was over; we felt we only had to fight.

We examined the gate and found a side entrance round the corner which was capable of being battered in. Through this I ordered the 1st Sikhs, under Colonel Pollock, and the Maxims under

SLUICE GATE WHERE THE BRITISH ENTERED.

Bland and Wakefield to advance, whilst the Fusiliers and some of the 24th followed me towards the sluice gate. The 12th Field Battery, escorted by the Hong Kong Regiment, I ordered to find their way to the Temple of Heaven. Whilst we were forming up prior to carrying out these orders, I dismounted a troop of the 1st Bengal Lancers, and directed them under Lieut. Macaulay to hold the bridge. These men were fresh, and only too eager to get a whack at the enemy, who from time to time reappeared the moment our fire slackened. My party reached the sluice gate without firing a shot, but the 1st Sikhs and Maxims were rushed the moment they appeared inside the gate. The gun detachments had to put down their carbines and take off their bandoliers whilst lifting the guns through the broken gate, and were not all prepared when the rush took place.

The Sikhs were partly on a ramp leading up to the wall, but there were quite enough men to meet the rush, determined as it was, for in a few minutes they cleared the square of every man, bagging between 60 and 100. Our casualties were few considering the circumstances, but curiously enough the enemy managed to carry off some six carbines and accoutrements! Barratt and Bainbridge, of the Sikhs, were very conspicuous all the time their men held the bridge, which was a very exposed position. It was an excellent day's work. The sight which met our eyes on reaching the Legations was very thrilling, women and children were offering refreshments to Tommy and Sepoys without distinction, all were deliverers. The scene beggars description; it was very bewildering, and one could hardly collect one's thoughts. It was difficult, after the strain, to realise that not a hair of those who had been shut up so long had been touched except in fight. We were all suffering from a burning thrist, to quench which was now our one object, and how gladly we seized any glass or tin-pot held out to us, regardless of the contents so long as it was liquid!

By the time I reached the steps of our Legation I am afraid to think how many glasses I emptied—water, milk, soda water, whisky and water went down alike. For the moment we were spoilt children, surrounded by lady attendants. What a babel of voices; every language of the West could be heard at once. What pluck was hidden behind those summer toilets! On the faces of the ladies you could only read "joy," not a sign of suffering did they let us see. Not so the men. Amongst them you saw many grave faces. It was quite palpable what they had gone through, not on their own

BAMBOO RAMP ON THE WALL FOR THE CHINESE GUN WHICH SHELLED THE LEGATION.

account; they were ready enough to face death in any form, but the thought of their wives, their children falling any day during those weary months must have been truly "awful," so was it surprising to find them grave? Lady MacDonald, assisted by her sister and other ladies, were doing the honours. Never shall I forget that beaker of claret cup she handed me as I dismounted. Her husband was with Gaselee on the wall, so I had to make off and report myself to the latter and take orders. There was plenty to do. Heavy firing was still going on to our right, where the Russians and Japanese were still trying to gain an entry. A few bullets were flying about, and one or two men were hit amongst us as we stood. It was decided to bring up two guns from the 12th Field Battery and place these on the walls in order to silence some snipers who were firing from the buildings in the Forbidden City.

As soon as these guns opened fire some of the "relieved ones" showed signs of "nerves" till it was explained to them it was only the fire of friends. Picquets were posted on the walls from the Marines and Volunteers who had lately formed the plucky garrison. They would not hear of handing this duty over to us for this last night. The Americans entered by the sluice gate shortly after us, and thus swelled our numbers till there was hardly room to move, for in addition to fighting men there were hundreds of followers and mules with our baggage. When darkness came on we managed to get a kind of wash, and later we were all seated at Sir Claude's hospital table, feasting on soup made out of a mule, whilst the choicest dish of the evening was Lady MacDonald's favourite pony, the last beast to be killed!) It was very sad, and she had all our sympathies. Whatever she felt she made light of it, her one thought was our comfort. During the night of the 13th Sir Claude had a narrow escape from a shell, which knocked a big hole in the roof of his room. It is now late, I must turn in.

15th. A real busy day getting men into quarters. The 1st Bengal Lancers, 24th Punjab Infantry, two guns 12th Field Battery, one section Field Hospital, and all the transport are at the Temple of Heaven, whilst the South Gate of the Chinese city is held by 50 men of the 24th P.I. and one Maxim, the S.E. gate being kept by the Naval Brigade. The rest of our troops are in and near the Legation.

Looting is going on in all directions, but our men and followers are in hand, with of course a few exceptions. One can't be in a dozen places at once, but once settled down it will be all right. The Russians seem everywhere, and what they can't carry off they burn. This morning I saw a splendid store of most beautiful silks and brocades blazing away merrily just outside the Chien-men (gate). By to-morrow I hope there will be less of this. Without doubt some of the relieved ladies know where to look for "trifles." A few of the Missionaries are inclined to magnify slight acts of familiarity into criminal offences. The Sikh, for instance, is an admirer of beauty, and when he begins to toy with the hair ornaments of some fair Chinese damsel, who happens to be a convert, he should not be at once condemned as a gay Lothario who in broad daylight is about to shock everyones morals. I was much annoyed to-day after receiving the third frivolous complaint, and had to express my view in most unmistakable language. The native soldier of India is the least likely man here to offend the morals of the white races.

The Russians and Japanese had some hard fighting yesterday on the walls they attacked. They report finding over 300 dead, whilst the latter lost a lot of men when trying to blow in a gate. Something more reliable than rumour has it their artillery fired over 5,000 rounds! It will be days before we know what really took place yesterday.

The hero and heroine of the Legations are Colonel Shiba, and the wife of the proprietor of the French hotel, who armed with rifles, spent many a day and night on the walls during the hardest fighting, accounting for not a few of the enemy, whilst Colonel Shiba's conduct during the entire siege was a record any man might be proud of. He is certain to be a great man some day. Am afraid there have been a few cases of cruelty. I hear of one horrid case where a soldier seized a little child by the legs and dashed his brains out against the parapet of a bridge in front of some of his own men and others, who nearly ran him through. There is endless work to be done.

16th. (This morning we sent out 200 Marines, 100 1st Sikhs, and the same number 7th Rajputs to assist the French under General Frey in the relief of some of their people at the Pehtang Cathedral, Bishop Favier and a number of Fathers, chiefly missionaries, nuns, and converts, who for months were protected by a handful of Marines. These persons must have had an even more anxious time of it than their friends in the Legations owing to their complete isolation in the heart of the city. They were nearly blown up on more than one occasion. For a long time it was a case of mining and counter mining, those outside having six to one the better of the struggle. Why these poor people were kept in suspense two extra days I can't conceive. The task was not a very formidable one, and I'm sure every man in our force would have volunteered for this duty on the 14th had they been aware of the fact that women and children were in danger whilst they were safe. All's well that ends well. The French could hardly have undertaken the relief on the 14th single handed, and were probably reticent about asking assistance at the end of a tiring day, but how about yesterday?

The opposition offered the Anglo-French relief party was trivial. Our men were under the command of Major Luke, Royal Marines. A Japanese column assisted from the north side.

The troops (British) in the Tartar city are under my command, whilst those in the Temple of Heaven are under Gartside Tipping, pending further orders.

17th. Cleaning and demolishing in all directions. Selwyn appointed D.A.Q.M.G. till Brooking arrives. Instead of promiscuous looting all units are ordered to send out organised parties under officers to examine abandoned houses and bring in all articles of value inside the Legation compound. Major Luke and his party, with Captain Bingley, of the 7th Rajputs, remain at Coal Hill, where the French troops under General Frey are in camp. This is the most northern portion of the Imperial City. I hear the French have a nice amount of loot in their camp! We found a large supply of ice in the Chinese city, over which I have placed a guard of the Welsh Fusiliers. The weather to-day is pleasantly cool, which is a nice change after the intense heat. The health of the troops is excellent. Our convoy to Tang-chou returned with seven days' supplies.

18th. At noon a report came in saying Boxers had been seen in numbers S.W. of the city, so two guns of 12th Field Batter, two Maxims, one company R.W. Fusiliers, and one company 7th Rajputs reinforced the Temple of Heaven.

Later in the day this news was confirmed by our cavalry, who reported they had seen a regiment of cavalry and battalion of infantry.

The Ministers and Commanding Generals met to-day, and the city was partitioned off for purposes of order and police supervision. Besides the Legation the British are to control a portion of the Chinese city and S.W. corner of the Tartar city from the Shun-shi-men gate in continuation of the

Americans and to the north till we come in touch with the French. In addition we have the lesser Lama Temple quarter east of the Imperial City besides of course the Temple of Heaven enclosure. Temporarily we hold Coal Hill with the Russians and French, with a small guard at Paytsung, so we are pretty well spread out. Rode out to Coal Hill; in two streets there were hundreds of Chinese corpses, and the stench was truly awful. The Russians were moving these with drag ropes manned by Chinese forced labour; it was a horrible sight. Corpses are to be found in nearly every empty house. Until all these are discovered and buried or burnt we run grave risks of an epidemic. Many of the wells have corpses in them, mostly females, who committed suicide on the approach of the armies. Whole families made away with themselves. In one out-house I saw five bodies hanging. At night there is a fair amount of shooting. I fancy sentries pass the time practising on dogs or other moving objects. No doubt there are many Boxers in the city, who hope to get a chance of polishing off the unwary "foreign devil," mooching about on the look out for spoil.

Our signalling posts are established, so can send messages in all directions.

I have now learnt the Russians reached Pekin

on night of 13th, and made a desperate attempt to enter the city by the Tung-pien-men, but withdrew after losing some 150 men. The Japanese attack was directed against the Chi-ho and Tung-chih Gates, where at first they received a check after attempting to blow them in, and were forced to retire, when they heavily bombarded the walls with every available gun, and effected an entry about midnight the 14th, after losing upwards of 200 men in the assault and street fighting which followed. Without doubt these Russian and Japanese attacks on the east face of the Tartar city enabled us to enter from the south without much opposition.

It will be seen the Russians completely stole a march on the other Powers, and perhaps it's just as well they did, otherwise the Chinese might have devoted their whole strength in a final attack on the Legations and overpowered them whilst we were still at Tang-chao. How the Russians were able to reach Pekin a day ahead of us without its being known I don't suppose I shall ever hear. Never has there been such muddling. Only abnormal good luck has pulled the Allies through.

It is difficult to form any correct estimate of what the losses of the Allies have been since leaving Tientsin, but I have reason to suppose that all told they will not be far off 1,000, of which the Japanese must have lost quite 500. The Russian losses are probably 350, and the Americans and ourselves 150 equally divided. Excepting inside the city of Pekin I never once saw any numbers of Chinese dead. So as far as casualties are concerned the Allies seem to have come off second best, due as I have more than once said, to the white uniforms and closer formations of the Russians and Japanese in the attack, the Russians forming a target which seemed impossible to miss, and the Japanese very little better in this respect, for although they did open out more than the Russians they were even "whiter," for with them all was white excepting their caps, accoutrements, and boots, which were black. A more unbusiness-like uniform for active service during a rainy season is hard to conceive, and it seems wicked that gallant fellows like them should have been sent out to slaughter as they were.

From time to time we heard of cruelties inflicted on the peaceful inhabitants during the march up, but personally I only saw one instance of this, which was quite sufficient. When passing through a village within a yard or two of our path we came on the nude bodies of two young Chinese girls tied to a stake, which had been horribly mutilated, quite recently, by whom God only knows. Had any of our men, European or native, been witnesses of this dastardly act, I feel convinced they would have shot the cowards down like dogs, irrespective of nationality. The officers persuaded the men to believe it was the act of Boxers, rather than allow them to think it was done by one of our "friends." In action we noticed that the Japanese did not spare the wounded or respect the dead, which was bad enough, but there was some excuse for this, as they had not forgotten their war with China some years previously, when neither side spared the other.

19th. A convoy left for Tang-chao this morning at seven escorted by cavalry, who were ordered to keep a sharp look out on their right flank.

The 26th Baluchistan Regiment arrived to-day, so now I have my Brigade in the country, but I don't suppose I will actually command it for a single day, certainly never if we remain an army of occupation in the city of Pekin.

I moved into quarters, and was more than pleased to have a room to myself.

Foraging parties are out daily. We hope to despatch the first batch of refugees to Tientsin next Wednesday, thus giving us more room, as at present we are very cramped in and about the Legations. We have an excellent building as a temporary hospital.

20th. The latest I have is Boxers and Regulars are collecting in the Deer Park, where I hope they will remain till we have more time to look them up.

21st. We are now beginning to get our letters from home and India. The news from South Africa does not seem to improve. If you hear good news one day you may expect some depressing items the next. I fancy the good people at home take no further interest in our doings out here.

Dorward seems to have had a very nice turn up with some Boxers outside Tientsin. The report says he has killed upwards of 300 and taken 60 prisoners, our loss being only some half-dozen wounded. Our native cavalry seem to have done very well.

The conservancy problem keeps one fully occupied. The Chinese work well and honestly. I fancy they are fairly surprised at getting any wages at all, so what must they think of the liberal sum we expend daily on cleaning up streets and lanes they never touched! Once things are shipshape we will begin to teach them western ideas and habits that will be irksome no doubt at first, but the "cat" soon brightens their ordinarily dull faces when they don't wish to understand. As a matter of fact they are just about as intelligent a race as you could find in any part of the globe. The Chinaman grows on you, at first I thought he was a horror. Every day he improves, and soon I expect to admire him, unless I'm much mistaken.

I'm beginning to realise Lord Wolseley's estimate of him. He is a fine built powerful man, capable of almost anything, and probably has it in him to be very staunch. Our officers of the Chinese Regiment swear by him. I see a good deal of Dent, who belongs to the Chinese Regiment, and from him I am picking up news which will assist me greatly in forming a correct opinion of their character which I trust will turn out useful later on. I must note a curious order published to-day. "The R.E. and Sappers and Miners are excluded from the Tartar City command!" Before I leave China I will probably have some more "curios!"

22nd. (Owing to heavy rain last night the convoy of men, ladies, and children could not start this morning.)

23rd. The above convoy, escorted by a squadron of the 1st B.L. and one company 26th Baluchis, left this morning, and I was glad to hear they reached Tang-chao in safety after 14 hours! They rested there for two hours and then joined the junks. With the stream they won't take long getting to Tientsin. Once there they will be quite safe. How thankful they must be after the experiences of the last few months. To-day an order was issued directing every officer in the force to submit a certificate on his word of honour as an officer and gentleman that he had given up articles of loot in his possession! If officers forget themselves they must expect degradation of this kind. Personally I would issue an order to the same effect, but leave out the "certificate," which to my mind is unnecessary. An officer who would keep back articles which he in a moment of weakness had taken, after an order to disgorge the same, would sign the certificate and retain the spoil. Some wags wished to know if the "issuing" authorities also signed the certificate!

24th. After the late rain it is now very close and stuffy, and the flies most objectionable. These pests are likely to carry disease, chiefly opthalmia, which is very prevalent amongst the Chinese.

25th. The escort of 60 R.W. Fusiliers and 240 men of the Baluchis accompanied the British Minister to the western gate of the Forbidden City, inside which it was rumoured there were several armed men who wished to be released. It ended, however, in smoke. This is how troops are harassed

26th. Our first church parade, which was held in the tinga facing the British Legation.

A regrettable occurrence took place to-day in the Chinese city. Two Pathans of the 24th P.I. were interfering with a woman, who screamed out. This attracted the attention of an American patrol, on seeing which the men decamped in the direction of their quarters at the Temple of Heaven. To stop them the patrol opened fire,. killing one man at once. His comrade dropped on his knee and returned the fire till he was knocked over. The firing attracted the guard over the entrance to the Temple of Heaven, and soon there was an excited crowd of Sepoys, who carried their comrades' bodies to their lines, for the second man died almost immediately. It speaks well for the discipline of the regiment that the men did not retaliate. They were sorely tried, but with such officers as Colonel Ramsay and Major Climo on the spot their soldierly instincts restrained them from taking action. General Chaffee stands no nonsense from his men, and it didn't take him long to court martial the offenders) Considering it was broad day light, and our men were recognised as armed soldiers the action of the patrol was

THE ENTRANCE TO THE FORBIDDEN CITY,

decidedly despotic. When the unwounded man returned the fire the Americans realised that our Sepoys are men not to be trifled with. I don't think they will repeat this.

27th. There is a certain amount of fever knocking about, which one must expect in the rainy season, when one moment it is chilly and the next boiling.

28th. The allied armies marched through the Forbidden City. It was a very impressive sight. The Russians in the van followed by the Japanese, British, American, French, Austrian, Italians, and Germans in the order given, which represents the different forces in the country. The march passed off without a hitch, which speaks well for the arrangements, as there wasn't too much room. Bowing and scraping *Eunuchs* were much "en evidence," but the buildings we hurried through were not very attractive, although many of them were piled up with priceless cloisonne. The carvings of the stone steps leading to each building were truly splendid. The wood work, screens, and ceilings were also very grand, but at the same time there was much that appeared gaudy. After a private view I will be better able to form an opinion. Refreshments were served in a tinga after the troops were ordered back to quarters.

Here all the beauty and fashion of the many Legations were mustered, and report, which is not always reliable, states several "objects d'arts" were lifted. Our Minister at least appeared to be very indignant, but I fear the culprits were not to be found entirely amongst the coarser sex, and it seemed wiser to retrace one's steps with "eyes front," and regale oneself at the mess. I am beginning to hate the sound of the word "loot." If you do happen to pick up an article which seems good, and for which you have paid the price you are at once asked "Where did you loot that?" Even those who ought to know better seem to doubt your honesty. Life under such conditions is a bit degrading.

29th. It has been raining continuously for the last 24 hours, so the odours are worse than ever. The roads are ankle deep in thick slimy black mire, which does not add to our comforts. Two companies of the R.W. Fusiliers relieved the Marines at Coal Hill, who go down with the Naval Brigade to-morrow. The Marines at the Lama Temple have been relieved by the Biluchis.

30th. Owing to the state of the roads after the continuous rain the Naval Brigade were unable to move this morning. Captain Selwyn, our Commissioner of Police, asked for 100 men yesterday to surround a house full of Boxers. All these men caught was a wetting! I forgot to note Captain Brooking joined my staff on the 23rd as D.A.Q.M.G., and during the week, with the help of Bobby Low, has done wonders in the matter of getting our quarter into a sanitary condition. He is an excellent officer; wish he had joined me sooner.

31st. The Naval Brigade, commanded by Captain Callaghan, including the R.M.L.I., under Major Luke, and the companies of the Chinese Regiment, left this morning, the former to join their ships and the latter to relieve the Marines at Tang-chao, Matao, and Ho-shi-wu, viz., one British officer and 30 men at Tang-chao, one B. O. and 20 men at Matao, and the remainder at Ho-shi-wu.

We established an important post at Fengtai this morning. Important because it is the junction of the Tientsin and Pao-ting-Fu lines, and might have been occupied by some other nation to our inconvenience later on. It is about five miles from the south gate of the Chinese city in a S.W. direction. Messrs. Van Someren and Bean of the Indian Postal Department, arrived this afternoon. The former is an old friend, and the latter, his brother-in-law, is a musician of no mean order, so we look forward to many pleasant sing-songs in our mess, as we intend appropriating them during their stay in Pekin. More of Bean's banjo later on I expect.

His experiences are much the same as my own, and corroborate my views as to the staff.

Why is it so many staff officers become "superior," when the superiority only consists in a brass bound head ornament?

This does not put more brains under the hat, at all events not sufficient to truthfully explain or account for the swollen condition of the head. The staff officer with the offensive-smell-under-the-nose-appearance is one of the abominations of our service, and I daresay every other service. He is invariably grovelling to his superiors on the staff whilst almost insulting to the regimental officer, who as a rule soars far above him as a component part of the machine at work. On this subject I can speak with a certain amount of authority, having served on the staff in cantonments and the field, and whenever I found the brim of my "chapeau" fitting tight the best antidote was immediate association with the nearest regimental officer, and the avoidance for the time being of brother brass hats.

Reduce the pay of the brass-bound ones, and I

think they will become more useful. On the other hand what a veritable blessing a really good staff officer is. In India an uncle or an aunt, a pretty wife, or numerous visits to Simla will secure you any of the fashionable billets going. Stay in the plains and do your work with your regiment, and you will remain a beast of burden to the end of your days unless you get a chance of distinguishing yourself on active service. Seize that chance, and in a moment you will be translated from the flat footed regimental officer to a study in "red and gold," for to give the devil his due, merit in the field is speedily rewarded, examinations and theoretical qualifications are brushed aside. Some of the best staff officers I have met have not been entitled to the magic letters P.S.C. after their names, whilst others possessing those letters have only been noted for their all-round incompetence. There are many heroes who are socially classed as fools, but wise men are not all heroes. "Manners" is a qualification which should be insisted on when choosing staff officers.

1st September. The rain has ceased, and it looks as if we are in for some fine weather. It is still very hot in the day time, but the mornings and evenings are very pleasant. The large quantity of loot taken from deserted houses of men who bolted with the court and those of well-known Boxers is now being sold by public auction for cash to anyone who chooses to bid irrespective of race. In this way something like $1,000 a day is coming in. How this money will eventually be distributed it is hard to say. Opinions vary. Some hope it will be divided amongst our troops who actually relieved the Legations. This seems to me highly improbable. I think every man in the force should have a look in. The honour of being, through sheer good luck, in the van is worth a great deal more than any money consideration, and once the point is definitely decided I don't suppose anyone will give the subject a second thought. A point which ought to be considered is the opportunity we have, which is denied to others, of procuring very interesting mementos of the country at, what I trust turns out, reasonable prices. It is quite possible some articles, the value of which we are in absolute ignorance of, may be picked up for a mere song. In this respect old residents score over us poor soldiers. Watching the sale to-day I'm inclined to think some bargains were picked up by the "knowing ones." When we are settled down I think I will trust it to the open market. The sale has left a nasty taste in my mouth!

We occupied Lia-ka-Chao this morning, a bridge head about three miles on the Pai-tang-Fu side of Feng-tai of some importance, as it commands in all three bridges, and thus we will be able to divert supplies coming in for our own use. The country people are beginning to see the advantages of bringing in all sorts of food stuff which they can at once sell in bulk for cash.

2nd September. The weather is absolutely perfect, and the health of the troops all that could be desired. We have no idle men, there is heaps of work for everyone up to 4 p.m., by which time all are free. The duties are fairly heavy, but this will improve. The men seem to enjoy wandering about the bazaars, where they can amuse themselves by looking at all the queer odds and ends exposed for sale on the sides of the main thoroughfares. It is quite entertaining to watch the "haggling" going on in a dozen different tongues. When the bargain is definitely closed the Chinaman's face beams, a sure sign *he* has not been done. Probably most of these articles are the proceeds of months of looting, and have cost the vendor nothing, so no wonder he beams!

3rd. Major Scott, D.S.O., attached to the 1st Sikhs, is appointed road Commandant line of Communications from Tang-chao to Ho-shi-wu, both places included, with his head quarters at the former, where he will be Post Commandant also when present. The appointment takes effect from the 6th inst.

Convoys to Tang-chao are now to run daily excepting Thursdays and Sundays, changing loads half way, i.e., they will go out empty and return full.

4th. With a view to wintering here inspected all available buildings with C.R.E. and Brooking. The Engineers will not be able to undertake all the work, so fancy the wisest plan will be to direct Commanding Officers to look after their own men. The Chinese are clever carpenters, and the necessary skilled work can be given out to contractors, whilst the Sepoys can do the carrying, demolishing, etc. No doubt sums of money will be allotted on rough estimates being submitted. When all is completed I feel sure the men will be very comfortably housed. There may be some difficulty about warming and lighting the buildings, so it's just as well this question is being tackled at an early date. If you leave work of this kind to the last moment it generally means waste in the end.

A convoy of ladies and children went off this morning, also Parsons, of the Burmah Commission, who up to date has been acting Brigade Interpreter. We will miss him in the mess.

5th. Every available man is now employed on work connected with winter quarters, by breaking down walls we will make new streets and thoroughly ventilate the place. The Germans in the N.W. quarter of the Chinese city appear to indulge in indiscriminate shooting at night, presumably at dogs. Rumour has it that Prince Ching arrived four days ago.

6th. Rain fell last night, and has made the place in a mess again. It is rather heart-breaking, but it can't be helped. We can't metal our roads, so must submit to muddy lanes after every shower.

The Russians must have had a scrimmage somewhere, as wounded were seen entering the south gate of the Chinese city. It is very difficult to get any reliable news of the doings of others. I hear, however, from a good source, they are closing their bank here and moving their Legation to their concession at Tientsin. This, of course, is magnified into a declaration of war against China! I don't suppose the Minister has any intention of moving, and beyond closing the Pekin branch of their bank there is no truth in the rumour. Their hands are full in Manchuria, and I expect very soon they will march their army across country via Shan-hai-kwan, and leave only a small detachment in Pekin and Tientsin. This friendly occupation cannot suit the Russian idea.

7th. Once more complaints have come in of further looting. Spread out as we are it is impossible to keep your eyes on everyone. Men followers and transport are continually on the move, and no doubt some of them do break away and wander through bye lanes instead of sticking to the main roads, but taking us as a whole we are too occupied to find time for this sort of thing except in isolated cases. There are a great many idle Europeans still here, who seem to spend their time roaming about with the intention of finding fault, and everything is put down to the unfortunate Indian. As a matter of fact we are far more particular than others, excepting possibly the Americans, and certainly we have fewer idle men.

We are expecting a convoy of mules, carts, and R.E. stores this afternoon. It rained again hard last night.

We sent 700 mules to Tang-chao this morning to bring up stores.

The O.C. Baluchis reports that a party of Americans, including some officers, released an

American prisoner from the custody of one of their guards on a city gate after assaulting the havildar in command. This man has been placed under arrest. Chaffee is the last man in the world to tolerate this sort of thing. Our men must be taught they are not to submit to treatment of the kind. It is a very difficult question. Probably the best plan is to put your prisoner out of sight, and call on the nearest guard of the nationality concerned to fetch their man away, and keep him a prisoner till a report can be submitted. This case will probably lead to European police being posted on all gates held by us.

8th. Our postal arrangements are a bit erratic. Last evening a mail came in which ought to have been delivered some time ago, probably the fault of some transport which carried this particular mail. To-day is dull, and looks as if we were in for more rain.

9th. We frequently hear of Boxers, but don't often see them. The troops in the Temple of Heaven made a reconnaissance this morning, but drew a blank.

10th. A lot of rain to-day, and towards evening it was too cold for summer garments, so hope our warm clothing will soon come up, as nothing causes sickness more quickly than these sudden changes if you can't meet them. The Chinese don't like working in the wet, they either keep away or turn up in reduced numbers, so our sanitary arrangements suffer. At present these coolies are under Dr. Dudgeon, of the Legation, who of course knows their language, but he seems to be weak with them, so the sooner we take them in hand the better. The Chinaman breaks all the laws of sanitation, but that is no reason for us to fall into his ways. He must be taught our ways, as we have had to do in other places. In Candahar we had the same kind of trouble. We pay them well and we expect good work in return, rain or no rain. To our minds they are absolutely filthy in their habits, but I really don't think cleanliness will cause them much disease, whilst their insanitary habits may bring about an epidemic. Anyhow we have no intention of running any risks, and a slight display of the "cat" which our provost establishment is armed with will soon do the needful.

11th. Once more fine and bright, but decidedly cooler. A telegram received this morning from Road Commandant reports two Sepoys of 26th Baluchis missing from a convoy between Ho-shi-wu and Matao, apparently on the 9th. Cavalry ordered to search.

12th. More Boxers in the air! Am getting

tired of this sort of thing. I don't suppose our men have ever had better food than they are getting. The meat supply is excellent and plentiful, and the commissariat is turning out just as good bread as the men get in cantonments in India. All this good food with a glorious climate will keep the men in fine condition. It has been warm, but with six months of cold weather ahead there is nothing to grumble at once our supply of warm clothing comes up.

13th. The meat eating natives are now getting two rations of meat a week. After dinner last night there was a fine blaze in the Russian quarter the other side of the street opposite the Baluchis. We all turned out and offered our assistance, which was not very promptly accepted, the Russians saying "the property was not theirs." We explained, however, that in a few minutes they would be without a roof, which apparently appealed to them. It was certainly a very fine sight, and although we couldn't save the buildings we managed to get all their personal effects out and pile them in the centre of the square, whence the Russians condescended to drag them into safety in rear. Our men thoroughly enjoyed the excitement, otherwise I think I would have ordered them back to quarters. A change of wind might have sent sparks across the road to our quarters, so it was wiser to stick to the job and see it through. After our men and officers had worked hard for some time the Russian officers also joined in. Fire is the most serious enemy we have owing to the inflammable material with which all Chinese houses are built, and these particular buildings were more so than most owing to their enormous dimensions. It was the old Chinese Revenue Office. At midnight we had to think of some means of confining the fire, so Colonel Scott Moncrieff suggested experimenting with gun cotton, which was very successful. We stood by till all the main buildings fell in. It was really a very grand sight, for the flames leapt up quite 100 feet into the sky. The heat was terrific, and the fire must have been seen for miles, but not a single soul came to the assistance of the Russians or even had the curiosity to send men to enquire what was up. The Russians declare it was the act of some incendiary, as the fire started in the roof of a low building, the tiles having been previously removed. Whilst they were looking at this without attempting to put it out, the whole of this smaller building burst out into flame, which no human power could battle with. We have gained some experience which I hope will prove useful, for fires we must expect.

14th. Warm and fine, a few showers in the evening. A Chinaman who insulted Mr. Backhouse has been sentenced to death by our Minister. Evidence proved that he had harboured Boxers during the siege, and when he insulted Mr. "B." he asked the "Sun" why the foreign devils had been victorious instead of the Boxers, at the same time boasting that he himself was one of that "ilk." The Americans are out scouring the country, and hope to relieve some missionaries who are shut up in a village not far off.

A mixed force is to proceed to some temples situated west of the Summer Palace at the foot of the hills, below which our Legation people generally spent the hot months of the year. I gather these temples are some 10 miles distant, and rumour has it that many Boxers are collected there.

A telegram was received this evening from Tang-chao reporting a serious explosion of gun powder, with 30 casualties, amongst whom is Captain Hill, of the Chinese Regiment, seriously injured. No further particulars. I suppose our men were employed destroying the large store of powder we discovered when passing through Tang-chao 12th and 13th last month.

15th. Further reports from Tang-chao state that by 8 a.m. 17 men had succumbed, and many more were in a hopeless condition. Medical aid was despatched at once. There is every hope that Hill will pull through. The force referred to yesterday will start to-morrow. If well managed we ought to be able to surround the temples and have all at our mercy, but I have not much faith in these mixed parties. Much wiser to hand the venture over to one nationality. It is again much warmer.

16th. The following troops rendezvous at the west gate of the Chinese city at 3 p.m. this afternoon under the command of Colonel Tulloch, of the Baluchis, with Brooking as D.A.A.G. and Stotherd and Leonard as gallopers. Goldingham, R.E., will survey the ground, etc.

Two guns 12th Field Battery, two Maxims, 70 1st B. Lancers, 90 R.W. Fusiliers, 200 26th Baluchis, 150 1st Sikhs, 150 7th B.I., 150 24th P.I., one company Bengal S. and M.'s, one Native Field Hospital, one section for Europeans, 200 rounds of ammunition per man, and 3 days rations for all. They march to Lu-ka-chao to-night, bivouac there, and attack in the morning. An American detachment also marches to Lu-ka-chao this evening, and the whole attack in the morning under the command of General Wilson, U.S.A. The Germans are to co-operate in the morning from the south, and the Japanese from the east, so all depends on good timing and secrecy. *If* our men occupy the hills in rear without being observed they ought to catch the entire gang in a trap, but it is a big "IF," and I hardly think it will turn out the success we hope. The Chinese as a rule kept an excellent look out and are very particular about securing their retreat. In this respect they are "masters."

Four Boxers implicated in the murder of some missionaries 21 days after we entered Pekin have been sentenced to death by Macdonald, and handed over to us for execution, which will be be carried out in the village where the massacre took place, some seven miles off.

17th. Slight rain fell during the night, and again this morning. So far no sounds of firing. Am afraid the Boxers have given us the slip, though, of course, finding themselves surrounded, they may have given in without firing. In the afternoon I visited our hospitals, and found all satisfactory barring the lighting. A message has come in saying the temples have been occupied, without any mention of fighting, which does not look promising.

18th. The temperature has suddenly dropped, and even at 11 a.m. the sun is only pleasant.

Won't be happy till the warm clothing arrives. The deaths at Tang-chao have now reached 25, and the latest news of Captain Hill is less hopeful. A lot of loose powder caught fire and burnt the men's clothing, on which they rushed in a body to the river, where they tore off their uniform, and then dropped on the bank stark naked. Few, if any, will recover, and this being the case I fear we will never discover the cause. Probably there was some carelessness in opening the tins of powder on shore, when this might have been done with security by men standing knee deep in the water. The casualties apparently are confined to the men of the Chinese Regiment.

A committee composed of S.M.O., D.A.Q.M.G. and Garrison Engineer assembles at once to finally select winter quarters for troops, followers and hospitals. If we do not use the Temple of Heaven ground for commissariat purposes there will always be the danger of fire. The distance, however, is against this, and I expect we will continue to use the carriage park, which is very handy, besides containing magnificent godown accommodation for perishable aritcles. The concentration of our transport requires careful consideration, for at the lowest computation we will have 600 mules and 200 carts, for which there is only room at the

Temple of Heaven, and besides these there will have to be lines for 400 cavalry, without counting the 12th Field Battery, which will, I presume, be located in the Tartar City, where the majority of the European troops will be quartered. One thing is very evident, we can't all fit in in the Tartar City, so the Temple of Heaven must be retained. Here the troops will score over the city garrison.

Captain Hill I regret to say died to-day. We are still without full particulars of this most deplorable occurrence.

Colonel Tullock and most of our troops returned this evening. The Germans are blamed for the failure of the operations. As far as I know every man Jack got away with a whole skin.

19th. At the temples they found workshops and an armoury, for the destruction of which the detachments R.W. Fusiliers, R.A., 100 Baluchis, and the Sappers and Miners remained behind. Two Gatlings and some 20 breach loading shoulder guns which required two men to manipulate fell into our hands. It turns out there were only some 400 Chinese in the place, who escaped by the hills in rear. Had our men been in position an hour earlier they would have trapped the lot, and as it was Turner, of the Baluchis, very nearly caught them. The Germans were not only late, but advanced in close formation, and gave the show away.

Glanders is knocking about, so every animal is being carefully inspected by Hazleton.

Have just seen Tulloch, and from what he tells me our intelligence department were not free from blame for the failure of yesterday. I am more inclined to think we employed too large a force. Our own was quite large enough for the job.

20th. Heavy thunderstorm last night, with torrents of rain, which put out both our incinerators and flooded the commissariat yard.

Tulloch's official report to hand. His dispositions seem to have been quite sound, and all the arrangements made by Bingley, commanding at Lu-ka-chao seem to have been excellent. The Baluchis under Turner very nearly succeeded in cutting off the retreat of the Boxers. It was a race between the two, and by the time our men did reach their position they were so pumped their shooting was erratic, so casualties were few.

21st. Another perfect day, as it invariably is after a storm. There is some friction about the control of the railway. Looking at the question generally the Russians seem to have a stronger claim than anyone else at the moment. They brought everyone as far as Tientsin at the most

LIEUT.-GEN. SIR A. GASELEE AND HEAD QUARTERS' STAFF.

critical time, and without them I don't know what we should have done. As regards ourselves, we have one R.E. officer who knows something about railways, two native engine drivers, and perhaps enough sleepers to carry rails half a mile! whereas the Russians can command a Railway Battalion some 2,000 strong. Our officers speak of the Russians with a great deal too much bitterness, whilst admiration for the Japanese is almost hysterical. One never hears a word of news from our head quarters people, which makes it very difficult to form an opinion on any international matter. This policy of secrecy is wrong, but I do not allow it to irritate me in any way. It must result in shaking one's confidence, for after all we are only human. It is very awkward when discussing the situation with foreign officers to have to admit absolute ignorance. Discussion is much freer with the other forces. This secrecy detracts from an otherwise interesting and unique experience of campaigning. The explanation may be, "There is nothing to tell," and on the whole I'm inclined to look at things in this light. It is certainly the excuse I make if asked a question from one of our own.

22nd. Visited the Chefoo Palace, which has been told off as Brigade Head Quarters and

General Hospital. Nothing better could be found in the city. The buildings which will be used as a hospital are brand new, and quite palatial in dimensions, with large paved court yards, where the convalescents can sit and sun themselves. Our one and only difficulty will be the question of heating, but even this can be overcome by building brick chimneys, for any quantity of really fine bricks are at hand. With large fire-places at each end of the wards and a few stoves dotted about on the floors I think all will be quite snug, even in the bitterest weather, as the walls are massive, and no sign of draughts. The Cefoo Palace is in the extreme S.W. quarter of the Tartar city, just under the walls, the top of which will form an excellent promenade with a glorious view of the surrounding country, to get at which it is proposed to cut an opening through the wall, a matter of some 70 feet. This will make life bearable, for through this opening one will be able to get a morning and evening canter without having to go through miles of filthy streets. Besides the Hospital I will have practically the whole of my command within five minutes' walk, barring the Baluchis, who will remain in the Legation portion near our Army Headquarters. We are all looking forward to our move with intense pleasure, and already officers are making up their minds where they will play tennis, squash racquets, etc., etc.

At last the surroundings are beginning to look clean, and as the Americans are to be our neighbours, I hope the entire route from Chefoo Palace to the Legations will be presentable. For walking purposes one always has the top of the wall to fall back on. Here you never see a Chinaman.

Vaughan, our Chief Commissariat Officer at Pekin, has gone out to Fengtai and Lu-ka-chao to inspect the coal stored in these places. I have seen samples of this coal, which weigh very heavy. The amount you could put inside a helmet is more than a man's daily supply, so we need not therefore regulate the quantity by weight now that we know what is wanted for a day's consumption. Camel caravans from the north east should soon be coming in. These only work when the weather is cold, but already we hear the Russians are trying to secure these for themselves. We will doubtless make use of these camels for bringing in coal. I have seen some of these, and they are certainly magnificent brutes, and much more docile than our Indian camel.

23rd. Found some Boxer proclamations on the walls of the West Tartar City, exhorting the people not to light their cooking stoves between the 23rd and 31st October, "between which dates all foreigners must be utterly exterminated." Sent a translation to the Chief of the Staff. It is considerate of these good people to give us a month's warning! Some wag's hoax.

Report from Tientsin has come in to say the forces there, excepting the British, had arranged to attack the Peitang Forts, and when the British expressed a wish to join the Russian, French and German troops they were informed the railway was not capable of carrying any more men, so Lorne Campbell, commanding our troops at Tientsin, collected a small force which he took down by river, to find he was too late. Hearing firing he sent a staff officer ahead to enquire, only to learn the fort or forts had been taken, and French, Russian, and German flags were flying over it or them! The firing lasted from 7 to 11 a.m., the Chinese being the first to fire.

24th. We are in for more rain I fear, as it is decidedly close to-day. Friction with the Russians over the railway continues. They object to our meddling as they are pleased to term it. Our contention is they have no claim to the Pekin-Tientsin section on the strength of the original agreement arrived at by the Admirals, which only referred to the Tag-ku-Tientsin section. As the entire line was built with English capital it is only right we should be consulted even if we are not in a position to work it at once. It would not take long to get hold of the staff which worked the line in the piping times of peace, and patch up the existing rolling stock, for whoever works the line, there must be considerable delay before new engines, etc., could be procured. Possibly these would come from America. Wherever there is friction between ourselves and the Russians the latter are sure of the support of the French and Germans, the Japanese looking on and thoroughly enjoying the discord. The Americans on the other hand would certainly join with us.

Macdonald goes to Japan as Minister, and Satow comes here in his place. He is a red hot "Jap." As far as one can gauge political secrets, our Minister in China is merely a figure head, who has to implicitly carry out any instructions sent by Lord Salisbury, who appears to let things slide.

General Richardson, commanding the Cavalry Brigade, arrived with the 16th Bengal Lancers to-day. He will take over command of our troops at the Temple of Heaven. We will soon have as many Generals as limbs here!

25th. Weather looks unsettled. Gaselee left for Tientsin; he has made up his mind to stick to the Legation section for the winter. Knapp, of the 1st Sikhs, arrived yesterday with our warm clothing. Reid's Brigade has landed, and I fancy his destination is Shan-hei-kwan, where he may see a bit of fighting.

The Chinese say the Empress Dowager and Emperor are only 300 li from here; this is about 100 English miles. If Li-Hung-Chang comes up she will probably try and make terms. The condition of Europe, however, is against any solid business being done, and on the Continent we appear to have no friends excepting Italy. If the reported rebellion of Soudanese troops is true, India is certain to be called on to furnish a division, which would prove a great strain on her resources. Things look black on all sides, and poor old Kruger's words may yet have some truth in them.

26th. Gaselee and Seymour are to meet at Tientsin to discuss Shanghaï affairs. Having landed troops there other Powers will certainly do the same. Our first post by road from Tientsin arrived to-day. It is carried on mules escorted by Sowars, and will take three days, as soon the days will shorten.

27th. Most of the troops have now got warm clothing, but not so the followers. It is now decidedly colder at night, the days being perfect. Many of the Legation people are leaving. We have now four Generals and about 3,000 men!

28th. Li-Hung-Chang is said to be at Tientsin, which is now full of celebrities! It is contemplated sending a German-British Force to "*some place*," under General Gaselee, to meet another force coming from Tientsin. Beyond this there is no news.

29th. The British portion of the force for "*some place*," will consist of four guns R.A., 16th B.L., 100 R.W. Fusiliers, 100 7th B.I., 200 1st Sikhs, 200 24th P.I., 200 Baluchis, a company of Sappers, and one Field Hospital, without tents, and under the command of Richardson, with the staff of the Cavalry Brigade. The mysterious "some place" is of course Pai-tang-Fu, but I am not curious enough to enquire.

30th. A nasty, dull, raw day, which improved considerably towards evening.

1st October. Coal Hill was evacuated by our troops this morning, leaving only a guard over the Rotunda palace in conjunction with the French. H.E. Field Marshal Count Waldersee assumed command of the Allied Forces in China on the 27th ult. What his powers are, God only knows. I fancy the troops of the two Republics will only be nominally under him. The Japanese, Russians, and Americans are stated to have received instructions as to the numbers which are to remain here. Some Americans are off in a few days to the Philippines. I expect they would prefer this to Manila.

2nd. Cold, bright, and dusty. There are persistent rumours of Chinese Imperial troops in the neighbourhood. This is quite possible if there is any prospect of negotiations, otherwise I don't think they would venture so near men who would probably "go" for them first and ask their business later.

Received orders to furnish a guard of 120 men from the R.W. Fusiliers and Baluchis under a subaltern to be at the British Legation 9 a.m. to-morrow with kits loaded, in case it is necessary to send these also. Another mystery! I suppose some of the Legation people are going out for a pic-nic!

3rd. Sixty men R.W.F.'s and 60 of the Baluchis left for the Summer Palace this morning with three days' rations. Now we know where the pic-nic is! Wrote to Scott Moncrieff asking him if he can supply lights for the streets, which would be a check on "prowlers" if carried out. A report from Feng-tai saying a Chinese force had been seen approaching, which caused reinforcements to be sent to the Temple of Heaven, turned out to be some practical joke on the part of a Russian officer to another Russian, and was misdirected to us. This sort of thing is most annoying, as our men have plenty to do without being fooled in this way. General Chaffee held a ceremonial parade of the men proceeding to the Philippines on the ground between the Temples of Heaven and Agriculture, with an "At Home" after in the Temple of Agriculture Grounds. The men looked very well, but I don't like cavalry in single rank, there is a "want of weight." The infantry march past at our "port," which is decidedly effective. Nearly all the "swells" turned out for this function, and did justice to the good fare provided. It was piping hot at the review. Gaselee returned in the evening, and has given out the occupation of Shan-hai-Kwan. Presumably this refers to Reid's Brigade.

4th. After the heat yesterday, to-day feels bitterly cold. At the review yesterday Chaffee wore a yellow silk ribbon over his blue coat. I quite forgot to ask what it represented. As far as I know the Americans don't go in for "orders" and "fall-lalls." It must have something to do with "the Dragon," the yellow was quite Imperial!

Late this evening it actually attempted to snow. These frequent changes of climate are most treacherous, and the wonder is we are free from sickness. It hits the men on convoy work harder than others. Was extremely annoyed to learn to-day that one of these had started without an escort. Someone must be dropped on to for this.

5th. Spent a most interesting afternoon watching our Engineers testing a supply of gun cotton in the western ditch. Hope to move into the Chefoo Palace on 7th. All Brigadiers have been given the local rank of Major-General, dating from 22nd of last month. As I am probably a pucca Major-General at the present moment the lift (?) does me no good. Gaselee is junior to me as a Colonel.

6th. Nothing to note. We are all busy packing for our move to-morrow.

7th. The last of our things moved into the Chefoo Palace just before the rain came down. As one of my rooms has a glass roof I won't get much sleep to-night. This is a trifle one soon gets accustomed to. It is ever so much fresher and nicer down here, where there is a sense of cleanliness. I have three nice rooms "en suite" with a cosy writing room, besides the glazed one, which will be charming in the winter with a bright sun.

8th. Rained heavily all night. As enquiries are being made for suitable quarters for Li-Hung-Chang, we may soon expect this wonderful old gentleman, who I fancy is as clever as paint, and quite capable of battling with the combined Ministers of the West. Our post now comes by rail as far as Yangtsun, which is a sign of the times, and soon I hope we will be relieved of this heavy escort work. It was so raw to-day that an issue of rum was sanctioned, but as this order only reached me at 7 p.m., and the godowns are two and a half miles off, not many of the men benefited by it.

9th. This is again a perfect day. The order regarding the issue of rum on account of the cold yesterday only reached the Baluchis this morning, and they are quartered next to the godowns!

10th. Weather perfect and crisp. The men look very cosy in their warm coats. The expedition to Peitang-Fu is again talked about, and will probably come off end of this week. They will find it cold at night without tents unless there is a sufficiency of Chinese houses.

11th. A complaint against the Germans stopping our work people coming in, and using them themselves, has just been made, so a guard has been placed on the Shun-chih-men gate to put a stop to this.

12th. A combined Anglo-German force started for Peitang-Fu this morning with three weeks' supplies and tentage. Our troops are under the command of Richardson, with Ramsay commanding the infantry and Gaselee the whole. Twenty miles from Peitang-Fu they are to meet the Tientsin force under a French General, with the British portion under Lorne Campbell. Richardson's command will be

Four guns 12th Field Battery.

Four squadrons 16th B. Lancers.

Two hundred 1st Sikhs.

Two hundred 24th P.I.

Two hundred 26th Baluchis.

Det. Mounted R.E.

Half company Q.O. Madras Sappers and Miners.

One section Field Hospital.

The weather is perfect, but cold at night.

13th. Count Waldersee on arrival is to be received with an International guard of honour. The streets will be lined along the entire route through the city.

14th. Bright sun, but air much cooler.

15th. Preparations for the winter in full swing. We had one death from enteric last week, and now there are three cases in hospital. I don't think we will have many more cases now that the men have been moved into better quarters. The "usual" scourge which creates so much havoc amongst soldiers has broken out.

Li-Hung-Chang arrived a few days ago quite quietly, and apparently has gone into his own house.

16th. A camp rumour says Gaselee met a Chinese force of 8,000 men the third march out. Li-Hung-Chang is interviewing Ministers in turn. There are numerous shaves knocking about, and fighting is certain to take place. Some Chinamen caught a transport duffadar coming in from Fengtai, and were dragging him into the millet when an escort appeared on the scene and secured five of them. I have been ordered to shoot one and flog three in front of the males of the village they belong to, and fine the village from $100 to $500, according to size. Have directed Tulloch, of the Baluchis, to carry this order out, and after flogging the three men to have them handed over to Captain Barrow for three months' work as coolies.

17th. All general officers with two staff officers each met Count Waldersee outside the N.E. gate of the Chinese city at 11 a.m. The streets were lined from the Ha-to-men up to his quarters, the Empress Dowager's Winter Palace, where there were guards of honour 100 strong of Germans, Americans, English, Italian, French, and Japanese. They marched past in fours, and although the Welsh Fusiliers were only in khaki, they looked about the best. H. E.'s staff, consisting of some 50 officers in brilliant uniforms, made a very picturesque group. The F. M. himself wore a light blue and silver lancer uniform, and behind him was carried the special colour presented by the Kaiser. After shaking hands with each General the procession started at a walk through the dusty streets. The Indian troops looked splendid. The American cavalry led, followed by the 1st B.L., and the rear was brought up by the Japanese cavalry, and a few Uhlans, who I presume are a personal body guard. Very fine men. The Field Marshal looks a soldier all over, has a nice seat on a horse, and carries his 70 odds years well, but I don't envy him his command! Some of the staff were poorly mounted; there were Arabs, Australians, and Chinese ponies. The absence of the Russians was a great pity. They seem to have completely cleared out of the place.

I was much struck by the appearance of some of the German officers, and pleasantly so. Was delighted to meet Grierson again, a little heavier, but the same cheery face, with fun sparkling in his eyes. What a wonderful experience he has had. He will be a great soldier yet.

18th. A nasty raw day with slight rain at intervals. The sentences on the men who assaulted the transport duffadar were carried out this morning, and the group of villages was fined $300, which is to be paid by Monday next or the head man's house will be burnt down. Another Boxer was shot this morning outside the British gate (or hole in the wall), by order of our Minister.

19th. Fine bright day. The Australian contingent won't arrive till to-morrow, and the Welsh Fusiliers will march out on 21st. Sent them a complimentary order. They are a very nice body of men, and their conduct has been exemplary. I hear the Chinese received the troops at Peitang-Fu with open arms. The French and Germans are inside the town whilst our troops are encamped outside.

20th. A raw, dark, dull, windy day. Nearly all the leaves have been blow off the trees, which gives a wintry appearance. Snow fell for half an hour this morning. Sir Ernest Satow arrived to-day. The Australian Naval Contingent Volunteers arrived this afternoon. They are a very fine body of *men*, not boys, commanded by Captain Gillespie, R.N.

21st. The Royal Welsh Fusiliers under Colonel the Hon. Bertie, and the 14th American Infantry marched out this morning, the former for Hong-Kong and the latter for Manila. Forty-three of the Fusiliers remain here for police duty. The private of the Chinese Regiment who was tried by general court martial for shooting at a corporal in his regiment, was sentenced to transportation for life. This was commuted to five years' penal servitude. I think the man is dotty. Last night in the Baluch guard room he asked another prisoner to cut his pig-tail off, which the Sepoy promptly did!

22nd. A lovely day. Once more we hear of Boxers in and outside the city. They have adopted a new watch-word, and have changed their uniform to a white girdle with a white thread in their hair. It's wonderful how we get all these details without seeing the gentlemen themselves. A large gathering is generally supposed to be in the vicinity of Tang-chao.

23rd. Have been asked to find quarters for Scindia.

24th. Scindia arrived this afternoon. Told off a house for him near the 24th P.I. Mess. He has with him Lieut. Spence, of the Central India Horse, Satiola, his brother-in-law, and Colonel Abdul Ghunny, who commands one of his Imperial Cavalry Regiments. He appears most keen to see some active service.

25th. Sir Claude Macdonald left to-day. He must be glad to turn his back on Pekin.

26th. Inspected all the works, which are getting on satisfactorily.

27th. A nasty raw day. Scindia started to join Gaselee's force. One of our posts was attacked by Boxers to-day, and driven off with a loss of 25.

28th. Delightful day. After church inspected the lines of the Battery and those of the Australians. There is much work to be done at the former, whilst the latter have shaken down and made themselves thoroughly comfortable. They are a superior body of men, but I noticed a few who seemed too old for active service. The officers seem very keen, and are more than satisfied with their quarters. They call their rooms "cabins," and partition walls "bulkheads." Most of our mess are spending the day at the Summer

Palace. Grierson, Pollock, and Tulloch lunched with me, and we spent a very pleasant afternoon. Grierson as usual was full of anecdotes. His news of the doings in South Africa up to the time he left was most interesting. He has the happy knack of condensing what would fill a volume into an intelligent history of events in the shortest time imaginable. I have seldom met a more clear-headed man. He had the advantage of eager listeners.

29th. A charming day.

30th. Raw and cold. All ranks are to be inspected with a view to picking out all men who are unlikely to stand the rigours of a severe winter. These men will be sent either to India or Southern China. We are now in telegraphic communication with Head Quarters, and it is proposed to connect all units and departments by telephone. This will be a great blessing, and save endless orderly duties which are so harassing to the men, especially in bitter or wet weather. Was to have lunched with Grierson, but had to put him off, much to my disappointment. He lives at the German Head Quarters, where they have some 70 members in the mess speaking every conceivable language. Count Waldersee has his own mess, but generally takes lunch with the others.

31st. Received orders to select quarters for the Ordnance Field Park, consisting of one British officer, five warrant officers, 23 Lascars and artificers, besides 1,500 maunds of stores requiring 2,000 feet superficial area, with 400 additional for work shops. Have decided to put them at Chang-wang-Fu, where they will be alongside the Field Battery. These sudden calls are not easily complied with. Every additional quarter we take up means extra guard duties.

The hat is going round for the unfortunate Green family to provide them with necessaries and passages, an expense which should be borne by their own Mission, but the call is sure to meet with a warm response, considering the awful experiences these poor delicate women and children have gone through, far too terrible for me to repeat. How one of them is alive to tell the tale is difficult to conceive.

The L.G.C. has returned from Paitung-Fu.

1st. November. I hear 247,000 taels of silver were seized at Paitung-Fu, which are to be divided amongst the allies.

2nd. The Japanese have made us a present of a large store of rice which they cannot consume. This entails a guard of ours in their quarter, which is not desirable. This will fall to the Baluchis, as they are nearest. Some of the followers are beginning to drink at Chinese liquor shops, so must see to this. We can easily stop the sale in our own section, but the difficulty will be in other sections.

3rd. Maharajah Bikanir is expected to arrive to-morrow. He must put up in the same compound as Scindia. Prince Koe with his ladies turned up without warning at the 24th P.I. mess yesterday, and asked permission to remove their valuables which had been buried under the floors occupied by the men, which was immediately granted. They dug up three places, drawing blank in one, much to the chagrin of one of the young Princesses. Climo tells me they must have recovered at least £20,000 in cash besides jewels. These he did not see as they were all in safes intact. Before the Prince and his party left he was asked what he thought of the "blank draw," when without hesitation he said it was the work of one of their own servants. Had the troops made the discovery of these valuables during the weeks they had been squatting on them I fear Koe would have gone away a sadder man!

The Chinese of this section presented me with an address and complimentary umbrella this evening. The procession consisted of about 100 men with a weird band that made the most hideous noises. I accepted the gift as a token of their good behaviour up to date, and trusted it would continue to the end, assuring them they would always be treated with fairness by the English, whilst any acts of treachery would entail the severest punishment. After presenting dishes of fruit they went, apparently quite pleased, excepting the band, which was very disconcerting, but here Duncan came to the rescue, and a few dollars got rid of them! It seems the rule for the musicians to be paid by the individual honoured!

General Pipon, commanding R.A., arrived. The last time I saw him was at Cabul, when he was a Captain in R.H.A. We are now five Generals!

It now freezes at night.

4th. After breakfast it was only 45deg., and sun too powerful for small caps. Bikanir arrived.

5th. A cutting wind with bright sunshine. Bikanir called on me with Major Watson, D.A.A.G. He has grown into a fine handsome young fellow. Looks very well in uniform, and most eager to take part in a fight!

Our sick list to-day is Europeans 23, natives 40, and followers 31. Barrow is off to Shan-hai-Kwan, where chaos reigns, whilst the Russians are doing nothing towards repairing the railway. The difficulty in landing stores is causing much anxiety, as work is at a standstill when there is any sea on. Labour is unprocurable, as those who have not bolted are in a state of panic.

6th. Cold and bright, 43deg. in my room at 7 a.m. The Paitung-Fu column has returned after a chukkur to the north and east by the Ming tombs. During a march heavy firing was heard ahead, so the mounted sappers and cavalry advanced and found a German company engaged with the enemy strongly posted in the hills, up which mounted men could not go. The Germans were running short of ammunition when our men took up the fire and drove the enemy off. Their loss was four killed and six wounded. Either they had very few rounds per man or the Chinese must have been in great force; the latter is improbable. A bird whispers that when first attacked they were marching in "fours." As usual the shooting was shocking. But talking of shooting reminds me of a yarn in connection with a trumpeter of the 16th B.L. On the way to Paitung-Fu our troops came across some Chinese troops; the General commanding them came out "to palaver" with Gaselee, but during the conversation his mount became restive, and eventually bolted. The trumpeter, under the impression that it was intentional, immediately gave chase, on which Gaselee and his staff shouted out "Mat maro, mat maro" (don't kill). All the trumpeter could hear was "Maro, maro" (kill, kill), so drew his revolver and shot the Chinese General dead! Another regrettable incident. I don't know how much truth there is in this tale.

7th. Spent the morning with Selwyn drawing up rules and regulations for new police scheme to be taken over by the Australians, thus allowing the Welsh Fusiliers to rejoin their regiment.

8th. The L.G.C. seems anxious about our hospital accommodation, so wrote and told him that with one R.E. officer specially told off to superintend the work there was no reason why everything should not be completed by the end of the month, and in the meantime there was ample for our requirements. The Madras Sappers and Miners left for Shanghai to-day, and excellent work they have done.

9th. Not so cold to-day, only 46deg. at 7 a.m. We are now getting Reuter's telegrams, so feel more in touch with the outer world.

10th. A nasty day, no sun and a nor'-wester blowing. A hard frost set in before nightfall.

11th. Bright but cold. It was 34deg. in my

bedroom at 7 a.m. with a fire burning in adjoining room, which is only divided by a paper partition. During the night I received a wire saying Staff Surgeon Steele, of the N.S.W. Naval Contingent, had been found lying on the floor of his room dead. A court of inquiry is sitting. Without doubt it is a case of an overdose of chloral, which apparently he was in the habit of taking for insomnia. The funeral will take place at 10 a.m. to-morrow.

Thirty R.W. Fusiliers (late police), under Lieut. Bainbridge, of the 1st Sikhs, started for Hong Kong this morning, also three of the N.S.W. Contingent considered unfit for a winter in North China, for return to Australia.

12th. Fine bright day and freezing hard. A German force started this morning in a north-westerly direction. Will probably visit the far side of the great wall (Kalgan), Wingate and Ryder accompanying it as intelligence and survey officers respectively. They have an escort of 16 Sowars and 6 Afridis, and expect to be away a month. Maharaja Scindia and Nawab Afsur Dowlah, of Hyderabad fame, left this morning for India. The Maharaja of Bikanir left yesterday. None of them liked the cold! Attended Staff Surgeon Steele's funeral, and later accompanied

General Gaselee round the quarters of the Naval Contingent and Hospital. He did not seem altogether pleased with the latter, but Rome was not built in a day, and I am quite aware the work cannot be completed before the end of this month. He does not approve of our fireplaces, but prefers stoves. Here I think he is quite wrong.

I get some quaint orders occasionally, the last one was to supply a party of Pathans with "rum!" I sent this on to Ramsay as I received it, which brought him over pretty sharp.

13th. Lieut. Jones, R.N., with an escort of seven Sowars, left this morning to catch up the German force. I hear this officer's object in going north is to try and obtain news of his brother, a Royal Engineer officer, who has not been heard of since the troubles began.

14th. Each infantry regiment is now supplying working parties of one B.O. and 200 men on the line near the Temple of Heaven.

15th.—Defensive schemes called for, as we are in the heart of a walled city with allies all round us this ought not to take long.

16th. Weather perfect. Captain Dent and the few recruits he has picked up for the Chinese Regiment, with Lieut. Meakin, I.M.S., left for Wei-hai-wei this morning. I will miss Dent very much. He is now in my old corps the 68th. The thermometer for the last few days has been 36deg. in my room at 7.

17th. Detailed the officers for the defence scheme, (a) the defence of quarters of each unit, (b) the defence of our section, the report to show what steps would be advisable, (a) in the event of a town rising, (b) a blockade in the event of our being alone without allies. Similar schemes to be drawn up for the Legation quarter and Lama Temple. Major Myville Thompson, I.M.S., sent to Hong Kong or India as being unfit to winter here. A draft of two B.O.'s and 100 men of 1st Sikhs and General Hospital arrived yesterday.

18th. Warmer to-day (40deg). I believe it has been settled we are to have control of the railway.

19th. Our probable strength in the Tartar City on 1st December will be: Europeans 616, natives 2,369, followers 1,326.

20th. An unpleasant day. The morning was quite warm, and by evening was freezing hard.

21st. Heard from Sir Power Palmer, asking for my views of Northern China. Low is expected this evening with our stores purchased at Hong Kong.

22nd. The Germans entertained all comers on

the racecourse. The attendance was not very good as it is rather an awkward place to get at. I think it was a mistake having it in the forenoon, when one could not do justice to the mulled port which was to be had for the asking. The Germans were in full force. Our officers were well represented, also Americans, and a few Japanese. Count Waldersee with a brilliant staff was present, and had a friendly greeting for everyone. He seems a charming personality. The racing was not up to much, but it was a pleasant outing, and helps to bring men together who would otherwise never meet. The German officers appear to be a particularly nice lot, who are in no way afraid of their limited knowledge of English when the supply is limited; so different to the Englishman, who will not attempt conversation unless he happens to be fluent. Unfortunately we have very few officers who speak German, but as every German knows French and most of them a smattering of English, there is no real difficulty in getting on with them if you only make up your mind to put aside mock modesty and dash boldly at it.

23rd. Whilst some of our followers were demolishing some old buildings outside the quarters N.S.W. Contingent, there was a small explosion, when two of their number were injured. The buildings formed part of an old Chinese magazine, and evidently a pick struck some loose powder which was so mixed up with the earth that the men did not recognise it as such. Immediate precautions were taken to prevent a recurrence.

24th. Weather continues bright and just cold enough to make men enjoy work.

25th. Wrote to Sir Power Palmer, and gave him all the news I could think of. The native troops are very satisfied with their lot, ditto the followers. They are well fed, well clothed, and saving, for them, large sums of money, so look forward to a year of Northern China with the utmost content. They are beginning to make friends with the Chinese, especially the children, who are particularly bright. It is most amusing to watch these youngsters playing at soldiers! For some time they watched the men drilling, and when they mastered the subject they formed squads of their own, and armed with sticks practice every morning, using our English words of command, German in the German quarter, and so on. They are wonderful mimics, and whilst at the game are quite serious. The squad is drawn up for inspection, and the "officer" goes down the ranks, corrects the dressing, etc., and when all is ready drills the squad by the hour, dismissing it at the end of the morning's performance with all the seriousness of the barrack square, and the moment they are dismissed they laugh and joke and go in for horse play as children should. The whole time they are being watched by sisters, mothers, grandmothers, and the men folk. In the German section you see the youngsters doing the "high step" with the utmost precision. If these youngsters were taken in hand what a wonderful army you could make of them in time. This has been well illustrated by the Chinese Regiment at Wei-hai-Wei, which is as smart as paint.

26th. There have been two or three fires lately, so have issued most stringent orders on this subject, pointing out that immediate action must be taken. A few minutes' delay might cause the destruction of a whole block. Fire will be a source of anxiety during our stay. On a windy night a few budmashes might burn us out of the city in a few hours. The origin of the most trivial fire must be traced with just as much care as the more serious ones. All beams in the vicinity of chimneys and fire places must be removed or protected. The Chinese themselves are apparently alive to the danger, for up to date there have been no cases in dwellings occupied by them, as far as I am aware. Every street and gully in our section is patrolled by our police at night, and no body of men could carry out this work more thoroughly than the police we now have from the N.S.W. Contingent. Being "Handy Men," they are full of resource, which is a great comfort.

27th. Strict orders have been issued about the wearing of uniform, which is always irksome to the British officer, accustomed to mufti, a full supply of which everyone possesses. This is a mistake, we ought never to have brought it with us.

28th. A case of small pox reported this morning amongst the Australians. On the voyage it was discovered that this man had never been vaccinated, so this was done at once.

29th. It is getting much colder. Last night we had 15deg. of frost. The villagers outside the city nearest us presented me with another umbrella, which is a sign of the times. The more you see of the Chinese the more you like them.

30th. News has come in from the German column of the tragic death of Colonel Commandant Yorck von Wartemberg, caused by the fumes of a charcoal stove whilst sleeping in a room with probably all doors and windows hermetically sealed. This is another matter which requires the most careful watching. However, most Indians know the dangers of a charcoal fire.

A Chinaman from a village three miles out on the road to the Summer Palace has complained of budmashes who have been blackmailing the village. A fortnight ago these rascals shot two of his brothers dead and wounded him, hence the delay in making the report. My interpreter, the Rev. Duncan, seems to be appealed to by the natives of the country more than anyone else. Bingley, commanding at Liu-ka-Chao, who came in to see me to-day, reports that this sort of thing is very general. Only a few days back he shot three of them who were recognised whilst attending a funeral. They were all Boxers. Many of these gentry must be in hiding in the city.

1st. The gymkhana which was to have been held to-day is postponed owing to Count Yorck's death.

2nd. Some weeks ago a Madras Sapper was reported missing, and later on a Chinaman was caught with his carbine, and as he turned out to be a known bad character he was sentenced to be shot after having been kept in confinement seven weeks without giving any satisfactory explanation as to how he came in possession of the carbine.

3rd. Nothing to note. Weather perfect.

4th. Nothing to note. Weather perfect.

5th. Looks as if we were in for a snow storm. The body of a Sepoy of the 24th P.I. was found in a small well this morning. The funeral of Count Yorck, which was attended by nearly every officer, took place at 11 a.m.

6th. Snow fell during the night, and there is a cutting wind to-day. Inspected the spot where the Sepoy's body was found. An evident case of murder, as some distance from the well we found a pool of blood in a dilapidated building, from which you could easily trace how the body had been dragged over bricks and stones to the mouth of the well, which was so narrow that it required some force to push the body through. This done a large slab of stone used as the well cover was replaced. The man's warm coat and pugaree are missing, and as he is supposed to have had $100 in his possession, I'm inclined to think the murderer is to be found in our own camp. Ordered a thorough search to be made in the lines of the 24th and regimental transport. The regiment also think it must have been done by one of our own men. The coat and pugaree may lead to the discovery of the culprit. No man has been found to possess so large a sum of money and enquiries at the post office regarding remittances to India throws no light on the subject. Ramsay and Climo will not relax in their efforts to find out the murderer, the native officers are also doing all in their power to assist.

7th. The coldest day we have had so far. Last night it went down to 2deg. below zero, and at 11 a.m. it was only 14deg. The water in our baths freezes solid! Visited the small-pox patient, who is getting on famously, was most anxious about his personal appearance, poor fellow. We procured a looking glass, and he seemed quite satisfied. Science and a perfect climate will soon put him on his legs again.

8th. Very windy and cold. Lunched at the Cavalry Mess, Temple of Heaven, and spent a very cheery afternoon. Grierson seems to think we will all get away by the end of March. I don't see how this is possible, for up to date we haven't advanced a step as far as we poor outsiders know. English mail in; my name in the Gazette as a Major-General from 19th October. Gaselee and the other Generals in our force are only Colonels! It seems odd, but it's a way we have in the British Army. I'm not quite sure how it would pan out with a "mixed force." The position is not altogether pleasing, but being on service one is less inclined to "bother" over personal matters.

9th. The cold seems to make the men fitter every day. Just ideal weather for marching and knocking about. Barring blizzards, it would be difficult to find a more perfect climate for men well fed and properly clothed.

10th. Outside thermometer in the shade 18deg. at 8 a.m.

11th. Another perfect day. The thermometer stood at 10deg. at 8 a.m., but in the sun it is glorious. Report says a reply has been received saying the Emperor accepts the terms submitted to him, and intends returning in March, the weather at present being too severe for a long march. Whether he comes in or not at least one brigade from each force is certain to remain till the question of indemnity is settled. The Americans and ourselves would probably accept promises of payment, but not so the others. We are to have a proclamation parade on 1st January after all.

12th. Went round the wards. There are not many serious cases. We must look out for pneumonia amongst the natives, as there are always some fools who will strip themselves and wash in the shade when by moving a yard or two they might carry out their ablutions in bright sunshine.

13th. Mr. Webster (a missionary), who has

just returned from Mukden, where he saw a lot of the Russians, who are now treating the Chinese with the utmost leniency, which they don't quite understand, after the severe handling of previous years. Someone has been tampering with the trestle bridge over the ditch outside the British gate. Have warned the nearest village it will be held responsible.

14th. The villagers caught two men removing planks from the trestle bridge. Traced them to their homes, where those previously removed were found. I think "the cat" will put a stop to this.

Ramsay reports the finding of the murdered Sepoy's coat and pugaree in a doorless hut close by the scene of the murder hidden under a pile of stones. The discovery was made by a party of his men who were at "fire drill." No Chinaman would have taken the trouble to hide these articles. The pugaree had traces of blood on it, and I'm inclined to think more than one man is implicated. It would have taken a single man some time to drag the body over the piles of debris the distance the body was dragged. Where the fatal blow was administered there were distinct marks of boots, which the Chinese do not wear. Amongst our transport followers I fancy there are many bad hats, who look upon murder as a trifle. Lieut.

Watts Jones has recovered his brother's body, which had been placed in a Chinese coffin some time after his murder by some better disposed Chinamen. The tortures the poor fellow was put to make one shudder. For four days he was mutilated and tortured whilst tied to a stake, and in the end beheaded when they saw they could not keep him alive any longer. The coffin was opened for purposes of identification, and is now being brought in for burial.

15th. The L.G.C. inspected the hospital, and was quite satisfied. He and his staff remained to lunch.

16th. Visited the Summer Palace with Jermyn, Low, Brooking, Scott-Elliot, and Duncan. It is certainly a wonderful place and must have cost a fortune, whilst every building seems to be full of priceless treasures in the shape of china, bronzes, and cloisonne, an immense amount of which must have been carried away or destroyed by Russians when in occupation judging from the broken pieces to be seen lying about in all directions. Every building and all the walks are lit up with electric lighting, which of course is not in working order as the machinery has been destroyed. The lake was frozen, and the whole scene was absolutely beautiful.

Tulloch and a party of his men have had a turn up with Boxers in a temple which they surrounded. No particulars to hand yet.

The transports in the Taku roads have been ice bound for some days.

18th. Young Macpherson, of the Baluchis, and Sebadar Kamardin, followed by a handful of men, scaled the walls of the temple, where the Boxers were busy going through some buffoonery, and jumped in on top of them, whilst one of the party unbolted a door and allowed others in. A hand to hand fight took place till most were killed or taken prisoners. The affair was well managed, and altogether it was a plucky act as the Boxers were armed to the teeth. Fortunately it was a complete surprise.

19th. Much warmer to-day, the outside thermometer is only 24deg. and the water didn't freeze in my rooms last night.

20th. The 12th Field Battery and an American Battery had some practice in the Hunting Park this morning. A cutting wind was blowing and the light was most treacherous, so the firing was decidedly poor. Many German officers turned out, and all were busy taking notes. Apparently the men have discovered some place where drink is procurable, for two Tommies were brought into the Native Field Hospital at the Legations in a helpless condition, one of whom died. I rather suspect the Italian quarter off Hatamen Street.

21st. Had a sumptuous lunch with General Chaffee. Generals Schwarzhoff and Von Gayl, of the German Army, were also guests. The former is Chief of the Staff of the allied forces, and the latter Quarter Master General. Both understand English, though I hear Schwarzhoff only studied it on board ship on the way out! What he doesn't know isn't worth knowing, I expect. Evidently a very shrewd man, who asked the most pointed questions. The other is a man of the world who enjoys life. It was a delightful function, and after the meal was over General Chaffee took us round his camp and showed us everything. They have excellent arrangements for heating tents, and stables made of canvas. The latter seemed to me far too hot. I much prefer our system of keeping the horses in the open with ample bedding and blankets. The American horses showed no signs of winter coats, and would undoubtedly suffer on the march. Their stores were a sight, perfect order reigned, and any mortal thing a soldier could possibly require was procurable, from a "pin" upwards. In

GENERAL CHAFFEE AND THE OFFICERS OF THE AMERICAN ARMY.

their hospital all was very much up-to-date, including nurses, but here again the wards seemed to me too warm; a thermometer I looked at registered 80 deg.! The hospital building itself wasn't a patch on ours, and their sick didn't look as well as ours, they were much more washed out in appearance. The Americans bury their dead in their enclosure, the Temple of Agriculture, which struck one as being rather uncanny, but this was explained by the fact they never leave the bodies of their soldiers on "foreign soil," all are taken back to America.

The officers have a very cosy little club house, where they have a festive time of it, and where all meet on equal terms as ordinary gentlemen. This appeals to me, for on service I'm afraid we are inclined to remember we are "in uniform" a little too much.

A court martial was sitting in a building close to the club and as I was asked if I would care to "look on," I took advantage of the offer for a few minutes. Their system resembles our Criminal Court. A series of "question" and "answer," so different to our system, where the witness is asked to make a statement of what occurred on such and such a date, etc., etc.

I wish we had General Chaffee's cook and some

of his excellent Chinese servants. He tells me all these were engaged for him by their Consul at Tientsin under orders of his Government. This is consideration we are not accustomed to.

22nd. All very sad owing to the latest bad news from South Africa. The telegram states that five officers and nine men were killed, 18 officers and 550 men missing, including four companies Northumberland Fusiliers, belonging to Clement's force, while a squadron of Brabant's Horse were surrounded and taken prisoners elsewhere. The proportion of prisoners to killed and wounded sounds shocking.

23rd. The Ministers appear to be very busy, and rumour has it there is more unanimity, without which there can't be much progress.

24th. The 7th Rajputs had their mess gutted by fire this evening. They estimate their losses at £300. Two officers' quarters were also destroyed.

25th. Christmas Day. Spent the morning visiting the different units under my command, attending church, etc. An ideal Christmas Day, everyone seemed full of good cheer!

26th. No post for some days, due no doubt to the frozen condition of the sea.

27th—30th. Perfect weather, nothing to note.

31st. Had a rehearsal of to-morrow's parade, and in the afternoon lunched at Richardson's mess and looked on at the burlesque which is causing a certain amount of "stir." It is decidedly clever, but not quite in good taste, for, after all, the Empress is "a woman."

We had just finished seeing the old year out and thinking of bed when to our surprise in walked Tulloch, Rowlandson and Du Boulay, who having ridden 2½ miles had to be entertained, and the consequence was we did not break up till 3 a.m. The snow is about 2 feet thick, so did not envy these light-hearted ones their ride home.

1st January, '01. The parade was taken by Count Waldersee in person, who called for three cheers for our Most Gracious Majesty. It was held in the courtyard in front of the Forbidden City, and was really a very fine sight. Our troops looked splendid, and were much admired by all the foreign officers, who seemed to turn out to a man. It is the first opportunity they have had of seeing our force to advantage, and it is very pleasing to think they are at last impressed. It being also the first day of Australian Commonwealth the occasion was quite unique, if not historical.

The Australian contingent dined with us, and a very cheery affair it turned out, entailing a good many speeches. We got Duncan on his legs, and in a speech of nearly an hour he gave our colonial friends an outline of the entire Boxer rising, which interested them immensely. He also told us with what fear and dread he and other missionaries accepted posts as interpreters to our different units. These gentlemen met as a body, and the general opinion amongst them was the British officer was a sort of wild animal no man calling himself a Christian could possibly associate with; but owing to the hard times and in the interests of their families they decided to run the risk! Speaking for himself and from what he had heard from others, he had come to the conclusion the British officer was a gentleman head and shoulders above others they had ever met, and that all had written to their respective missions saying how proud they felt of having served with the Army, and that it was with feelings of shame they looked back to that hour when they sat in judgment on men who were far more worthy than themselves! He will never hear the end of this. Commander Connor, who is old enough to be Gillespie's father, was in great form. I would be afraid to say how many speeches he made. He has two of his sons in the ranks of the contingent, and very proud he is of this.

2nd. After two late nights spent a quiet day.

3rd. The following cable was despatched on 1st to Private Secretary, Her Majesty the Queen, by General Gaselee:—"The force in China to-day held parade in Her Majesty's honour. Field-Marshal Count Waldersee at my request, as the representative of the Queen's grandson, gave the Royal salute and led the cheers for Her Majesty.

"The New South Wales Naval Contingent, in honour of Federation, headed the Infantry Brigade, and the New South Wales Marines formed the guard of honour at the flag staff."

To which the following reply was received from Sir Arthur Bigge, Osborne:—

"Queen interested and gratified by your telegram, and wishes all under your command a Happy New Year."

Tulloch with a small force started for Kowiloon.

4th and 5th. Weather continues perfect; temperature 19deg.

6th. Bright, but colder. The column under Tulloch returned, found the place deserted as far as men of position are concerned.

7th. Very bright weather, thermometer 5deg. at 8 a.m.; am not feeling very fit.

8th—11th. Confined to bed with fever;

weather perfect; lots of snow has fallen. Regular convoys to Tang-chao have now ceased.

12th. I hear there is some hitch in the negotiations, but as Li Hung and Prince Ching are urging the Court to sign and not trouble about small details at this stage, we hope for progress. Influenza of a mild type is very prevalent.

13th—15th. Ideal weather; at night we generally experience 25deg. of frost. There is still some friction with the Russians about the railway, which will probably continue until they receive orders from St. Petersburg.

Orders have been issued stopping the printing of the burlesque written by Fane. It seems some busybody cabled home on the subject, quoting a verse supposed to be sung by the Empress-Dowager.

16th. Am afraid we are in for some bad weather, a dark threatening day. Just got hold of the peace conditions, which were submitted on the 23rd December by the Ministers to the Chinese Plenipotentiaries.

"In the course of the months of May, June, July and August of this year disturbances first broke out in the Northern Provinces of China, and crimes were committed under peculiarly outrageous circumstances, which have no parallel in the history of the world, crimes against the laws of humanity and civilisation. The principal of these crimes are the following:—

"1. On the 20th June H.E. the Imperial German Minister, Baron von Ketteler, was, whilst in discharge of his official duties, on his way to the Tsungli Yamen, murdered by soldiers of the Regular Army, who acted on the command of their leaders.

"2. On the same day the Foreign Legations were attacked and besieged, and these attacks were continued without interruption until the 14th August, on which date they were brought to an end by the arrival of the foreign troops. The attacks were carried out by Regular soldiers, who united with the Boxers and obeyed the orders sent out to them from the Imperial Palace. During this time the Chinese Government caused to be explained to the Powers, through its representatives, that it undertook to provide for the safety of the Legations.

"3. On the 11th June Mr. Sugiyama, Chancellor of the Japanese Legation, was murdered at the gates of the city by Regular soldiers, whilst he was engaged in the discharge of an official mission. In Peking and in different Provinces foreigners were murdered and martyred. Others were attacked by Boxers and Regular troops, and owe their safety only to their own obstinate resistance. Their dwellings were plundered and destroyed.

"4. Foreign cemeteries, especially in Peking, have been desecrated, the graves opened, and the bones scattered abroad.

"These proceedings compelled the Foreign Powers to send their troops to China in order to protect the lives of the representatives and of their fellow countrymen, and to restore order.

"On the march to Peking the Allied troops met with resistance from detachments of the Chinese Army, which they were compelled to repulse by force. Since China now acknowledges her responsibility, expresses her remorse, and has made known a wish to bring to an end the situation created by the disturbances in question, the Powers have decided to give effect to her desire, upon the following detailed irrevocable conditions, which they regard as essential for the expiation of the crimes committed and the prevention of their repetition:—

"1*a*. The dispatch of an Extraordinary Embassy, headed by an Imperial Prince, to Berlin, in order to express the regret of His Majesty the Emperor of China and of the Chinese Government for the murder of H.E. the Imperial German Minister, Baron Von Ketteler.

"*1b*. The erection of a memorial monument in keeping with the position of the deceased, on the site of the murder, with an inscription in the Latin, German and Chinese languages expressive of the regret of the Emperor of China for the murder committed.

"*2a*. The infliction of the severest punishment applicable to their crimes upon the parties mentioned in the Imperial edict of the 25th September, 1900, as well as upon those persons whom the representatives of the Powers may later on indicate by name.

"3. The granting of suitable compensation on the part of the Chinese to the Japanese Government for the murder of Mr. Sugiyama, Chancellor of the Japanese Legation.

"4. The erection of an expiatory monument by the Chinese Government in each of the foreign or international cemeteries which have been desecrated or the tombstones destroyed.

"5. The maintenance of the prohibition of the importation of arms and such material as is exclusively used for the manufacture of arms and ammunition under conditions to be later on determined and communicated by the Powers.

"6. Suitable compensation for the States, companies and individual persons, as well as for those Chinese who during the recent events suffered injury to their persons or their property on account of their being in foreign employ.

"6*b*. The adoption of financial measures on the part of China, in a manner acceptable to the Powers, in order to provide for the payment of the aforesaid indemnities, and in order to provide security for the loans.

"7. Authority to the Powers to maintain standing guards for their Legations and to place the Legation quarters in a state of defence; and the withdrawal of the permission for Chinese to reside in this quarter.

"8. The razing of the forts at Taku, as well as of those forts which might interfere with free communication between Peking and the sea.

"9. The right of military occupation of certain places, to be indicated by agreement among the Powers, in order to keep open communication between the sea and the capital.

"10*a*. The promulgation of an Imperial edict by the Chinese Government in all district cities by means of placards, during two years, of the following purport:—

"Permanent prohibition, under pain of death, to belong to any anti-foreign society;

"Recital of the punishments which have been inflicted upon the guilty parties, including the suspension of all official examinations in towns in which foreigners have been murdered or ill-treated.

"10*b*. The issue of an Imperial edict, to be published throughout the whole Empire, stating that all Viceroys, Governors and Provincial and local officials will be held responsible for the maintenance of order in their respective jurisdictions; and in the event of renewed anti-foreign disturbances or other offences which are not immediately punished by those responsible, the officials concerned are to be removed without delay, never being allowed to accept new offices or to receive any distinction.

"11. An obligation on the Chinese Government to enter upon negotiations regarding the conditions considered suitable by the Foreign Governments for trade and shipping regulations, as well as other matters affecting mercantile transactions, with a view to facilitating the latter.

"12. An obligation upon the Chinese Government to reform the Ministry for Foreign Affairs, and to change the Court ceremony for the reception of Foreign Ministers in a manner to be indicated by the Powers.

"So long as the Chinese Government has not complied with the foregoing demands to the satisfaction of the Powers the undersigned are not in a position to take into consideration the conditions of the evacuation by international troops of Peking and the Province of Chihli.—(Signed) Mumm, Czikann, Joosteus, Cologan, Conger, Pichon, Satow, Saloago, Nishi, Knobel, Giers."

17th. The railway question still hangs fire, and apparently the correspondence is becoming a little strained. There does not seem to be much inclination for give-and-take. The Russians have to refer every point to Alexieff, who likes having his own way in everything.

18th. It goes down to zero every night, but in the absence of wind the climate is charming; on the coldest day you can sit in the sun in your shirt sleeves. Finished the outdoor work of candidates for admission to the Indian Army.

19th. Major Cox, attached to the Imperial Service troops, with Lieutenant-Colonel Dhip Sing, who commands the Bikanir Regiment, are staying with us for a few days.

20th. So long as the frozen snow lasts the

place remains clean; it is such a treat having no dust.

21st. A small local paper, under the title of "The China Times," was published to-day for the first time. It says: "The Court, in its sorrow, has to accept the 'Terms,' but urges Prince Ching and Li Hung to continue their efforts to have many modifications made!"

22nd. Reuter gives us most alarming news of our Beloved Queen's health.

23rd. The cable this afternoon regarding Her Majesty has cheered us all up. Dined with the Australians, when the Queen's health was drunk with the most profound feelings of affection. It was easy to see what was in the minds of everyone present.

24th. Received wire from headquarters announcing the death of our Beloved Queen as having occurred at 6.30 p.m. the 22nd. We are a grief-stricken Army. The natives are just as affected as ourselves; without doubt they truly loved "Their White Queen."

25th. Shone has been ordered back to India to succeed Turner, deceased, as Director-General Military Works.

26th. Nothing to note.

27th (Sunday). Attended German birthday

parade "by order," which was most distasteful to us, considering our Beloved Queen lies still unburied. I expect the Germans were more surprised than others to see us turn up.

28th. A painful tragedy took place at the Hotel-du-Nord this evening. The guests at the hotel were finishing dinner and still seated at their tables when three shots were heard close to the dining-room. The manager at once ran to the spot where the shots appeared to have been fired, and was met by Lieutenant Dening, of the 3rd Bombay Cavalry, who came from one of the private rooms staggering, and exclaiming, "I am wounded."

The manager then entered the private room, where a dreadful spectacle presented itself. A husband and wife were lying prostrate on the floor, still living, but on the point of death. Nothing could be done for them, and they shortly afterwards expired.

It appears that three rooms had been engaged for Dening, the Lindbergs and a maid. Captain Lindberg, a Danish officer well known at Tientsin, and formerly engaged there as Military Instructor for the Chinese troops, arrived from Tientsin during dinner, and that meal over repaired to his wife's room, showing no indication of what was to come.

Hearing the first shot, I suppose Dening rushed in to see what was up, and was then fired at and wounded, whilst with the third shot he blew his own brains out. Dening's wound is only slight. Captain Lindberg, I hear, was much troubled about money matters, as his employment ceased with the Boxer rising last May. The bodies of Captain and Mrs. Lindberg will be sent to Tientsin for interment.

29th. The snow makes riding unpleasant, but along the Wall one can enjoy a brisk walk in comfort, with a fine view of the surrounding country. What labour must have been expended on these same walls, strong enough to defy even modern guns! The perimeter, including the Chinese City, is some twenty miles.

30th. General Cummins, commanding a Brigade at Tientsin, arrived this evening. Was so pleased to see him again. He has a son in the 24th P.I., who will naturally take up most of his time.

31st. It is now 5deg. below zero, with every prospect of being colder!

1st February. The Chinese plenipotentiaries Prince Ching and Li Hung Chang having signed their agreement to the twelve demands presented to them by the foreign Ministers in Peking, and an Imperial edict having been issued confirming their action they now request the Ministers to meet them in joint conference with a view to settling minor points and drawing up treaties between China and the Powers.

The Ministers, in reply, have requested the plenipotentiaries to put in writing the points they wish to discuss, so that they may arrive at an understanding as to the answer to be sent them.

On receipt of this the Chinese representatives drew up a memorandum suggesting "that the forces at present in occupation of Peking and the Province of Chihli should be withdrawn in accordance with the final clause of the agreement," further "that hostile operations should cease, movements of troops should be suspended, and no further expeditions should proceed into cities and towns, thus causing alarm to the populace."

In other words, they say "We will do anything you wish, but withdraw your troops!"

Their comments upon the demands for the punishment of high officials concerned in the recent outrage are anything but satisfactory. As regards indemnities they suggest the Chinese be permitted to increase the custom tariff, mining duties, etc., or in other words the foreigner should pay his own indemnity!

They admit the necessity for Legation guards, but want to know where the Legation quarter begins and ends.

Lastly they urge a date be fixed for the withdrawal from Peking, Paitang Fu, Tientsin, and Tang-chao!

When the Chinese have carried out every clause they possibly can it will be time enough to discuss the question of withdrawal. We are hardly likely to even commence this on promises alone. At this rate we will be here this time next year!

2nd February. Have just returned from the funeral service of Her Most Gracious Majesty. Every man off duty was on parade. The service was most impressive. The entire Diplomatic Corps and every European in Peking paid this last tribute to the most revered Sovereign in Europe. Strong contingents were present from the forces of Germany, America, France, Russia, Italy, Austria, and Japan. Our nation's sorrow was certainly shared by others this day.

The troops were under my command, and all presented arms with our men. The little Japanese in the lowest of tones chanted a " dirge " whilst they remained at the present. When I gave the order to march to quarters the troops of the Allies remained at attention till the last of our men had left the courtyard. This is indeed a day of mourning.

The cold was intense, but no one gave this a thought.

3rd and 4th. The last three days we have had high winds, which seem to cut you in two.

5th. H.E. the Field Marshal started for Shan-hai-Kwan. I trust he will be able to settle the disputes about the railway, which seem to be almost undignified: it is playing into the hands of the Chinese, who take advantage of it.

6th. Cummins returned to Teintsin. I have promised to pay him a visit the moment I can get a few days' leave. The Tientsin garrison have a much better time of it than ourselves. The Ministers have come to the conclusion they are only wasting time with Prince Ching and Li-Hung-Chang, and have decided on sending a draft edict in Chinese to the Emperor with a note saying he must either publish it or take the consequences.

7th. I have just heard of a German column which went out on the 4th, but in what direction I have no idea. Army orders are not sent to

Brigades! Attached to the Japanese is an extraordinary character known to us as "Tapioca," who in his cups tells the most wonderful tales, which turn out to have absolutely no foundation. His latest was a naval engagement off Chemulpo between the Russians and Japanese!

8th to 11th. A blizzard has been blowing for days, and to-day, the 11th, it seems to have reached its height. We now know what Northern China can be. The hospitals are filling, chiefly chest complaints. A party of 60 Zouaves met some Chinese Regulars near Tientsin whom they dispersed, losing three men.

12th. One of our transports attempted to reach Shan-hai-Kwan, but failed owing to the ice. Two passengers, however, made up their minds to do so on foot, and left the ship at 1 p.m., thinking they would reach the shore after a walk of an hour or two at the most. They did reach, but not till late the next evening, and then only through the efforts of some Chinese, who went out and carried them the last mile. They had a small supply of brandy and a few biscuits. The former they sipped during the night and in the morning discovered they were on "floe" ice. Three times during the day they were immersed, and as a consequence their garments froze. In this condition the Chinese found them, brought them ashore, and sent a telegram from the nearest railway station to say two foreigners in a dying condition were found on the ice. Medical aid was sent, and they were discovered to be Lieut. Mahon, R.E., and a Mr. Pratt, of Reuter's. They are both alive, but I hear one is down with double pneumonia. I believe when they left the transport the Captain put the distance at five miles, and thinking the ice was solid to the shore, put out to sea. Under any circumstances it was a very foolish thing to attempt, especially as they were wearing only the lightest garments on account of the walk. How they expected to get clothes when they landed I don't know. There are few of us who possess too much. Colonel —— who was also a passenger, should have at once put his foot down on so senseless a venture.

13th. The blizzard blew itself out last night, though there is quite enough wind to make it unpleasant.

14th. Have heard of Boxers and other blackguards who are robbing villages right and left, so have suggested a party being sent out, as they are reported to be inside the British sphere.

15th. Have sent 30 Mounted Infantry from the 24th P.I. and 1st Sikhs, six Australians, and

25 Sowars 16th B.L. under Lieut. Cummins, 24th P.I., with Duncan as interpreter, to scour the country for a week.

16th. We hear the Emperor has approved of the execution of the persons named by the Ministers, but there is no mention of "catching" them. The whole of these negotiations seem to be most puerile. The Field Marshal has issued an Army order for the whole force to be ready to move on 1st March. A copy of this no doubt has been sent to Prince Ching and Li-Hung-Chang, who are quite cunning enough to see it is all bluff, and in forwarding the same to the Empress Dowager will probably write across it the Chinese equivalent for "RATS."

17th. Reid, commanding the Brigade at Shan-wai-Kwan and posts on line to Tientsin, is here on leave. He doesn't seem to trust the Russians. This feeling seems to be infectious. If some of our Generals only spoke the Russian language there would be a better "understanding."

18th. An ideal spring morning. Can it possibly mean the winter is over? Football is the most popular game with our men. We have found an excellent field just behind the International cemetery. Considerable numbers of foreign officers look on, and with tents pitched for refreshments and a band playing, we spend many pleasant afternoons. Being a sheltered spot makes it all the more popular. Another advantage is we get to know something of our "friends," or at all events the sporting element.

19th. The Chinese New Year, when all have to wear new clothes.

20th. Inspected the 7th Rajputs at the Temple of Heaven. They are a fine regiment, and have stood the winter wonderfully well. It is again very cold to-day and windy. Made a round of calls in the American camp.

21st. A football tournament is in full swing. Watched the match between the N.S.W. Contingent and 7th Rajputs. The latter were victorious owing to better combination. The sailors were very amusing, and at times a bit rough, but all was in good temper.

22nd. Inspected the N.S.W. Contingent. Found everything in first-class order. These men are pining for a fight.

23rd. Inspected the 1st Sikhs.

24th. The party under Cummins returned, and of course had seen nothing of Boxers. He, however, picked up some useful information.

25th. Inspected the 24th P.I.

26th. Inspected the 26th Baluchis. Two noted Boxers, Chi-Shin and Shin-Cheng-yi were executed this afternoon at 3.30, when without any warning a tremendous storm came on which lasted for seven hours. Both these men were Chinese Government officials. A very large crowd watched the execution. From their demeanour I expect both had been well drugged, and from what Duncan tells me these men will always be looked upon as martyrs. The storm breaking at the moment of execution, caused the Chinese to think the sentence was unjust.

27th. Another blizzard, which keeps all self-respecting persons indoors!

28th. General Gaselee entertained the Field Marshal at the International Club, and a most enjoyable dinner it was. General Chaffee was in great form, and told us how Wilson, his second in command, 30 odd years back commanded a force of some 20,000 cavalry. "None of your —— mounted infantry," added he, much to the amusement of all, and more particularly the guest of the evening, who whispered to me, "I like plain speaking." The other guests were the American and German Ministers with their attaches, General Chaffee, General Von Gayl, Colonels Grierson and Powell, Messrs. Rockhill and

Squires, Captains Hutcheson, Pell, Philipps, Steele, and Dick, Generals Barrow, Pipon, and myself, besides three A.D.C.'s of the Field Marshal.

1st March. We hear the Court have ordered carts to be sent from here on 6th to meet them at Taian Fu, as they intend travelling via Honan, and thus avoiding famine stricken districts.

2nd. Submitted inspection reports on my Brigade and units attached thereto. It is once more beautifully fine.

3rd. Lunched with Grierson at the German Head Quarters Mess, which is always a big affair on Sundays, lasting as a rule to the dinner hour! The German staff do not like our system of breaking up a number of units to furnish men for our numerous posts, they think one battalion should be detailed for this work. They also find fault with "centralisation," and cannot understand why a field force order should be necessary for the supply of "a pair of socks woollen" to a follower or Sepoy! and very pointedly said, "Have you as a General Officer commanding a Brigade no authority?"

This would almost appear so from our F.F. orders, which they are picking to pieces in detail. Nothing apparently escapes General Schwarzhoff, the Chief of the Staff. He remarked that our F.F. orders reached our Brigades and detachments at Tientsin, Shan-hai-Kwan, Wei-hai-Wei, and Shanghai. Did it interest them to know church service would be at such and such an hour on the following Sunday in the Tartar City? Satisfactory replies to these and other equally small details were not easily forthcoming at a social function surrounded by eager listeners. As regards expenditure I pointed out the Imperial Government had to pay the piper, and therefore a F.F. order probably simplified matters, and as regards church parade it was in the hopes of drawing some of the officers of the German Army to our services, as our F.F. orders were posted daily on their notice board! They are inclined to be "cynical" when discussing professional questions, but you can always put a stop to this by catching the eye of one of their number and raising your glass to him. A good deal of this goes on, and the consequence is you are mixing champagne, hock, läager beer, and red wine to a dangerous extent. I noticed this particularly in the case of two Japanese officers, who before they left the table were decidedly uncomfortable. On the whole I think they are charming companions and hosts, and enjoy chaff as much as we do, the thing to avoid is too much familiarity, which only leads to regrettable incidents. Count Waldersee seems to enjoy these Sunday meals, and takes a real pleasure in chatting with the numerous guests from other armies.)

I wish I could speak their language as Grierson does. I fancy he gives them a good deal more than he gets, and withal appears to be the most popular man in the mess. It is quite delightful to see him, and hear him conversing fluently in French, German, Italian, and possibly Japanese, as he seems to be able to pick up a language in a few weeks. We certainly couldn't have a better representative of the Field Marshal Staff, and it is easy to see he is a "persona grata" with H.E., and all others, outspoken as he is.

4th. The finals of the football tournament came off this afternoon between the 24th P.I. and the 1st Sikhs, and a capital game it was to the end, when the 24th won by two goals to one. The French paid us a great compliment by sending one of their bands down, which was much appreciated by our men. They also turned up in force and followed the game with the greatest keenness, and appreciated the way a Sepoy banged into a British officer without favour or affection, proving to them the excellent feeling existing between officers and men in spite of colour. I really think the French have a higher opinion of us than any of the other allies excepting the Americans, with whom we are naturally on the most friendly terms. Dick and others mix a good deal with the French officers, and the result is improved "camaraderie." The bitter cold and short days of the winter months have interfered with friendly intercourse, which without doubt will all change with the most delightful of all seasons, Spring.

5th. Nothing to record.

6th. At night it only just freezes, and in another few weeks I suppose we will be longing for snow. Such is man! Lunched with the Whittalls, and again met Morrison, of the *Times*, who was very full of the supposed secret understanding between Russia and China, which he thinks must lead to endless trouble. An alliance of the kind could only be "aimed" at Japan, and Japan is not likely to put off "settling day" with Russia till China recovers lost ground. These two Powers (Russia and Japan) must fight it out some day, and many think very soon. In regard to results opinions differ. The majority favour the Japanese at sea and the Russians on shore, whilst the Japs themselves are absolutely confident of their Army. Their Army officers also hint at an early increase to their sea power.

7th. All sorts of shaves are knocking about. An early rupture between "the Bear" and the "Rising Sun," due to the supposed secret understanding above referred to.

8th. Had a visit from Satow, who evidently has a very high opinion of the Japanese.

9th. To-day we performed the sad duty of transferring to the International Cemetery the bodies of all persons buried in the Legation grounds during the siege, in all 14 coffins, including three children. It was a very solemn affair, the impressiveness of which was much marred by a blizzard which came on just as the procession emerged from the British gate.

10th. Captain Paddock, of the American cavalry, died to-day. Sent off letter to A.G. in India in reply to his regarding the advisability of raising another battalion of men.

11th. Attended the funeral of the late Captain Paddock, 6th Cavalry, and had a long chat with Colonel Windt commanding the 6th.

12th. Grierson, Powell, Bond, Pollock, and Bainbridge dined with me, the first three also sleeping. The return trip at night through the

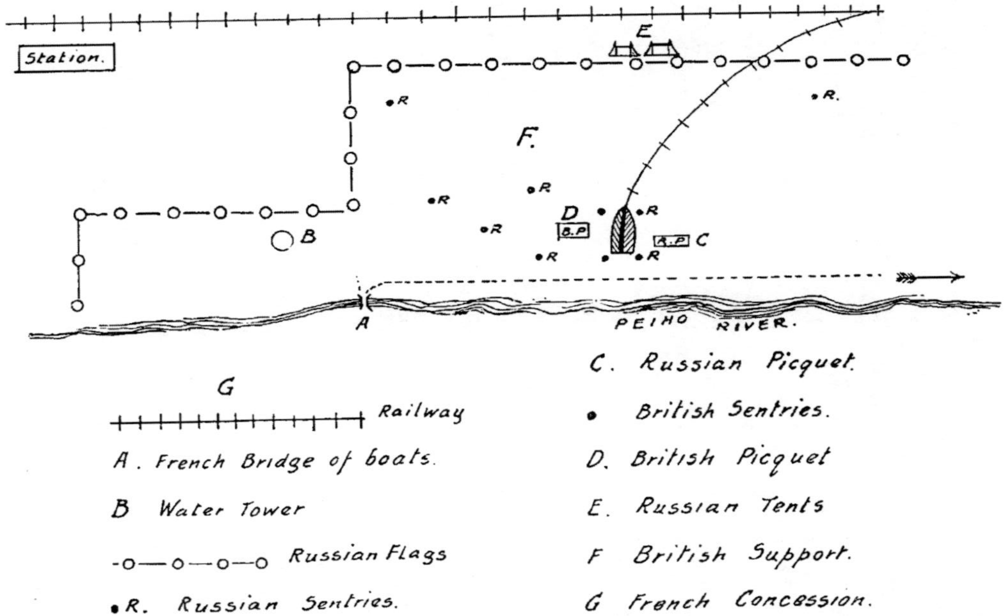

"WHAT DO YOU THINK OF THAT?"

city is no joy, and men fight shy of dinners unless you can put them up for the night.

13th. Increased the detachment of the 1st Sikhs at the Summer Palace to a double company. Visitors are beginning to arrive from all parts of China.

14th. Weather very pleasant. Very pleased at the thought of a few days' leave.

15th. Brooking and I are off for a few days to Tientsin. On arrival at the Tientsin station I was met by McSwiney, of the 7th D.G.'s, who, pointing to some broken ground near the station, said, "What do you think of that?" My eye followed the direction indicated, and to my astonishment I saw "two picquets facing each other composed of Cossacks and Madras Sepoys," separated by some nine feet. It didn't *look* well, whatever the cause. Passing over the bridge and going through the French concession on my way to General Cummins, it was plainly evident something disagreeable had occurred, as French and German soldiers we passed barely saluted us. Later on I heard more particulars, and came to the conclusion we were in the wrong. The whole trouble is over the wretched siding we wished to cut on disputed ground without consulting the Russians. We are working the line, and are responsible for the safety and comfort of all. Unfortunately, however, that portion of the line in the vicinity of the station the Russians some time ago marked out with their flags, and Macdonald, who is in charge of the railway, finding the goods traffic congested, wished to cut a series of sidings down to the bank of the river. This necessitated a considerable amount of cart traffic with material passing through the portion "flagged" by the Russians, which resulted in a certain number of these flags being knocked down and cast to one side. On the Russians seeing this they apparently imagined their flag had been insulted, and the consequence was they placed an armed picquet on the ground, and later we placed one of ours (the Madras picquet we saw on arrival). These two picquets very unfortunately are in full view of the French concession, and apparently the French are for the Russians and against us, whilst the Germans are also inimical towards us.

It seems to me all we had to do was to point out the flags were knocked down by our carts accidentally, and had nothing whatever to say to the "disputed ground," which at the moment was "sub judice." No doubt I will hear more about the affair from Lorne Campbell, who I hope to see this evening or to-morrow. In the meantime posting these picquets as they are is undignified. You don't want to put two armed parties so close to each other that each time the sentries meet they "jostle" each other, as I witnessed with my own eyes.

Called on Lorne Campbell, but he was out.

16th. Saw Lorne Campbell this morning. I could see he was disinclined to speak about the picquet question. Later on we met General Wogack, commanding the Russians, to whom Cummins introduced me. His first question was, "Have you come from Pekin, and are you senior to Lorne Campbell?" I answered both in the affirmative, but added I was only paying a friendly visit of a few days. After some general conversation he referred to the picquet episode, and said all he expected was a little courtesy, which he felt he had not received. A reference to him about the siding would have met with his immediate approval, but under existing circumstances he declined to negotiate with the British, and was awaiting orders from Admiral Alexieff. In the meantime the French and Germans are openly slighting every British officer they meet. How different it is to Pekin, where all is courtesy and politeness. There must be faults on both sides, and from what I have heard I can't help thinking we are more to blame, more especially as we have a large force behind us compared to the handful of men at General Wogack's disposal, and perhaps it is fortunate this is the case, for the Russians are not in the humour to stand on ceremony now that they feel they have been discourteously treated. If our picquet was considered a necessity I think it would have been wiser to make the selection say from the Australians.

Some restrictions about entering the British concession owing to horse play indulged in last Sunday have annoyed the French, who are now only allowed to enter our concession on duty or in small parties of two or three men.

17th. This evening French and German soldiers have been openly insulting British officers, and in some cases even assaulting them. Am afraid this unfortunate affair of the railway siding will cause serious friction so long as the picquets remain. The river only separates these from the French concession, and hundreds of French and German soldiers are grouped on the opposite bank eagerly watching events. The British and Russian sentries at the head of the cutting nearest the river jostle each other every time they meet, as they turn on their respective beats. A more unsoldierly sight you can't conceive. Our picket has only posted two sentries, whereas the Russians completely surround us. The prod of a bayonet accidental or intentional would put the fat in the fire, and both French and German soldiers would rush to the rescue of the Cossacks. I think there is no doubt about this. As I rode along the bank of the river through the French concession I saw dozens of foreign officers and civilians taking snap shots at the two picquets, copies of which are sure to appear in all the Continental papers. Fortunately the Cossacks appear to be well in hand, and barring the sentries "shouldering" each other when they meet, there are no further outward signs of enmity. In fact I noticed the men of each picquet conversing across the small cutting, apparently quite amicably. If these pickets don't come to blows it speaks well for both, as the position is a very trying one when you realise our men are practically surrounded.

18th. I again met Wogack accidentally in the street. He was more communicative, but looked very upset. Even now he declares he would remove his men if a polite and official reference were made to him. I pointed out to him the siding under dispute was for the public good, and was only one of a series intended, so as to give a separate siding for each nationality. This seemed to surprise him, as he was under the impression we were making this one cutting for our own use. As regards the positions taken up by the pickets he claims having placed his men on unoccupied ground, and the British coming in close contact with his men he could not be held responsible for. Here he is undoubtedly in the right. Our picket might have been posted at the railway station seeing the Russians had no tools with which they could fill in the work executed by us. Wogack resents Lorne Campbell's action in not having interviewed him personally instead of through a staff officer. Before forming an opinion I should like to hear Campbell's version, for as a rule we are not discourteous. At the Club I noticed German officers studiously avoiding British officers. No one can support the action of the French and German troops, who throw stones at every passing tonga containing British officers. Grierson was stoned in his tonga driving from the station, and he may be trusted to put the case very clearly to the Field Marshal when he arrives this evening.

19th. Count Waldersee arrived last night in a terrible dust storm, so determined to break his journey. He was met at the station by Lorne Campbell and Wogack amongst others, and left this morning by special for Pekin, where he will probably settle this dispute about the sidings. The discipline here is not what it should be.

20th. Marines arrived during the night and relieved the native picket. This will improve matters. Had the Victorians supplied our picket in the first instance much friction would have been saved. The foreign element imagine native troops were employed to purposely slight the Russians! This I won't believe. A French General has come up from Paitang-Fu to enquire into the general conduct of the French soldiers, and a strong party of gendarmes from Pekin have arrived on the scene, and are doing excellent work at the end of our concession nearest the French, where they are hustling their men properly! Wogack left for Pekin this morning.

21st. The air is much clearer to-day. The French General and Campbell have settled matters, and now the French are to be allowed freely inside the British concession on Saturdays and Sundays, whilst the unruly French regiment is to be moved to some jungle outpost. Returned to Pekin and passed Wogack at Fengtai on his way to Tientsin. I hear both pickets are to be withdrawn at once.

22nd. The British and Russian pickets were removed to-day simultaneously after presenting arms to each other, so here ends the most puerile and undignified affair I have ever seen or heard of. In all armies you must find men who are wanting in tact. This affair quite spoilt my short holiday, for at any moment Cummins and his Brigade might have been called out to perform some uncomfortable duty which would have proved most distasteful to him. He has a number of nice friends amongst the civilians, who to a man sided with the Russian commander as far as it was possible for me to judge.

23rd. To-day we buried the body of Captain Watts Jones, R.E., which had been brought in by his brother from Kalgan in a Chinese coffin. It was a very sad duty, as all who attended were aware of the brutal manner in which this poor fellow had been murdered. Every officer of the garrison off duty was present.

24th. The report of the murder of the Rev. Stonehouse, of the London Mission, by armed robbers or disbanded Chinese soldiers, was brought in to-day. I also saw in the papers the death of poor Parsons in Burmah from small-pox.

25th. Seven officers and 226 men of the R.W. Fusiliers under Major Everett arrived this evening in relief of the N.S.W. Contingent.

26th. The N.S.W. Contingent left this morning, and had a great send-off. They are a very fine body of men, and the Colony that sent them out may well be proud of them. Their conduct has been exceptional, and the manner in which they have performed their duties has been most creditable to all concerned. With the greatest regret I said good-bye to them. They made ideal police, and will be much missed by the Chinese themselves, whilst their very "bulk" was sufficient to "sober" the light hearted foreigners bent on adventure in pastures under British control. There is a rumour knocking about that the Russians are purchasing from the Americans the Hankow Canton Railway concession, which seems too absurd to be true.

27th. The weather is perfect, and all the fruit trees are in blossom. There is still considerable friction between ourselves and the French at Tientsin. In the British concession there are certain attractions which appeal to the foreigner, and to be deprived of these excepting two days in the week must be irritating. On the other hand we can't put up with riotous living day and night simply because the best drink shops and places of amusement happen to be in our quarter. Our force of white troops could not possibly stand the strain. and our natives are not the men to deal with elated foreigners. Now the Victorians have left Tientsin the "chucker out" element is scarce! Each Victorian could comfortably handle two foreigners, and it seems a pity they could not have been retained to the end. They were better adapted for this kind of work than even the N.S.W. men at Pekin, as they were particularly tall and powerful. Some day there will be a brawl, and as all men are armed, lives will be lost, and another "regrettable incident" for the Foreign Office to worry at, besides advertising those who would otherwise never be heard of! There are too many idle men in Tientsin. With plenty of work all this unpleasantness would disappear.

28th. We can hear no news of the Court, so fancy we are stuck here for some months.

29th. Jermyn left this morning on eight months' leave, and Parr, of the 7th Rajputs, has been appointed D.A.A.G. in his place.

30th. The German troops were reviewed by Count Waldersee in the Hunting Park to-day. They looked very well, but made as many mistakes as troops could. Artillery and cavalry ignored infantry fire from entrenched positions. whilst infantry attacked infantry in position without attempting to open out, and from what I hear the F.M. gave all a thorough good slating.

31st. After a few raw days with much wind it is now beautifully fine.

April 1st. Yesterday, Sunday, Barnett, of the 6th Burma Regiment, was violently assaulted in the French concession, Tientsin. As he must have been in uniform the assault must have been most deliberate.

2nd. There is some hitch in the negotiations, as Satow thinks a fortified Legation quite unnecessary, and impossible for the Chinese to agree to. Other Ministers, however, are strongly opposed to him, and some are indifferent! The Field Marshal's patience is being sorely tried, and he is about to call a meeting of Generals to discuss the question of carrying out the 8th and 9th clauses of the "Terms," without further delay. These refer to the destruction of the Taku and other forts, and the occupation of certain places between Pekin and the sea. It has blown a perfect hurricane all day, quite the worst we have had. No wonder the F. M. is a bit bellicose.

3rd. There has been some sniping at Tientsin, and one of our sentries shot, so have despatched a party of two N.C.O's and 20 picked men of the 24th P.I. under a native officer, all Afridis, to put a stop to this.

4th. Gaselee returned from his tour of inspection.

5th. Good Friday.

6th. The 1st B.L., 14th Sikhs, and eight pom-poms are to come up as L. of C. troops, which is a sign of the times, and gives us some hope of getting away soon. We have had quite enough "city" work to last us a life time. There was a meeting of Generals under the F.M. which only lasted an hour. Another good sign.

7th. The Generals yesterday discussed the question of the reduction of the forces, the strategical places to be held and the destruction of forts, and came to an unanimous decision. The papers are now with the Ministers, who have to deal with the political side of the question.

8th. Count Waldersee's birthday, so called on him. As usual he was very charming. He was very proud of a carriage clock he had received from the Kaiser, besides numerous telegrams from all parts. Guards of honour were posted along the approaches to his quarters to salute all visitors of rank. The way these guards and sentries handle their arms is a revelation.

9th. Gaselee inspected the 1st Sikhs, 24th P.I., R.W. Fusiliers, and hospital, after which he and his staff lunched with me.

10th. The body of a German officer was found this morning on the side of the road leading to the Summer Palace; a clear case of murder. If officers roam about at night without escorts in disobedience of orders they must expect to come to grief sooner or later, for although we can't put our hands on them, the city and surrounding villages are full of Boxers and budmashes, who will always take advantage of an unarmed man. This officer was probably returning late from the Summer Palace. The F. M. called on me to-day, but at the time he hadn't heard any particulars regarding the murdered officer. He told me he was more than pleased at the pipers of the Baluchis serenading him on his birthday, and declared he enjoyed the "music," but I noticed some of his staff "squirmed" at the very remembrance. This is our first day of the races and assault-at-arms. I hope all goes off well, for we are doing it on a large scale, and practically all Pekin and Tientsin are our guests for the six days they last. The weather, however, is not very promising, as there is a strong wind blowing.

11th. The more uninteresting events took place

yesterday. The driving of the 12th Field Battery to-day impressed all spectators. The Americans turn out to a man, and a good many French and Japanese soldiers, but not so the Germans. As regards officers, there is nothing to complain of, nearly every one in the garrison turns out, and the fellowship is exactly what it ought to be amongst gentlemen. All are delighted, and many of the French officers are competing, especially in all the mounted competitions, whilst some of the Germans are taking the plums in the horse racing line.

The Americans won't compete at all, which is very odd, as they are on such particularly good terms with us. However, so long as they all enjoy themselves and are content to watch us, we are quite ready to cater for them in every way. A number of ladies have come up from Tientsin to brighten the scene. Sir Pertab Sing is in great form, and is sure to win some of the best races. I wish we could get up an international "Tug-of-war," but there is no chance of this. The air was so laden with fine dust to-day that we had to abandon the tent pegging. It increased everyone's thirst, and drove all to the refreshment tents more frequently. French was the Court language. and it was quite remarkable how eloquent even

OFFICERS AND NON-COMMISSIONED OFFICERS 12th FIELD BATTERY.

the British officer became. May the dust continue if it forces him to speak some other tongue than his own.

12th. Helping to do host becomes more attractive each day, where all are determined to enjoy themselves. Foreigners are really much easier guests to entertain than our own people. They make themselves comfortable and help themselves in a rational manner without ever forgetting their inborn politeness, and they are certainly all there with the ladies. Our fellows are of course busy looking after the different competitions as well as the guests generally. When our Horse Artillery from Tientsin turned out for "driving" the tents were absolutely deserted, and never did our horse gunners show to greater advantage than to-day. The applause was hearty to a degree and well merited, and the admiration was without doubt genuine. The majority of the spectators had never seen such a sight, and they openly admitted this.

When they saw the 12th Field Battery a couple of days ago they thought they had seen the best we could show them, and were delighted, but to day's performance literally took their breath away, every moment they expected to see the guns topple over and complete teams come down.

I think all will respect British troops more from this date. The faces of the little Japanese were a study, they must have thought our men had suddenly become "possessed of devils," and the lady spectators were absolutely frantic with delight, and clamoured for an encore! I only wish we had had the full battery up for the day.

13th. The racing to-day was quite good, and one of the German officers has a smart string that takes some beating. Sir Pertab is well to the front, and riding in nearly every race in spite of an attack of fever; I must say he is a wonderful old sportsman. The F. M. seems to be enjoying this week as much as anyone. So far all the competitions have been most keenly contested. especially the tent pegging, tugs-of-wars, and bayonet exercise. Amongst the infantry the honours will rest with the 24th P.I. and 26th Baluchis. The foreign officers are rather surprised at the physique and stamina of our men, and are beginning to form a more correct estimate of our Native Army. They are much struck with the bearing of the native officers, most of whom have many medals and decorations, and would give a good deal to be able to converse with them. I introduced many native officers, especially to the Germans, who put most searching questions, and were apparently delighted with the quick replies given. I have never felt prouder of our native soldiers than I have during the last nine months. I don't think they would mind tackling any European foe, led by their British officers, but curiously enough they still fear the Japanese least of all. This, of course, is entirely due to their diminutiveness.

Orders are out for the return of the 4th Brigade to India, so my friend Cummins must be pleased. The Americans have instituted a new order to be known as "The Military Order of the Dragon," to commemorate this unique gathering of nationalities under arms, and to-day I received notice of having been elected an honorary member of the same.

The Germans have caught the Chinaman who murdered Captain Birtsch on the road to the Summer Palace; the captain's horse was found in his possession, and he has confessed to the crime. He poses as being a captain in the Chinese Army, and only shot the officer to get his horse!

14th. All the semi-finals took place to-day.

15th. The last day of the assault-at-arms and racing. All went off without a hitch. As I expected, the 24th P.I. and 26th Baluchis did best. The final tug-of-war between these teams was excellent. After the prize giving there was the usual rush for refreshments and light talk, and I think our friends went away full of regrets the week had come to an end. I have never seen a better managed show, and the credit of it falls on General Richardson and his committee of assistants. The officers of the "Chasseur d'Afriques" put up a team for the jumping competition which were hard to beat.

General Chaffee gave a dinner to-night in his quarters at the Temple of Agriculture which could hardly have been surpassed in New York. It was such a brilliant affair that I feel I must reproduce a copy of the artistic menu and its accompaniments. Yesterday was the General's birthday, but he very considerately thought it advisable to keep it the last day of the sports, which being a Saturday leaves us Sunday for recovery! Chaffee made a short speech, to which the F. M. responded, both in English, and after the guests departed a few favoured ones remained behind till there was sufficient light for the drive home through the tortuous streets of Pekin. I have spent many enjoyable evenings, but never one to touch the 15th April, 1901. Chaffee made a charming host with much dignity, but at 1 a.m. when he had said good-bye to his last guest, he threw aside all reserve, and was the youngest of the select few who remained behind to drink his health over and over again. Song followed song, intermingled with recitation and anecdote, so natural to our cousins across the Atlantic. There must have been something very exceptional in the fun to have kept us all standing in a passage till 5 a.m. without signs of fatigue. Our one regret was that daylight put an end to the happiest and most cheery evening any of us had ever spent. It must not be forgotten that this entertainment came at the tail end of a very heavy week of festivity.

16th. Orders are out for the 1st Sikhs to proceed to the Summer Palace to be followed by the Baluchis, 24th P.I., and possibly the 12th Field Battery. Why, I have no idea. Have sent Brooking and Rainsford out to report on the accommodation. A German force from Paitang-Fu under General Van Gayl is going out to smash up a Chinese force which has shown itself, and which is being closely watched by the French stationed at Paitang-Fu. No doubt the French will co-operate with the Germans.

17th. As we were leaving the mess to turn in for the night we saw a fire in the city, which turned out to be a big blaze in Count Waldersee's quarters, so sent off all our engines, but on arrival they were told further assistance was not needed.

18th. The fire at the F.M.'s was a very serious affair. The Count's asbestos house was burnt to ashes in a few moments, and Waldersse himself was only helped out through a window with much difficulty. He has lost all his possessions, including, I hear, medals and decorations, only saving his baton, whilst General Von Schwarzhoff, the Chief of the Staff, has lost his life. It appears the fire broke out in the kitchen behind the chief of the staffs quarters, and before there was time to notice the danger the whole place was ablaze. General Schwarzhoff, after rescuing some valuable documents with the assistance of his A.D.C. made a further attempt to save his terrier, which was tied to his bed, and whilst doing this the roof of his quarters fell in without hope of any human power being able to reach him. In fact some time elapsed before it was known he was missing. The flames leapt into the air to a great height, and the smoke was so great that no one could approach the building, and all attention was directed to neighbouring buildings. Had there been any wind the entire block known as the Empress Dowager's Winter Palace must have been reduced to ashes if not the entire

Imperial City. The general's death is a terrible loss, and the circumstances make it truly tragic. He was the most able man in the German Army out here, and a very fine character, though not too popular, due probably to the fact you could not humbug him, and he took care to let all know this. The force has lost a strong man, and I expect the Field-Marshal will not find it easy to fill the gap. He was certainly the right man for the mixed "crew" he had to deal with. He favoured no one, listened to all, and sent many away with a flea in their ear, richly deserved. His comments were not always complimentary, but they had the merit of being "honest." Some called him "crooked," but I expect his actions bore investigation, and if at times he appeared "crooked," it was only when dealing with men who were still more "crooked." Anyhow, he was capable of "riding off" the many generals who tried to ride round him in vain. He knew no English when he left Germany, but by the time he reached Pekin he *understood* quite enough "not to be taken in." During the Franco-German War he proved himself a gallant man, and rose to his high position through "merit," and lost his life whilst attempting to save that of a dumb animal, which speaks for itself. It is difficult to realise that three days ago one was speaking to him full of life and energy at General Chaffee's dinner, where every utterance of his was eagerly devoured, for when he spoke he spoke to the point.

19th. The Ministers have agreed to Count Waldersee's scheme for the reduction of the forces and are on the point of settling the indemnity question. The Franco-German expedition near Paitang-Fu has been most successful. They encountered a force of Chinese, said to be 18,000 strong, and utterly routed them. The Germans mustered 5,000 and the French 3,000, and their losses all told were only 50 killed and 150 wounded. We may never hear details of the fight, which is a pity; but I gather the French were always a bit ahead of the Germans, having started with an advantage which they retained to the last. At the opening of the fight the French were entrenched, facing the Chinese, also entrenched. The latter had their backs to the hills, and always had their retreat secured. The Chinese force was composed of Regulars, so it may be assumed they were fighting "by order." The situation is a peculiar one, as we are supposed to be here as the "Friends" of China, with whom "we are not at war!"

20th. General Schwarzhoff's funeral took place at 10 a.m.; a most impressive scene; each force sent a guard of 100 men, whilst the Germans turned out in strength—every officer was present, and made a wonderful display of uniforms.

Brooking returned from the Summer Palace, and reports accommodation for 3,000 troops, after cleaning and clearing up.

21st. There has been a small skirmish on the line near Shan-hai-Kwan, in which Major Browning and six men have been killed, and a few wounded. Apparently it was an affair with a gang of armed robbers who infest that part of the country.

22nd. Further details from Shan-hai-Kwan put our losses at Browning and one sepoy killed, one sepoy dangerously and one seriously wounded, with Lieutenant Stirling and four sepoys wounded. Our detachment only consisted of 100 Rifles, marching along without any advanced scouts. The old story—carelessness!

23rd. More signs of an early break up. Vaughan started for Tang-chao this morning to decide on what stores should be left there and what brought in here. The 1st Sikhs and 12th Field Battery will go out to the Summer Palace next week. This change is merely on the score of health. A company of Baluchis and squadron of 3rd Bombay Cavalry form the escort of a survey party which starts on the 25th.

24th. It looks like rain to-day, which is badly wanted. The Ministers declare they are not to blame for the slow progress of negotiations.

25th. Rain fell last night, so it is quite chilly to-day. The proposed Franco-German advance on Hailu has fallen through, due probably to insufficient transport. At the fight referred to on the 19th, it is now stated the Chinese numbered 20,000 men, with 25 guns, whilst the French and Germans had eleven and eight battalions of infantry, besides cavalry and artillery, respectively. The affair at Shan-hai-Kwan leads me to suppose the detachment of the 4th P.I. did not behave too well, as Major Browning's body was left on the ground. Subsequently Colonel Radford with 400 of his men, some Zouaves, Lancers and Japanese, went out and killed 50 the first day, and completely broke up the gang the following day.

26th. Nothing.

27th. Further details of the fighting S.W. of Paitang-Fu show that the French and Germans followed the Chinese for some distance beyond the Great Wall and took a number of guns. The narrow hill tracks were so blocked with carts and baggage of the fugitive Chinese that further progress was impossible, and the Chinese got clean away.

28th. Nothing to note. Still getting the summer quarters ready.

29th. The 1st Sikhs left for the Summer Palace. The 12th Field Battery paraded this morning for the benefit of General von Trotha, who expressed a wish to see something of our British troops' equipment and interior economy. The generals met this morning to discuss the following points:—

a. The exact numbers each force is to leave behind.

b. The continuance or discontinuance of the local government at Tientsin.

c. The entertaining of police for Pekin.

d. The question of whether the Legation Guards are to be under the orders of the Ministers or the Generals.

What decision they arrived at I know not; all I do know is "they were unanimous," which is something.

30th. General von Trotha and his staff lunched with us after inspecting the quarters of the 12th Field Battery, R.W. Fusiliers, and our hospital. He professed to be very pleased with all he saw, and was profuse in his thanks. He is a particularly pleasant man, and told me of his intention to pay India a flying visit, promising to look me up at Bolarum, where I would be able to give him a thorough insight to all matters connected with our native troops.

1st May. Privilege leave is now open to officers to visit Japan. I wish I could avail myself of this grand opportunity of really seeing the Japanese Army and its organisation, a most interesting study, for it cannot be long before these ideal little soldiers will have their hands full. Their next war will be a fight for their very existence, and no one knows this better than themselves. They are full of confidence, which is half the battle, and all they hope for is that they may be allowed to fight it out without interference. That they can ever take Port Arthur seems to me quite impossible. Beyond mentioning war with Russia "as a certainty," they are not inclined to be communicative. They have made up their minds that the struggle must come, and the sooner the better pleased will they be. If they can put 300,000 or 400,000 men in the field of the same class as they have here, they may have a chance of doing something surprisingly great; but it is inconceivable to me they possess so many really fine soldiers.

Their infantry is nearly perfect, but their cavalry is the poorest I have ever seen, and their artillery, though well trained, is quite deficient in weight, unless they have something very superior up their sleeves. Only a visit to Japan could possibly enable one to form anything like a correct estimate of their "power." It is with deep regret I cannot seize this opportunity. I have a very high opinion of the Russian soldier, but their army lacks good officers, and judging by what we have seen and heard they are half-a-century behind the rest of Europe.

2nd. We have discovered some stupid printed notices on red paper, one of which was posted outside the Chin-men, reminding the people that to-morrow is the day all "Foreign Devils" are to be massacred! Horrible nuisance this, as I want to go to the races!

3rd. Received notice that two M.L. bronze guns, about 2.375 calibre and 4 feet long, mounted on a single carriage, had been put aside for me. I will present these to the contingent mess. The Pekin races commenced to-day, and were quite good.

4th. Admiral Seymour is here on a short visit.

He attended the races this afternoon, which turned out quite a fashionable gathering, as all the Ministers and their families were present and a large contingent from Tientsin.

5th. The American cavalry, artillery and transportation (!) marched off this morning; the British officers turned out in force to wish them good-bye. Quite a festive day, lunched and dined at German headquarters with Grierson and attended the races.

6th. The last day of the races; all our horses seem to be "crocked"; we hadn't a single entry. On the whole, the meeting was a great success, though we did not carry off the Field-Marshal's cup. We hear of a Russian officer having been shot at Tientsin by a German sentry, the result of some midnight altercation between the Russian and a German officer. I also hear that our railway staff officer at Tientsin has offended some German officers. There must be something in the "air" of Tientsin that makes men truculent.

7th. The shooting affair has been put down to "accident"! The story goes the two officers were quarrelling, and the sentry fired a shot over their heads, on which the Russian drew his sword and went for the German officer, who in turn drew his revolver and shot the Russian officer dead; but as it has been decided to call it a case of "accidental shooting by a sentry," we must accept that verdict.

8th. Captain —— came in and made some absurd report to the L.G.C. about the hospital quarters at the Summer Palace, which is causing a small "flutter." As he is certain to be wrong, I don't intend losing my wool!

9th. As I expected, —— report had no semblance of fact in it. This is not the first time this young officer has drawn on his imagination. The Chief of the Staff has ordered a guard to take over to-morrow the American quarter of the Tartar section, with an intimation he will give the guard orders *personally*! Poor chap! he must be very hard up for something to do. It is raining hard.

10th. Took over the civil police duties of the greater portion of the American quarter in the Tartar City. This will give Du Boulay plenty of work. The young Chinese Prince who is to proceed to Europe to apologise to the Kaiser paid me a visit with two younger brothers at 11 a.m., and washed down numerous buns and cakes with port wine, after which they went round the hospital, saw the X rays and soda water machine working, and were eventually photographed. It seems the palace (?) we occupy is their private property, and anxiety or curiosity rather than politeness was the cause of the unexpected visit. With them was a very intelligent English-speaking Chinese doctor, who had travelled the world over. He preferred whisky and soda to port wine at 11 a.m. These young Princes seemed quite nice boys; the "apologising" one said he felt very nervous about his trip to Europe. I explained that the apology over, he would probably have a most enjoyable time of it, and was certain to be treated with the greatest kindness.

11th. General Voyron gave a big dinner to several Chinese Princes and Li Hung Chang, and in his speech referred to "Les crimes abominables," whilst later he took them outside to witness the "Foreign Devils," male and female, dancing on ground only used for the funeral ceremonies of Emperors! It is to be assumed he was quite ignorant of this, or he would never have turned it into an open-air ballroom. It led to a bit of a "Frost" amongst the Chinese group.

12th. A Chinese force near Paitang-Fu have been repulsed by Boxers, so appealed to the French, who gave them the necessary assistance.

13th. I think our warm weather is not far off.

The Germans can get no definite orders about leaving the country, and we are not likely to move before they do. I expect the command in Northern China when Gaselee goes will be offered to O'Moore Creagh. None of the generals on the spot would accept this; their experience has not been too pleasant. If centralisation has ever been carried to an extreme it has been here, where generals have been turned into letter-boxes. We have had quite a number of visitors lately in Pekin, including a batch of young "middies," also Lady Bruce, Mrs. O'Moore Creagh and Mrs. Edwards.

14th. Soon we may expect to hear some news of the breaking up of the forces.

15th. Two sections of pom-poms arrived to-day. One of these will join the 12th Field Battery at the Summer Palace and the other with the 3rd Section, when it arrives, will remain at the Temple of Heaven.

16th. Skeen, of the 24th P.I., sent in a report of a scrimmage with some Boxers in the Hunting Park. He lost one man killed and bagged six. They, however, carried off their wounded.

17th. The French troops are detained at Tanku, and General Voyron has made Tientsin his headquarters, with a view to watching the

Germans, who are suspected of only moving to Peitaho! We are all real friends! The "Daily News" (of Tientsin) announces the departure of the Court yesterday on the favourable report of the Ennuch T'sui. By departure, I, of course, mean with reference to their return to Pekin.

18th. Duncan informs me an Imperial edict has just been received from Hsian-Fu to the effect "that up to date the Ministers have been addressing the Emperor, and have taken no notice of the Empress Dowager, so the time has arrived for her to openly proclaim to China there is no Emperor, and that she alone rules and with a firm hand." If this is true, and there is no reason to doubt it, it means the defiance of all Europe, so war should be declared at once, the Woosung Forts should be attacked without delay, and Yuan-shih-kuis Army called on to surrender or be smashed. The Ministers on the spot are not likely to take this view, their game is "Diplomacy."

19th. The news of yesterday is not looked on seriously. They say the Empress Dowager often makes these statements; and, again, it is quite possible the edict (?) has been wired by some evil person without the old lady's knowledge!

20th. In spite of perfect weather we have a

good many men in hospital suffering from chest complaints.

21st. Reuter tells us it has been arranged by the Powers to let China have a loan of £60,000,000. If this is the case we ought soon to be taking our hats off to this country.

22nd. The 9th Infantry (American) left this morning at 7.30 and General Chaffee and his staff at 10.30. Every British officer turned out to "speed the parting guest," and the regrets were sincere and mutual. The 7th Rajputs furnished a guard of honour for Chaffee, who appreciated the attention. The Field-Marshal was on the platform with a large number of foreign officers, but the British made *the* show. No troops ever hit it off better than the Americans and British, and if we ever meet on the field of battle may it be side by side. I think Chaffee all round is the finest man we have had as a fighting general and a friend one would like never to lose sight of. There is a feeling of depression in our force to-day which is quite genuine. The Americans did not rush for us—I don't think they even hoped to like us—so the affection which sprung up between the two armies is all the more valuable.

23rd. The Ministers are very busy; but, of course, they don't let us know their secrets!

24th. The Germans are dispatching to Kiao-chao one battery, two battalions infantry, one company Engineers, and all Maxim guns, and bringing their Paitang-Fu troops to Pekin. The French troops from Paitang-Fu are marching on Tientsin, via Cheirg-ting and Hokien, clearing up all Boxers en route. The first of our lot to go will probably be the 16th Bengal Lancers, 12th Field Battery and Biluchis; but until German transports appear I do not think ours will be ordered! The Russians say they intend keeping some troops in Tientsin and increasing their Shan-hai-kwan garrison. General Wogack declines to receive any official correspondence from the British military authorities, and will only accept the same through Admiral Alexieff at Port Arthur. On our side we have refused to give them the balance of the $\frac{2}{5}$-in. rolling stock which was agreed, internationally, to hand over, until they hand us over all material they are holding on to, including sheds, buildings, etc., etc. Our departure depends more on the home authorities than any suggestions likely to be offered from here. That 18 Krupp guns were discovered buried at Tonchau was due to a Mahomedan Chinaman. He told his secret to a Moslem sepoy of the 20th P.I., and they may one day appear as a trophy!

General Fakushima proceeds on leave to Japan, and his place will not be filled on the F.M.'s staff.

25th. The Ministers are unable to agree about the indemnity. Germany and Japan want cash down, but are not inclined to accept payment from other Powers willing to advance the money, for once accepted they would have no "locus standi."

26th. The British headquarters announce a gradual reduction of the force, and propose sending the Baluchis to Wei-hai-wei! adding, "We cannot expect to get much transport under a month." They also ask for the names of officers who would like to remain in China. The first C.O. I mentioned this to, asked, "Who is going to remain in command?"

27th. A continuous reduction, till the 2,800 men limit has been reached, has been sanctioned. This reduction will take place simultaneously with the German withdrawal, and as transports for the latter are now preparing for sea, I presume our programme will soon be out. General von Trotha has protested against German soldiers being arrested by sepoys, which, of course, is absurd. It seems one man was arrested in the Hunting Park on a charge of rape by two sepoys of the 24th P I.

28th. Elderton, our marine transport officer, has arrived, which looks like business. Grierson expects to get away next Sunday, and intends going home via Japan. He is quite the best man the authorities could have selected to represent us on the Field-Marshal's staff, and right well has he performed his duties, which must, at times, have been anything but pleasant. The Germans do *not* love us.

29th. Transports were wired for to-day.

30th. The 1st Brigade will be the first to go. General Gaselee told me to-day he thought I would get away at the end of two months! He is full of mirth to-day!

31st. After a very close day the rain came down in torrents during the evening. The Baluchis and Grierson dined with us last night; for the next month it will be nothing but "good-byes."

1st June. The rain continues, so all sensible people are under cover and doing as little as possible!

2nd. The Baluchis started this morning for Wei-hai-wei, and considering the state of the roads they drew a large number of friends to see them off. As they have a number of men out on detached posts they only mustered five companies.

They are a grand regiment from the colonel to drummer boy. It is now practically settled that O'Moore Creagh will command the British contingent remaining, which will probably consist of 14th Sikhs, 4th Goorkhas, 6th Burmah Regiment and the Hong Kong Regiment.

3rd. Count Waldersee left this morning by special at 8.45. A large force of Germans, Italians, and Japanese paraded north of the station, whilst on the platform there were guards of honour. British, German, and Japanese officers mustered in force, and the send-off was most hearty, the British cheers knocking sparks out of the Hocs! The Count is a man of great charm, and all respected him. I wish he could have led us in the field. He felt his departure a good deal, whilst he was evidently pleased to turn his face homewards. To a man of his rank and history, I fear this command must have turned out a disappointing one to him. As the train moved off the Japanese artillery fired a salute. We hear of another emeute from Tientsin, in which French, German, Japanese and British were mixed up. This took place yesterday, the usual "sabbath" affair. As one French soldier was killed and 10 men have been wounded it seems to me some drastic measures should be taken to put a stop to this disgraceful state of affairs. It is most discreditable to us that these disturbances should take place in the British concession. It is very difficult to get hold of the "truth," as the inclination is to hush matters.

4th. Count Waldersee's farewell orders are out. They are quite short, and read a bit "cold." At 11 p.m. there was a big blaze in the Forbidden City, which I will doubtless hear more about to-morrow.

5th. The heavy rain of last night prevented the fire in the Forbidden City spreading. The buildings consumed contained nothing but records. Duncan tells me that he heard *yesterday morning* that an edict had been received from the Dowager Empress directing the immediate destruction by fire of all records in the store rooms of the Forbidden City. It is curious these very buildings should have been destroyed the same night, by lightning, if you are to believe the statements of the eunuchs in charge. Li-Hung-Chang says the loss is irreparable, whilst others declare the papers were of no value. If Duncan's information is correct all the sacred edicts and papers connected with the present dynasty have been destroyed, in which case the loss must be serious to someone! Scott Elliot, who has just returned from Tientsin, tells me the body of a Frenchman was found stabbed, the night before he left, just outside the barracks of the Hong Kong Regiment. Have received official notice that our transports are expected to arrive the end of the month, and that all heavy baggage of units should be sent off to Sinho under guards from each unit the moment orders are issued for their despatch. Heard the cuckoo for the first time.

6th. It has rained heavily all day. Rather a nuisance as there is a considerable amount of shuffling of detachments in consequence of our approaching departure. The roads are in a terrible condition.

7th. The rain has ceased, and looks as if we were in for a very desirable break.

8th. Another party of the Baluchis under Rowlandson and Ashburner left this morning. A number of young officers have started for Japan, where no doubt they will thoroughly enjoy themselves! Selwyn has taken over the police duties after a short trip to Japan, and Du Boulay has gone to the Summer Palace, where he will collect what remains of the exquisite cloisonne and china, and make an inventory of the same, and in this way prevent further vandalism. The destruction of works of art out there has been appalling. Met O'Sullivan, who tells me he knows absolutely nothing about the details of the withdrawal which the C. of S. keeps entirely to himself.

9th. The *China Times* publishes news of the murder of 13 Belgian missionaries on the Mongolian Frontier at a place called Ning-Hshia-Liang, also all male converts, whilst the females were carried off into Mongolia. Supposed to be the work of those scoundrels Tung-Fushang and Tuan. Duncan has been asked by Li-Hung-Chang to join a party leaving here on the 15th for Tayan-Fu and Hshian. He seems inclined to accept.

10th. Some of the detachments are proceeding as far as Tientsin by junks, which will relieve the railway considerably. The line of communications report that nothing is gained by sending heavy baggage ahead of troops, from which I gather there is not too much room at Sinho for storage, so will now send it with each party, which seems a safer plan. The latest news from the Court is they make a start on the 1st September. Prince Ching has asked permission to take over all the Royal Palaces, as it will take considerable time to put things in order. Barrow looked me up this evening re the departure of the 1st Brigade, which ought to commence embarking about 4th

July. The 7th Rajputs will be the last unit to get away.

11th. Mr. Moir Duncan has made up his mind to accompany the mission proceeding to Tai-an-Fu to enquire into the condition of the country. He appears to think it will not turn out very risky, as there will be so many prominent persons with him in the shape of Chinese officials.

12th. It rains hard for some hours every day, much to our discomfort. However, the air is cool so we must not grumble.

13th. Brooking started for Sinho to superintend embarkation arrangements. I will miss him very much. With Low, Leonard, and Parr working for all they are worth we will jog along merrily.

14th. Barrett, with an advanced party of the 1st Sikhs, left for Sinho. They will meet the regiment to-morrow and be ready to unload the heavy baggage.

15th. Saw the 1st Sikhs off this morning, and right glad they seemed to be turning their backs on Pekin. Gaselee addressed the N.O.'s before entraining, and thanked all for the good work they had done. On the way to the station we passed the procession accompanying the remains of the late German Minister, Baron Von Kettler, who was murdered at the commencement of the disturbances. The body is being taken back to Germany.

16th. Barrow came down to say good-bye. He is going to Shanghai to talk over affairs of State with O'Moore Creagh and then home. He is undoubtedly a very able officer, but has a weakness for centralisation which always interferes with "initiative," and "creates" positions which are undesirable, a very common complaint in our Army, where jealousy reigns supreme.

17th. Unarmed Chinese Regular troops are beginning to arrive in the city.

18th. Nothing.

19th. In addition to the regiments I have already named for garrison duty in Northern China there will be five sections of pom-poms. The Shanghai garrison under Richardson will consist of some pom-poms, the 2nd Rajputs, and 30th Baluchis, a poor sort of command for a cavalry officer.

20th. There is a considerable amount of sickness, chiefly bowel complaints, due probably to the wet weather, followed by hot intervals.

21st. Visited the Summer Palace for the last time, and said good-bye to the 12th Field Battery with many regrets. They are a fine body of men, and nothing could have been better than their conduct; but all our gunners are fine and well conducted. Pipon fired some experimental rounds from the pom-poms, which did not impress either of us very much. He will not be sorry to find himself on board ship again. His artillery command has been, I fear, a most disappointing one with his batteries spread all over the country. For a man with a record such as his, his position must have been at times "galling." Barrow started for Shanghai this morning. I have received orders to embark at Sinho on 3rd July, so will return to India with the 24th P.I. I almost wish now I were staying behind, just to see the thing through; at the same time I have a great longing to get back to the contingent. Duncan and his party left to-day. I wish him the best of luck. He has rendered me the most valuable services in my dealings with the Chinese, and as a companion and friend we will all miss him greatly. The formal approval of the home Government to our withdrawal has arrived, so now he have nothing to do but pack up and be off.

23rd. I am glad to see Colomb, of the 4th Goorkhas has been appointed D.A.A.G. Shanghai. O'Sullivan, Grimston, and Drake-Brockman make up O'Moore Creagh's staff. Am afraid Creagh will find Tientsin a very different place to Shanghai, and he will have endless trouble. However, he will stand no nonsense, and soon clean that stable!

24th. Heard from Grierson, dated Tokio, where he seems to be enjoying himself.

25th. Fane goes to Tientsin as Police Commissioner and Provost Marshal. General Gaselee's despatch has appeared in the papers of 15th May.

26th. Leonard has elected to remain behind as Treasure Chest Officer. Financially he has been a considerable loser, but he always takes his knocks with a smile. I wish he could have secured something better.

27th. The weather is very oppressive. Reminds one of the march up a year ago. Thank goodness we have the train to take us away.

28th. Received wire saying the 24th P.I. and my staff have been told off to the Patiala, sailing 4th July. This is final. We are to hand over the British gate to the Chinese on the 1st.

29th. Gaselee with a party has gone off for a few days to the Western Hills, where the Legation people usually spend the hot months. Sir E. Satow presented a "gallantry" medal to Signalman Swannell, of H.M.S. Orlando, for conspicuous bravery on the occasion of the death of David Ollivant during the siege last year. The troops were turned out, and the presentation took place on the spot where Ollivant was shot. Swannell must have felt a very proud man. I wish there had been more sailors present.

During the whole time we have been in China I had not one authenticated case of outrage brought to my notice, nor do I believe such a case occurred.

The temptations were great, but our men never forgot themselves as far as I know, and I hardly think cases of the kind could or would have been hushed up where all were so opposed by nature against acts of the kind. Amongst large bodies of men there must be some black sheep, but my experience of British and native troops on service makes me feel that outrage is a crime the officers have least to fear. All classes know what the punishment would be if brought home, which is quite sufficient deterrent to make the knockneed scoundrel think twice before he turns himself into a beast. These sort of things more often occur in the piping times of peac, where idleness and drink are generally the cause. No men respect the infirm, the women, and the children of an enemy's country more than the British and native soldiers of our Army, if they err it is usually on the side of kindness, for they are too ready to forget past deeds, and become friendly and therefore careless of their own protection.

30th. Busy packing up all day.

1st July. Handed over our heavy baggage to the 24th P.I. Hauled down our flag on the British gate, which was handed over to the Chinese, who presented arms and looked beaming. The Chinese officials and police were most respectful in their demeanour.

2nd. Devoted the day to paying visits. Dined last night with the Robertsons at the Temple of Agriculture. Mrs. Robertson and her daughters seem quite pleased with the idea of a long stay in Pekin. Major Robertson is to command the American Legation Guard.

3rd. Said good-bye to Pekin with mixed feelings. General Gaselee and his staff and the remainder of the officers saw the last of us, whilst the 7th Rajputs and Americans furnished guards of honour, and away we steamed amidst cheers. Saw Whittall at Tientsin station and some other friends, and reached Sinho about 5.30 p.m. Had an excellent dinner with Elderton and the officers Royal Indian Marine, and slept on board the tug Shanking.

4th. Got alongside the Patiala 7 a.m., and weighed anchor 3.30 p.m. As we passed the

Orlando their band struck up, and they signalled "A pleasant journey to you," whilst we gave them a hearty cheer. Just before starting I received a wire from General Gaselee "thanking the 1st Brigade." Our party on board consists of the 24th P.I., Ramsay, Climo, Whitchurch, Skipwith, Ellis, Cook, Morton, Furnie, Lobilliere, Wilson-Johnson, and Soady, Ball-Acton, of the R. W. Fusiliers, with Parr, Brooking, and Low of my staff. We passed Wei-hai-Wei on the morning of the 5th, and after a most enjoyable passage reached Hong Kong on the morning of 10th, where a number of old friends came off to see us and drag us ashore, each and all claiming us as guests, but in the end we accepted the invitation of the R. W. Fusiliers on "the Peak," for dinner. It was quite a treat to be once more seated at a well-appointed table. After dinner Colonel Bertie sprung a surprise on me in the shape of a very kindly speech, which I had to respond to, after which we all moved to the Regimental Theatre, where an Australian Theatrical Company were giving a performance.

On entering the theatre the entire audience rose and cheered vociferously. Thinking this was meant for the performers, I joined in heartily, when to my surprise I discovered it was a personal compliment, and the men were much tickled at my mistake, and were not to be quieted till I addressed them, an opportunity I gladly seized to once more thank those who had upheld the honour of the British Army as the Welsh Fusiliers had done on the march to Pekin and during their stay there under very trying circumstances, surrounded as they were by many temptations, which they resisted like men. No regiment could have behaved better than these gallant Welshmen, and it was a real pleasure to be able to speak to them as a body. During the interruption the performers remained on the stage, and accepted the "upset" with the utmost grace. On leaving the theatre the Sergeant-Major said a few words on behalf of the men, far too flattering for reproduction, which necessitated a few more words in response, and so a very happy evening came to an end, with a few minutes' halt at the mess, where we finally said good-bye to the officers of one of the finest regiments in the British Army.

Never shall I forget all that was done for me by Colonel Bertie, his officers, and men. On the morning of the 11th we called on the messes of the 22nd Bombay Infantry, 3rd Madras L.I., and 5th Hyderabad Contingent Infantry, all stationed at Kowloon, breakfasting with the latter. The 5th H.C. Infantry being one of the regiments belonging to my Indian command, I was more than pleased to see them again. Soon after our return to the Patiala she weighed anchor, and we continued our journey to Calcutta, only anchoring for a few hours in the lovely harbour of Singapore, where we were infested by boatmen selling every conceivable article, from a monkey to a kimona. Before reaching the Hooghly we experienced a few days of monsoon weather, but by this time we were all "sailors," and spent most of the time at quoits, bull, and other games of the ocean, not forgetting the lottery on the "day's" run, which I won four or five times, the proceeds of which helped to provide fruit and ice for the men of the 24th P.I. at certain stations on the line during their hot railway journey up country to Pindee. The afternoon of 23rd saw us in dock at Calcutta, and our first visitor was General Woolfe Murray, commanding. The next morning we commenced unloading, and in the evening we all moved to the Grand Hotel, after saying good-bye to Colonel Ramsay, his officers, and men of the 24th P.I., with feelings of deepest regret. To have been associated with this regiment was a high honour. Most of the officers were carried off by corps in garrison, but I managed to secure Brooking, Parr, Wetherall, Furnie, Johnson, Soady, and Skipwith for dinner.

After breakfast on the 25th came the saddest duty of all, the final farewell to those who had served me so faithfully, the members of my staff, and the few officers who could get away to say good-bye. Never shall I forget saying good-bye to such men as Ramsay, Climo, Brooking, Parr, and Whitchurch. No General was ever served with greater loyalty than I was by my staff and the regimental officers of the 7th Rajputs, 24th P.I., 1st Sikhs, and 26th Biluchis, which formed the 1st Brigade of the China Field Force as it started from India just one year ago. Bobbie Low was a fellow traveller with me as far as Bombay, and very comforting his presence was after the final parting from those I had learnt to love as comrades in the field.

Only those who have been on active service can realise what my feelings were on that Howrah platform on the morning of the 25th July, when parting with that small band of officers who for twelve months had vied with each other to see how much they could do to lessen the troubles and anxieties of their General. After a couple of days' rest at Bombay I continued my journey to Bolarum via Aurangbad. There I picked up my old friend Mason, who travelled with me to Bolarum, where Lushington was the first to greet me, with other

JAPANESE GUARD AT THE GATE OF THE FORBIDDEN CITY.

friends. I took over at once from Dening, who had been commanding during my absence, and was once more in harness tackling "files" with Herbert, who I was pleased to find still at his post as A.A.G., and therefore able to coach me in all that had taken place during my absence. Four months of routine work slipped by when the usual cold weather tour of inspection commenced, followed by three months' China leave, which I put in at Khandalla, at the top of the Poona Ghats, and then eight months to England, where I arrived in time for the coronation of His Majesty, which was at the last moment postponed under circumstances which are historical, but which ended to the joy of the nation so happily. Before going further it seems to me not out of place to put on record one's impressions of the men of foreign armies one met during an association of 12 months in the field under peculiarly interesting and unique circumstances. It is a subject I often heard discussed, but the impressions are purely personal, and in forming them I am in no way guided by the opinions of others, or do I expect others to agree with me, I am speaking for myself, and myself alone, and reproducing them from notes made at the moment.

The Japanese. Judging from what we saw,

they appeared to me absolutely fearless, and would show the same bravery against any foe. The infantry is second to none; their artillery seemed to me lacking in weight, but without doubt they handle their guns well, and thoroughly understand the "role" of artillery; their cavalry is most unattractive, but I fancy the "spirit within" is the same, and this branch of the service will never disgrace itself. As regards shooting, they are, I should say, decidedly indifferent, but I fear most European Armies are little better than "indifferent" when being peppered. The interior economy seems very good, whilst their medical and sanitary arrangements are excellent. Their transport of "one man to one pony" seemed to me most wasteful, but the man is a soldier rather than a follower, and as such "useful."

The Russians. In appearance the men are magnificent. They look capable of anything, and ought to be invincible, but their officers seem to be not only too few, but behind the times in all respects. Whilst the men are calm and collected, the officers seem to be excitable and boastful. Their Cossacks struck me as being inferior mounted infantry, who hovered about all over the shop in an aimless, though fearless, manner without any attempt at "system." With good officers and plenty of them the Russian forces would be grand. They struck me as being behind the times in every department, whilst as shots I should say they are about as bad as you can make them. The men stand like rocks, and fire volleys by word of command, but you might just as well arm them with gas pipes, as "taking aim" seems unknown to them. Their gun carriages look weak, as also their transport wagons, but in spite of this I didn't notice many breakdowns. All their work appeared to me "casual," but they have "stuff" in their ranks any nation might be proud of, and it seems cruel to think how painfully these grand specimens of humanity are neglected, and what terrible losses they must sustain when face to face with an earnest and warlike foe.

Thousands of miles away from the authorities in Europe the Russian Army in the East spells nothing but "neglect" of the worst type. A nation possessing such an asset as the Siberian Army should take trouble to see to its wants or be deprived of it. With good officers they ought to be capabls of sweeping the board, once brought "up-to-date."

The Italians are not in sufficient strength to give one any idea of their Army. The Bersaglieri are without doubt a fine body of men.

The French. On the march to Pekin the forces of France were represented by marines chiefly, and troops from Saigon and Tonquin, more or less washed out in appearance, but after the arrival of the Zouaves, Chasseurs d'Afrique, mountain batteries, and others from Europe they formed a corps worthy of their great country and traditions as soldiers. Excepting one battalion of volunteers from the Paris district, which gave a considerable amount of trouble at Tientsin, the French troops were splendid, and justly admired. In all respects they seemed very much up-to-date, and their officers excellent.

The Germans. Possessing probably the most highly trained officers and N.C.O.'s in the world, and men "set up" as no other soldiers are, they must at once catch the eye. There is an air of "superiority" about the German soldier, which is unmistakable, and if this is "real" I think they must bear the palm. Everything they do seems "thorough," and the men look soldiers born. In the field they seem to stick to closer formations than they ought to, but I expect they know the dangers of this as well as anyone, and can "teach" others how to work in open order, if the truth were known. What they don't know is probably not worth knowing. Nothing seems to escape the eye

AMERICAN GUARD.

of the German officer, who is never tired of picking up information, good, bad, or indifferent, they probe all. Without doubt the great name they have won is well deserved, and they have every intention of living up to it. In the matter of shooting I don't suppose they are any better than ourserves, if as good.

The Americans are much the same as our own British soldiers though more matured. I noticed no youths in the ranks. In their movements they seem a bit slow, but every man appears to *think for himself*, and form his own opinions. The private soldier is well set up, very cool and calm, with an excellent opinion of himself without being boastful, and strikes one as being extremely intelligent. They are most methodical, and there seems to be an excellent "understanding" between officers and men which at first sight might be mistaken for familiarity. The N.C.O. and private soldier seem capable of acting in the absence of the officer, which shows an independence which is absent in our army. All their arrangements are very good and their officers are extremely keen and confident. Nothing seems to be beyond the powers of the American, who is a very fine fellow.

Our Native troops have come out of this ordeal

with flying colours, and I have come to the conclusion that with their British officers they would stand up to any army in the world, whilst I think our native cavalry would do much more than hold its own against the cavalry any nation could put in front of it. Much as our native troops admired the Japanese and their undeniable pluck, they in no way fear them, due no doubt to the smallness of their stature. If it came to war I believe our native infantry would prove better shots than the troops of any nation, and taking them all round our officers ought to feel very proud of the soldiers India has produced and can produce to the end. It is very gratifying to feel that the native troops we had in the field were not what you could term "picked," they were a fair representative body, and all did well, both in the field and quarters, and if there is any fairness in this world I think the foreigners who saw them must admit they were a body of men any nation might well be proud of.

British Infantry were represented by the Royal Welsh Fusiliers, a regiment so well known and distinguished that no remarks of mine are necessary beyond saying they would always uphold the honour of "the thin red line" in any part of the world under any conditions.

As regards our artillery, no words of mine can

add to their fame, and comparing them with the artillery of other nations, as seen in China, they stand head and shoulders above all in every respect. The more you see of our gunners the more fascinating they are. In this branch of the service I honestly think we have reached perfection. The British battery seems to be a machine that never gets out of order, and in spite of the high standard our artillery has attained, the absence of "side" is truly remarkable.

The contingents furnished by New South Wales and Victoria were splendid specimens of manhood, but as they were unfortunate in the matter of seeing actual fighting one cannot speak of them from experience as soldiers; however, if looks and physique count, there was nothing in Northern China that could beat them, and had the opportunity come I feel sure they would have proved irresistible; in keenness they were second to none, whilst their conduct was exceptional.

The infantry of all armies seem to be sadly deficient in good shooting "when under fire," and it makes one wonder "if all musketry training in peace time is not so much money and time thrown away?" The closer the quarters the worse the shooting! Until our boys are taken in hand during their school days I don't believe we will have a really good "shooting" army. A man who can put in 15 consecutive "bulls" on a target at Bisley at 1,000 yards would probably miss a haystack at 300 if he were being fired at! It is at the closer ranges all infantry soldiers seem to fall to pieces. When you compare the "hits" to "rounds fired" on active service, you almost wish for the old days when you couldn't hit a man more than 100 yards off!

On my return to India, February '02, I found to my bitter disappointment the Hyderabad Contingent was on the eve of being broken up, and myself transferred to the Madras command, in which position I completed my service in September, '04.

The Madras command was and always had been a three-cornered one of little interest to its commander or the troops which composed it. These last days were a mere "picnic" in the midst of delightful surroundings, and a society hard to beat for sociability and good fellowship, where the stranger was made at home from the first. I was delighted to find my old friend Forbes as A.A.G., and have Brooking once more on my staff as D.A.A.G., with Sir George Wolseley as my Commander. Under such favourable conditions it is needless to say my last 20 months of the service were about the pleasantest and most peaceful in my experience. Just as my "harness" days were closing a change to "Ooty" to officiate for Sir George Wolseley practically ended my Indian career.

With the lead given to society at Madras and Ootacamund by such a host and hostess as Lord and Lady Ampthill, is it to be wondered at all were happy? Not once did I hear a note of discord, and when society declared it worshipped its Governor and its Governor's wife it spoke from its heart.

I was not much taken with the Native population, for here you saw the effects of English and education more pronounced than in any other part of India known to me, and the result appeared anything but complimentary to the West.

Drunkenness among the lower classes could be seen daily, whilst the swaggering youth and street urchin alike have taken to the everlasting cigarette, the smoke of which is blown in the faces of the European with the same objectionable freedom and equality as one is growing accustomed to in the streets of London. Soon all respect for the European will have vanished.

The Marina, which at one time was the fashionable promenade for Europeans, is now practically deserted by those who are known as being "on the Government House List." In fact it is "difficult" for "the Sahib" to walk through the streets of Madras, and impossible for the English lady. The ruled races here are as good as the rulers, unless you stoop to using the cane or stick to clear the way. As soon as night comes on the Madrassi hooligan thinks nothing of assaulting the British soldier walking or cycling alone. Assaults of this kind were frequent during my stay in Madras. The half educated English-speaking Madrassi youth is the most objectionable creature I know. Away from the towns it is quite different, and you feel there is some respect left for the white man, but it is a mere matter of time; education will penetrate the jungles, and the respectable and respectful ryot of Southern India will become as objectionable as the townsman. This I don't think would ever be the case, to the same extent, in other Presidencies where the so-called "Christian" is rare, for it is at the hands of so-called Christians in Madras you expect to find the greatest amount of impertinence and see the greatest amount of drunkenness.

I don't mean to imply there are no good men amongst the more highly educated classes, for there are many, but the half-educated ones are so greatly in the majority that you almost imagine the whole are impregnated with disrespect.

Speaking personally, I could see no redeeming features to recommend the Madras youth to the Englishman, and to cultivate whom was a hopeless task which he only took advantage of, and attempted to become your equal, in a most objectionable manner. So long as there is a very wide gulf between the races, there will be respect on both sides; narrow it, and all respect will vanish on one side. No one understands the Native of India better than the Englishman who devotes the best part of his life in trying to improve the country and the lot of the dwellers therein, and to them rather than to the Statesmen who come out to govern for a few years, should the treatment of the Natives be left, if we are to hold the country and make the most of it for the permanent good of all classes. Rarely indeed do you ever hear of a case of wilful disrespect from a native soldier to his officer; equally rare, no doubt, is disrespect shown by the native to a civil official, but the impertinence of the native of the City of Madras to the military man and non-official European is growing daily. These are my sentiments; I wish I could think otherwise.

In most parts of India natives are to be found who equal and often surpass the European in sport such as polo, cricket, racquets, riding, tennis and shooting, but here only a very few attempted any of these, excepting polo, which was indulged in by one small group led by a sporting Raja. However, to witness a polo or football tournament the whole town seemed to turn out, and from their applause appeared to recognise all the best features of the game or bout, proving that they understood the theory of the contest without any desire to take up a game in which the element of danger enhances its popularity with true sportsmen. I verily believe most of them looked on in the hope of witnessing a serious accident! The centres of education in this Presidency may be making the youth learned, but I could see no signs of turning them into men.

To compare the Native Army of '04 with that of '72 is like comparing the steam driven plough with the ox drawn one; the improvement *as a fighting machine* is beyond recognition. Whether the Army of to-day is more loyal and more contented is a matter of grave doubt.

In my humble opinion you could get our Native Army to do anything and go anywhere so long as the supply of the British officer is sufficient. For a campaign such as we have lately watched in the Far East our Indian Army is lamentably short of officers, and how gaps could be filled up is beyond my conception. For it must never be forgotten that our danger, when the bulk of the Army is far across the Frontier, is in India itself. A severe reverse at the front might be the signal for an upheaval all over the country, which would be made a hundred fold worse now that we allow the Native States to keep up large partly disciplined troops which are not officered by British officers.

On the outbreak of a war no doubt every Native State in India would put her men at the disposal of the Government, for I believe the Chiefs are, as a body, loyal to the backbone, but as these troops could never be put in the fighting line without a full complement of British officers, I only see in them a source of danger in the event of reverses. No doubt the Government have given this careful consideration, and are quite satisfied with their policy, but the man in the street who cares to take the trouble to think out the problem is not in "the know," and would not be satisfied with the present state of affairs.

To bring the Native Army up to date and make it capable of facing any contingency, it seems to me an absolute necessity that the British officers should be at least doubled in each and every unit. The first step in this direction should be the abolishment of the "military civilian," an article that is neither "flesh, fowl, nor red herring."

Take a case which, please God, may never occur, of an Army employed 300 miles beyond our Frontier which has received a check so serious that trouble starts in India itself. Who would be the first to feel this? The unprotected European. These would soon be slaughtered, and what would follow? The mob now steeped in blood would go for the families of those men who were at the front, and when the news reached these what would happen? Could these men be depended on?

In keeping the European Army in India at such a low strength we are tempting Providence. The money we are throwing away in educating the Natives up to Western ideas, and which the people don't want, might well be devoted to putting the house in order to an extent we might look to India *for* help in any part of the world instead of having to cry out for protection at a moment we could least spare a man.

India is the brightest jewel in our Crown; it possesses wealth sufficient for more than its needs if properly handled, so I don't see why an extra 50,000 British soldiers should not be added to its forces, the cost of which would go back to the people of the country, and similarly the extra charge of additional officers for the Native Army proper as well as for the forces kept up by the Native Chiefs, the personnel of which in many cases is admirable, and which could very soon be utilised for keeping order "at home," so to speak, on "the line of communications," or even the front.

The Army is as much a huge business concern as the largest company ever floated. Why should it not be run on business lines, and be able to show a balance sheet attractive to the investor—the Public?

Now that India is increasing its railways all over the country why shouldn't the British forces out there be increased by even 100,000 men, where climates fit for the white man are abundant, and make it pay?

Had India been in the hands of say the Russians for the past century would you see the rotten tumbled down bazaars to-day which we are pleased to term towns and cities? Would you see *all* enterprise in the hands of the Natives; would you hear of sedition; and would no Indian word have been forged for gratitude ere this, a word that is unknown to the languages of Hindustan?

It seems almost dangerous to make such a statement, but nevertheless it is true that during the whole of my Indian career I never once attended the funeral of an officer serving in any station I was quartered at. By this I do not mean I never attended a funeral, for, with much sorrow, I admit having attended many, but it was always on occasions when I was on leave or the deceased was on leave.

During the 33 years I served in the country I think I only once came in contact with a really "objectionable" man, so can look back to those years with unalloyed pleasure, and can conscientiously advise any man adopting the profession of arms, to seek his fortunes, as a soldier, in the East, where opportunities spring up like mushrooms "in the night." Given a good constitution every man should succeed to a lesser or greater degree according to "luck," which after all is said and done comes to each man in turn, who waits, in some shape or form. To some it sticks and never deserts, to others it comes early in life and then forsakes, and lastly it comes late in life, possibly at the end of a man's career, but whenever it does come, recognise it as such, accept it as such, and *never* allow it to cause that most disastrous of all diseases, "Capital inflation."

FINIS.